MAC® OS8 FOR DUMMIES®

by Bob LeVitus

Foreword by Steven Bobker

IDG Books Worldwide, Inc.
An International Data Group Company

Foster City, CA ◆ Chicago, IL ◆ Indianapolis, IN ◆ Southlake, TX

Mac® OS 8 For Dummies®

Published by
IDG Books Worldwide, Inc.
An International Data Group Company
919 E. Hillsdale Blvd.
Suite 400
Foster City, CA 94404
www.idgbooks.com (IDG Books Worldwide Web site)
www.dummies.com (Dummies Press Web site)

Copyright © 1997 IDG Books Worldwide, Inc. All rights reserved. No part of this book, including interior design, cover design, and icons, may be reproduced or transmitted in any form, by any means (electronic, photocopying, recording, or otherwise) without the prior written permission of the publisher.

Library of Congress Catalog Card No.: 97-80123

ISBN: 0-7645-0271-9

Printed in the United States of America

10 9 8 7 6 5 4 3 2 1

10/RR/QY/ZX/IN

Distributed in the United States by IDG Books Worldwide, Inc.

Distributed by Macmillan Canada for Canada; by Transworld Publishers Limited in the United Kingdom; by IDG Norge Books for Norway; by IDG Sweden Books for Sweden; by Woodslane Pty. Ltd. for Australia; by Woodslane Enterprises Ltd. for New Zealand; by Longman Singapore Publishers Ltd. for Singapore, Malaysia, Thailand, and Indonesia; by Simron Pty. Ltd. for South Africa; by Toppan Company Ltd. for Japan; by Distribuidora Cuspide for Argentina; by Livraria Cultura for Brazil; by Ediciencia S.A. for Ecuador; by Addison-Wesley Publishing Company for Korea; by Ediciones ZETA S.C.R. Ltda. for Peru; by WS Computer Publishing Corporation, Inc., for the Philippines; by Unalis Corporation for Taiwan; by Contemporanea de Ediciones for Venezuela; by Computer Book & Magazine Store for Puerto Rico; by Express Computer Distributors for the Caribbean and West Indies. Authorized Sales Agent: Anthony Rudkin Associates for the Middle East and North Africa.

For general information on IDG Books Worldwide's books in the U.S., please call our Consumer Customer Service department at 800-762-2974. For reseller information, including discounts and premium sales, please call our Reseller Customer Service department at 800-434-3422.

For information on where to purchase IDG Books Worldwide's books outside the U.S., please contact our International Sales department at 415-655-3200 or fax 415-655-3295.

For information on foreign language translations, please contact our Foreign & Subsidiary Rights department at 415-655-3021 or fax 415-655-3281.

For sales inquiries and special prices for bulk quantities, please contact our Sales department at 415-655-3200 or write to the address above.

For information on using IDG Books Worldwide's books in the classroom or for ordering examination copies, please contact our Educational Sales department at 800-434-2086 or fax 817-251-8174.

For press review copies, author interviews, or other publicity information, please contact our Public Relations department at 415-655-3000 or fax 415-655-3299.

For authorization to photocopy items for corporate, personal, or educational use, please contact Copyright Clearance Center, 222 Rosewood Drive, Danvers, MA 01923, or fax 508-750-4470.

Trademarks: All brand names and product names used in this book are trade names, service marks, trademarks, or registered trademarks of their respective owners. IDG Books Worldwide is not associated with any product or vendor mentioned in this book.

 is a trademark under exclusive license to IDG Books Worldwide, Inc., from International Data Group, Inc.

About the Author

Bob LeVitus (pronounced Love-eye-tis) was the editor-in-chief of the wildly popular *MACazine* until its untimely demise in 1988. Since 1989, he has been a contributing editor/columnist for *MacUser* magazine, writing the "Help Folder," "Beating the System," "Personal Best," and "Game Room" columns at various times in his illustrious career. In his spare time, LeVitus has written 25 popular computer books, including *WebMaster Macintosh,* Second Edition, the "everything you need to build your own web site on a Mac" book and CD-ROM; and his latest book/CD before this one, *WebCaster Macintosh,* the "'everything you need to create a cool webcast on a Mac" book.

Always a popular speaker at Macintosh user groups and trade shows, LeVitus has spoken at more than 100 international seminars, presented keynote addresses in several countries, and serves on the Macworld Expo Advisory Board, He was also the host of *Mac Today,* a half-hour television show syndicated in over 100 markets, which aired in late 1992.

LeVitus has forgotten more about the Macintosh than most people know. He won the Macworld Expo MacJeopardy World Championship an unbelievable four times before retiring his crown. But most of all, LeVitus is known for his clear, understandable writing, his humorous style, and his ability to translate "techie" jargon into usable and fun advice for the rest of us.

He lives in Austin, Texas with his wife, two children, and dogs.

ABOUT IDG BOOKS WORLDWIDE

Welcome to the world of IDG Books Worldwide.

IDG Books Worldwide, Inc., is a subsidiary of International Data Group, the world's largest publisher of computer-related information and the leading global provider of information services on information technology. IDG was founded more than 25 years ago and now employs more than 8,500 people worldwide. IDG publishes more than 275 computer publications in over 75 countries (see listing below). More than 60 million people read one or more IDG publications each month.

Launched in 1990, IDG Books Worldwide is today the #1 publisher of best-selling computer books in the United States. We are proud to have received eight awards from the Computer Press Association in recognition of editorial excellence and three from *Computer Currents'* First Annual Readers' Choice Awards. Our best-selling *...For Dummies®* series has more than 30 million copies in print with translations in 30 languages. IDG Books Worldwide, through a joint venture with IDG's Hi-Tech Beijing, became the first U.S. publisher to publish a computer book in the People's Republic of China. In record time, IDG Books Worldwide has become the first choice for millions of readers around the world who want to learn how to better manage their businesses.

Our mission is simple: Every one of our books is designed to bring extra value and skill-building instructions to the reader. Our books are written by experts who understand and care about our readers. The knowledge base of our editorial staff comes from years of experience in publishing, education, and journalism — experience we use to produce books for the '90s. In short, we care about books, so we attract the best people. We devote special attention to details such as audience, interior design, use of icons, and illustrations. And because we use an efficient process of authoring, editing, and desktop publishing our books electronically, we can spend more time ensuring superior content and spend less time on the technicalities of making books.

You can count on our commitment to deliver high-quality books at competitive prices on topics you want to read about. At IDG Books Worldwide, we continue in the IDG tradition of delivering quality for more than 25 years. You'll find no better book on a subject than one from IDG Books Worldwide.

John Kilcullen
CEO
IDG Books Worldwide, Inc.

Steven Berkowitz
President and Publisher
IDG Books Worldwide, Inc.

Eighth Annual
Computer Press
Awards ≥ 1992

Ninth Annual
Computer Press
Awards ≥ 1993

Tenth Annual
Computer Press
Awards ≥ 1994

Eleventh Annual
Computer Press
Awards ≥ 1995

IDG Books Worldwide, Inc., is a subsidiary of International Data Group, the world's largest publisher of computer-related information and the leading global provider of information services on information technology. International Data Group publishes over 275 computer publications in over 75 countries. Sixty million people read one or more International Data Group publications each month. International Data Group's publications include: **ARGENTINA:** Buyer's Guide, Computerworld Argentina, PC World Argentina; **AUSTRALIA:** Australian Macworld, Australian PC World, Australian Reseller News, Computerworld, IT Casebook, Network World, Publish, Webmaster; **AUSTRIA:** Computerwelt Oesterreich, Networks Austria, PC Tip Austria; **BANGLADESH:** PC World Bangladesh; **BELARUS:** PC World Belarus; **BELGIUM:** Data News; **BRAZIL:** Annuário de Informática, Computerworld, Connections, Macworld, PC Player, PC World, Publish, Reseller News, Supergamepower; **BULGARIA:** Computerworld Bulgaria, Network World Bulgaria, PC & MacWorld Bulgaria; **CANADA:** CIO Canada, Client/Server World, ComputerWorld Canada, InfoWorld Canada, NetworkWorld Canada, WebWorld; **CHILE:** Computerworld Chile, PC World Chile; **COLOMBIA:** Computerworld Colombia, PC World Colombia; **COSTA RICA:** PC World Centro America; **THE CZECH AND SLOVAK REPUBLICS:** Computerworld Czechoslovakia, Macworld Czech Republic, PC World Czechoslovakia; **DENMARK:** Communications World Danmark, Computerworld Danmark, Macworld Danmark, PC World Danmark, Techworld Denmark; **DOMINICAN REPUBLIC:** PC World Republica Dominicana; **ECUADOR:** PC World Ecuador; **EGYPT:** Computerworld Middle East, PC World Middle East; **EL SALVADOR:** PC World Centro America; **FINLAND:** MikroPC, Tietoverkko, Tietoviikko; **FRANCE:** Distributique, Hebdo, Info PC, Le Monde Informatique, Macworld, Reseaux & Telecoms, WebMaster France; **GERMANY:** Computer Partner, Computerwoche, Computerwoche Extra, Computerwoche FOCUS, Global Online, Macwelt, PC Welt; **GREECE:** Amiga Computing, GamePro Greece, Multimedia World; **GUATEMALA:** PC World Centro America; **HONDURAS:** PC World Centro America; **HONG KONG:** Computerworld Hong Kong, PC World Hong Kong, Publish in Asia; **HUNGARY:** ABCD CD-ROM, Computerworld Szamitastechnika, Internetto online Magazine, PC World Hungary, PC-X Magazin Hungary; **ICELAND:** Tolvuheimur PC World Island; **INDIA:** Information Communications World, Information Systems Computerworld, PC World India, Publish in Asia; **INDONESIA:** InfoKomputer PC World, Komputek Computerworld, Publish in Asia; **IRELAND:** ComputerScope, PC Live!; **ISRAEL:** Macworld Israel, People & Computers/Computerworld; **ITALY:** Computerworld Italia, Macworld Italia, Networking Italia, PC World Italia; **JAPAN:** DTP World, Macworld Japan, Nikkei Personal Computing, OS/2 World Japan, SunWorld Japan, Windows NT World, Windows World Japan; **KENYA:** PC World East African; **KOREA:** Hi-Tech Information, Macworld Korea, PC World Korea; **MACEDONIA:** PC World Macedonia; **MALAYSIA:** Computerworld Malaysia, PC World Malaysia, Publish in Asia; **MALTA:** PC World Malta; **MEXICO:** Computerworld Mexico, PC World Mexico; **MYANMAR:** PC World Myanmar; **NETHERLANDS:** Computer! Totaal, LAN Internetworking Magazine, LAN World Buyers Guide, Macworld Netherlands, Net, WebWereld; **NEW ZEALAND:** Absolute Beginners Guide and Plain & Simple Series, Computer Buyer, Computer Industry Directory, Computerworld New Zealand, MTB, Network World, PC World New Zealand; **NICARAGUA:** PC World Centro America; **NORWAY:** Computerworld Norge, CW Rapport, Datamagasinet, Financial Rapport, Kursguide Norge, Macworld Norge, Multimediaworld Norge, PC World Ekspress Norge, PC World Nettverk, PC World Norge, PC World ProduktGuide Norge; **PAKISTAN:** Computerworld Pakistan; **PANAMA:** PC World Panama; **PEOPLE'S REPUBLIC OF CHINA:** China Computer Users, China Computerworld, China InfoWorld, China Telecom World Weekly, Computer & Communication, Electronic Design China, Electronics Today, Electronics Weekly, Game Software, PC World China, Popular Computer Week, Software Weekly, Software World, Telecom World; **PERU:** Computerworld Peru, PC World Profesional Peru, PC World SoHo Peru; **PHILIPPINES:** Click!, Computerworld Philippines, PC World Philippines, Publish in Asia; **POLAND:** Computerworld Poland, Computerworld Special Report Poland, Cyber, Macworld Poland, Networld Poland, PC World Komputer; **PORTUGAL:** Cerebro/PC World, Computerworld/Correio Informatico, Dealer World Portugal, Mac*In/PC*In Portugal, Multimedia World; **PUERTO RICO:** PC World Puerto Rico; **ROMANIA:** Computerworld Romania, PC World Romania, Telecom Romania; **RUSSIA:** Computerworld Russia, Mir PK, Publish, Seti; **SINGAPORE:** Computerworld Singapore, PC World Singapore, Publish in Asia; **SLOVENIA:** Monitor; **SOUTH AFRICA:** Computing SA, Network World SA, Software World SA; **SPAIN:** Communicaciones World España, Computerworld España, Dealer World España, Macworld España, PC World España; **SRI LANKA:** Infolink PC World; **SWEDEN:** CAP&Design, Computer Sweden, Corporate Computing Sweden, Internetworld Sweden, it.branschen, Macworld Sweden, MaxiData Sweden, MikroDatorn, Natverk & Kommunikation, PC World Sweden, PCaktiv, Windows World Sweden; **SWITZERLAND:** Computerworld Schweiz, Macworld Schweiz, PCtip; **TAIWAN:** Computerworld Taiwan, Macworld Taiwan, NEW ViSiON/Publish, PC World Taiwan, Windows World Taiwan; **THAILAND:** Publish in Asia, Thai Computerworld; **TURKEY:** Computerworld Turkiye, Macworld Turkiye, Network World Turkiye, PC World Turkiye; **UKRAINE:** Computerworld Kiev, Multimedia World Ukraine, PC World Ukraine; **UNITED KINGDOM:** Acorn User UK, Amiga Action UK, Amiga Computing UK, Apple Talk UK, Computing, Macworld, Parents and Computers UK, PC Advisor, PC Home, PSX Pro, The WEB UK; **UNITED STATES:** Cable in the Classroom, CIO Magazine, Computerworld, DOS World, Federal Computer Week, GamePro Magazine, InfoWorld, I-Way, Macworld, Network World, PC Games, PC World, Publish, Video Event, THE WEB Magazine, and WebMaster; online webzines: JavaWorld, NetscapeWorld, and SunWorld Online; **URUGUAY:** InfoWorld Uruguay; **VENEZUELA:** Computerworld Venezuela, PC World Venezuela; and **VIETNAM:** PC World Vietnam.   3/24/97

Dedication

For Jodie, Andy, Robyn, Dad, Cousin Nancy, and all my other friends and relatives with new Macs. Now you can stop calling me at all hours.

Author's Acknowledgments

Special thanks to my friends at Apple, who were there for me every step of the way: Tim "the shortstop" Holmes, Doedy Hunter, Keri Walker, and everyone on the Mac OS 8 development team; the Apple evangelists; and the Apple fellows. Thank you all. I couldn't have done it without your help.

Thanks also to superagent Carole "Swiftier-than-ever" McClendon of Waterside Productions, for dealmaking beyond the call of duty. You're a wonder!

Big-time thanks to the gang at IDG Books: Mike Kelly, Diane Steele, Milissa Koloski, and the big guy himself, John Kilcullen. Nobody does it better.

Extra special thanks to my editor, Tim "the Whipcracker" Gallan, who has been better than great.

Thanks to my family for putting up with my all-too-lengthy absences during this book's gestation.

And finally, thanks to you for buying it.

Publisher's Acknowledgments

We're proud of this book; please send us your comments about it by using the IDG Books Worldwide Registration Card at the back of the book or by e-mailing us at feedback/dummies@idgbooks.com. Some of the people who helped bring this book to market include the following:

Acquisitions, Development, and Editorial

Project Editor: Tim Gallan

Acquisitions Editor: Mike Kelly

Copy Editor: Felicity O'Meara

Technical Editor: Dennis R. Cohen

Editorial Manager: Leah P. Cameron

Editorial Assistant: Donna Love

Production

Project Coordinator: Valery Bourke

Layout and Graphics: Maridee V. Ennis, Todd Klemme, Drew R. Moore, Heather N. Pearson, Anna Rohrer, M. Anne Sipahimalani, Deirdre Smith

Proofreaders: Renee Kelty, Christine Berman, Kelli Botta, Michelle Croninger, Rachel Garvey, Nancy Price

Indexer: Sherry Massey

General and Administrative

IDG Books Worldwide, Inc.: John Kilcullen, CEO; Steven Berkowitz, President and Publisher

IDG Books Technology Publishing: Brenda McLaughlin, Senior Vice President and Group Publisher

Dummies Technology Press and Dummies Editorial: Diane Graves Steele, Vice President and Associate Publisher; Judith A. Taylor, Product Marketing Manager; Kristin A. Cocks, Editorial Director; Mary Bednarek, Acquisitions and Product Development Director

Dummies Trade Press: Kathleen A. Welton, Vice President and Publisher

IDG Books Production for Dummies Press: Beth Jenkins, Production Director; Cindy L. Phipps, Manager of Project Coordination, Production Proofreading, and Indexing; Kathie S. Schutte, Supervisor of Page Layout; Shelley Lea, Supervisor of Graphics and Design; Debbie J. Gates, Production Systems Specialist; Robert Springer, Supervisor of Proofreading; Debbie Stailey, Special Projects Coordinator; Tony Augsburger, Supervisor of Reprints and Bluelines; Leslie Popplewell, Media Archive Coordinator

Dummies Packaging and Book Design: Patti Sandez, Packaging Specialist; Lance Kayser, Packaging Assistant; Kavish + Kavish, Cover Design

◆

The publisher would like to give special thanks to Patrick J. McGovern, without whom this book would not have been possible.

◆

Contents at a Glance

Cartoons at a Glance

By Rich Tennant

page 219

page 343

page 135

page 377

page 5

Fax: 508-546-7747 • E-mail: the5wave@tiac.net

Table of Contents

· ·

Foreword

• •

Some people say that Apple's Mac OS 8 is just a pretty face on old software. Some people say Bob LeVitus is just a pretty face. This book conclusively proves both sets of people wrong.

Mac OS 8 adds cosmetic improvements to the best interface in personal computing, but it's what it adds under the skin that really makes it worth your time and money. There's a whole bunch of new functionality and speed. A lot more of the code is optimized for Power Macs. And as usual, Apple only sketches out the new features and power in their documentation. Fortunately, there's no one better at analyzing and explaining the works of Apple than Bob LeVitus.

Bob's name is a working definition for Not Dull. No matter where you run into Bob — in conversation, around the poker table, or in his writings about the Mac — you are not going to be bored. You will pay attention, not that he'll give you much of a choice. And that's good. His opinions tend to be provocative and well thought out, his poker playing skilled enough to empty your wallet if you're not both good and lucky, and his knowledge of the Mac and ability to communicate it to readers unparalleled.

You need this book because Apple manuals are Apple manuals; you won't get a lot of explanation or help from them. To get at the new power, you could hire a consultant, but that's expensive and not at all necessary: Just read this book. It's a wonderful guide to all of Mac OS 8.0.

Like its System 7.x cousins, this book, *Mac OS 8 For Dummies,* might be better called The Best Mac System Software Book Ever. Bobby has gone past his usually really good writing level here, and taken a dry subject (who really gets excited about an operating system? A game, sure; and maybe even that exceptional productivity application, but the system software?) and created a book that makes you want to learn and use this important advance in Mac software.

He's also achieved the difficult trick of writing a book that works for first-time users as well as power users who have been using Macs since January 1984. That's no mean accomplishment. I've been writing for and editing Mac magazines since 1985 firsthand and understand (and stand in awe of) the magnitude of Bobby's achievement here.

This book is not free; Apple manuals come with the product. Why buy this book? Why not stick with the oh-so-pretty Apple manuals? Surely, they have everything you're going find here? Well, no, that's not so. The Apple manuals are pretty. But readable? I don't think so. They're so dry that they should be declared a fire hazard. They're very full of themselves and at the same time so carefully worded that it seems certain their final editing was at the hands of Apple's legal staff.

They tell you the good parts, not the bad parts. And they'd choke before allowing that there are power tips that can really make you productive. Their "avoid all risks; take no shortcuts because it might not be perfectly 100-percent safe" approach means that the Apple manuals are incomplete.

You can't accuse *Mac OS 8 For Dummies* of being incomplete. It goes beyond the too-dry manuals and the too-brief magazine articles and tells you everything about Mac OS 8. After you digest it you have the choice of doing things the Apple manual way, or really using and enjoying your Mac.

Here's an example of manual dry versus Bob LeVitus: backing up. Apple tells you to do it. Period. Bobby tells you why you must back up frequently, the absolute best hardware and software tools, the tools to use if you can't afford the best tools, and the absolute need for multiple backup sets.

With wonderful and refreshing attitude for a person who didn't grow up (or even ever live) in New York, Bobby gets vital information like his instructions on backing right in your face. He's never been shy, and if something is important, he makes sure you get it.

The greatest strength of *Mac OS 8 For Dummies* is the breadth and depth of its content. Mac OS 8 opens a lot of new ground for Mac users and this book covers it all. You're not going to find a better helper as you move into Mac OS 8.

The second greatest strength of *Mac OS 8 For Dummies* is its solid dose of in-your-face attitude. This is a readable helper that cares. All too many computer books today are either chores to read or in a couple of cases, simply unreadable because they seem to think dry seriousness is a "business-like" virtue. They're wrong. Readability counts big-time, and *Mac OS 8 For Dummies* can be as hard to put down as the latest potboiler. You not only learn from it, but you enjoy the process.

Mac OS 8 For Dummies jumps right to the top of the class in Mac system software books. Any book that surpasses it is going to have to be awfully good. And it wouldn't surprise me if Bob LeVitus is the author.

Introduction

*Y*ou made the right choice twice: Mac OS 8 and this book.

Take a deep breath and get ready to have some fun. That's right. This is a computer book and it's going to be fun. What a concept! Whether you're brand spanking new to the Mac or a grizzled old Mac-vet, I guarantee that learning Mac OS 8 my way will be easy and fun. They couldn't say it on the cover if it weren't true!

Why a Book for Dummies?

Because there wasn't a *...For Dummies* book about the Mac OS (though *DOS For Dummies, Windows For Dummies,* and *Windows 95 For Dummies* are huge hits), and because the nice folks at IDG Books asked me if I wanted to write one. The result was the international bestseller *Macintosh System 7.5 For Dummies,* an award-winning book so good it was offered by Power Computing instead of a system software manual.

And now I'm back with the all-new, totally revised, *Mac OS 8 For Dummies,* which combines all the old, familiar features of my earlier book with totally updated information about the latest, greatest offering from Apple.

So why a *...For Dummies* book about Mac OS 8? Mac OS 8 is a big, complicated personal computer operating system. *Mac OS 8 For Dummies* is a not-so-big (about 9 x 7 inches and not very thick), not-very-complicated book that shows you what Mac OS 8 is all about without boring you, confusing you, or otherwise making you uncomfortable.

In fact, you'll be so darned comfortable that I wanted to call this book *Mac OS 8 Without The Discomfort* but they wouldn't let me. There are apparently some rules we *...For Dummies* authors have to follow, and using the word "Dummies" in the title is one of them.

And speaking of dummies, remember that it's just a word. I don't think you're dumb. Quite the opposite. I wanted to call this book *Mac OS 8 For People Smart Enough to Know They Need Help,* but you can just imagine what IDG Books thought of that. (If you're reading this in a bookstore, approach the cashier with your wallet in your hand, buy the book, and I'll think you're even smarter!)

This book is chock full of information and advice, explaining everything you need to know about Mac OS 8, plus how to do it and why, in language you'll understand.

It is supplemented with tips, tricks, techniques, and steps, served up in generous quantities. It all adds up to the only book in the world that makes learning Mac OS 8 both painless and fun. Can your beer do that?

How to Use This Book

We're gonna start off real slow. The first few chapters are where we get to know each other and discuss the basic everyday things you need to know to operate your Mac or Mac-compatible effectively.

The first part, in fact, is so basic it will probably bore you old-timers to tears. But hey, it's my sworn duty to show you all there is to know in the most painless manner possible. And I can't do that without a solid foundation. So long-time Mac users should feel free to skip through stuff they know to get to the better stuff faster.

A word of warning: If you skip over something important, like why you absolutely *must* back up your hard drive (see Appendix B), don't come crying to me when you lose all your valuable data in a horrendous disk crash. In other words, it's probably not a bad idea to read it all, even if you think you already know it all.

Another thing: We learn by doing. Perform the hands-on tutorials while sitting at your Mac. They're much less effective if you read them anywhere else.

Here are a couple of conventions I use in this book:

  ✓ When I refer to an item in a menu, I use something like File⇨Edit, which means "Pull down the File menu and choose the Edit command."

  ✓ For keyboard shortcuts, something like Command-A means hold down the Command key (the one with the little pretzel on it) and press the letter A on the keyboard. Command-Shift-A means hold down the Command and Shift keys while pressing the A key.

Finally, there are extensive cross-references throughout the book and a better-than-average index at the back. Use them freely.

How This Book Is Organized

Mac OS 8 For Dummies is divided into four logical parts, logically numbered parts one through four. It's better if you read them in order, but if you already know a lot or think you know a lot, feel free to skip around and read the parts that interest you.

Part I: Basic Training

The first part is very, very basic training. From the mouse to the desktop, from the menus to the tricky-for-beginners Open and Save dialog boxes, it's all here. Everything you need to know to operate Mac OS 8 safely and sanely. Old-timers can skim through it; you newbies should read every word. Twice.

Part II: Making It Purr

Here, I discuss hands-on stuff, with chapters on organizing, printing, sharing (files, that is), and memory management. By the time you finish Part II, your system will be a finely tuned and running like a champ.

Part III: U 2 Can B A Guru

Now we're cooking. This part is about how things work and how to make them work better.

Tips, tricks, techniques, control panels, scripts and much more, plus the most useful chapter in the whole book, Chapter 14, "What Can Stay and What Can Go," which details each and every gosh darn file in your System Folder and why you need it or don't. If your Mac runs like a champ after Part II, wait'll you see it after Part III.

Part IV: The Infamous Part of Tens

Last but not least, it's the Part of Tens, which is mostly a Letterman rip-off, though it does include heaping helpings of tips, troubleshooting hints, and optional software and hardware ideas.

And that retires the side . . . almost.

Icons Used in This Book

 Put on your propeller beanie hat and pocket protector. This is truly nerdy stuff. It's certainly not required reading, but it must be interesting or informative or I wouldn't have wasted the space.

Read these notes very, very, very carefully. Did I say "very?" Warning icons flag important information. The author and publisher will not be responsible if your Mac explodes or spews flaming parts because you ignored a Warning icon.

Just kidding. Macs don't explode or spew (with the exception of a few choice PowerBook 5300s). But it got your attention, didn't it? It's a good idea to read Warning notes carefully.

This is where you'll find the juiciest morsels: shortcuts, tips, and undocumented secrets. Try them all; impress your friends.

This icon warns you that a hands-on tutorial with step-by-step instructions is coming. It's best to be at your Mac when you read these and perform the steps as you read them.

Me, ranting or raving about something. Imagine foam coming from my mouth. Rants are required to be irreverent, irrelevant, or both. I also try to keep them short, more for your sake than mine.

Mac OS 8 is chock full of new features. For those of you old-timers out there who remember Mac OS 7.*x*, this icon will alert you to something you've not seen before.

One Last Thing

I'm thrilled at how this book came out — I think it's the best thing I've ever written. But I didn't write it for me. I wrote it for you and would love to hear how it worked for you. So please drop me a line or fill out the registration card at the back of the book for me.

Did it work for you? What did you like? What didn't you like? What questions were unanswered? Did you want to know more about something? Could you have stood to have learned less about something? Tell me!

You can send snail mail care of IDG Books (they'll see that I receive it), or send e-mail to me directly at LEVITUS@cis.compuserve.com

I appreciate your feedback and try to respond to all e-mail within a few days.

Bob LeVitus
Summer 1997

P.S. What are you waiting for? Go enjoy the book!

Part I
Basic Training

"Well, the first day wasn't bad—I lost the 'Finder', copied a file into the 'Trash' and sat on my mouse."

In this part . . .

Mac OS 8 sports tons of new goodies and features. I'll get to the hot new goodies soon enough, but you have to learn to crawl before you walk.

In this part, you discover the most basic of basics, such as the de rigueur-for-books-with-*Dummies*-in-the-title section on how to turn your Mac on (it's very short). Next I acquaint you with the Mac OS 8 desktop: icons, windows, menus, disks, and trash — the whole shmear.

So get comfortable, roll up your sleeves, fire up your Mac if you like, and settle down with Part I, a delightful little ditty I like to think of as "The Hassle-Free Way to Get Started with Mac OS 8."

Chapter 1

Mac OS 8 101
(Prerequisites: None)

. . . .

In This Chapter

▶ What is Mac OS 8?

▶ A safety net for beginners

▶ A pop quiz on mousing

▶ Acronyms you can use to impress your friends

▶ The startup process revealed

. . . .

Choosing Mac OS 8 was a good move. It's more than just a System software upgrade; Mac OS 8 includes dozens of new or improved features that make using your Macintosh easier, and dozens more that help you do more work in less time. In other words, it'll make you more productive, give you fewer headaches, reduce your cholesterol level, and make you fall in love with your Mac all over again.

I know you're chomping at the bit, but we're going to start at the very beginning. This chapter mostly talks about Mac OS 8 in abstract terms. Don't bother to turn your Mac on yet, as there's no hands-on stuff here. What you'll find is a bunch of very important stuff that will save the beginner from a lot of headaches.

If you already know what System software is and does, how to avoid disasters, what a startup disk is, and how the startup process works, I suggest you read those sections anyway — to refresh your memory — and skim the rest.

Everyone else: Please read every word.

What Is System Software?

Along with the code in its read-only memory (ROM), the System software (often called the *operating system* or *Mac OS*) is what makes a Mac a Mac. Without it, your Mac is a pile of silicon and circuits, no smarter than a toaster. It's got a brain (ROM), it's got memory (RAM), and it's got ten fingers and toes (other stuff), but it doesn't know what to do with itself. Think of System software as an education, and Mac OS 8 as an Ivy League education. (A PC clone with DOS or Windows dropped outta high school in the 10th grade and flips burgers for a living.)

With Mac OS 8, your Mac becomes an elegant, powerful tool that's the envy of the rest of the computer industry. (Or so we Macintosh lovers like to think!)

Most of the world's personal computers use either DOS or Windows. Poor schmucks. You're among the lucky few with a computer whose operating system is intuitive, easy to use, and, dare I say, fun. Windows — even Windows 95 — is a cheap imitation of the Macintosh System software. Try it sometime. Go ahead. You probably won't suffer any permanent damage. In fact, you'll really begin to appreciate how good you've got it. Feel free to hug your Mac or give it a peck on the floppy drive opening. Just try not to get your tongue caught.

What Does System Software Do?

Good question. It controls the basic (and most important) operations of your computer. In the case of Mac OS 8 and your Mac, the System software manages memory; controls how windows, icons, and menus work; keeps track of files; and does lots of other housekeeping chores. Other forms of software, such as a word processor, rely on the System software to create and maintain the environment in which the application software does its work.

When you create a memo, for example, the word processor provides the tools for you to type and format the information. The System software provides the mechanism for drawing and moving the window in which you write the memo; it keeps track of the file when you save it; it helps the word processor create drop-down menus and dialog boxes and communicate with other programs; and much, much more.

Now you have a little background in System software. Before you do anything else with your Mac, take a gander at the next section.

A Safety Net for the Absolute Beginner — or Any User

If you're a first-time Macintosh user, please, please read this section of the book very carefully. It could save your life. Well, now I'm just being overly dramatic. *It could save your Mac* is what I meant to say. I deal with the stuff that the manual that came with your Mac doesn't cover in nearly enough detail, if at all. If you're an experienced Mac user, read this section anyway. Chances are, you need a few reminders.

✔ **If you don't know how to turn your Mac on, get help.** Don't feel bad. Apple, in its infinite wisdom, has manufactured Macs with power-on switches on every conceivable surface: the front, side, back, and the keyboard. Some Macs (most PowerBooks) even hide the power-on button behind a little plastic door.

In *Macs For Dummies,* David Pogue devotes several pages to locating the on switch for every current model of Macintosh. If you're having trouble, it'll be worth your while to check out the latest edition of his book. Or you can always look in the manual that came with your Mac.

Like personal fouls in the NBA, authors are only allowed so many weasel-outs per book. I hate to use one so early, but in this case, I think it's worth it for both of us. I promise this is the first and only time I'll say, "Look in the manual." Maybe.

✔ **Always use the Shut Down (Special menu) command,** or press the Power key once and then click the Shut Down button, to turn off your Mac. Turning the power off without shutting your Mac down properly is one of the worst things you can do to your poor Mac. It can screw up your hard disk real bad, or scramble the contents of your most important files, or both.

Of course, most of us have broken this rule several times without anything horrible happening. Don't be lulled into a false sense of security. Do it one time too many and your most important file will be toast.

Mac OS 8 actually scolds you if you don't shut down properly. If you break this rule, the next time your Mac is turned on, it will politely inform you that your Mac was shut down improperly, as shown in Figure 1-1.

If you find the little "This Mac was shut down improperly" reminder annoying, you can turn it off in the General Controls control panel. I actually like it and leave the warning enabled. You should too.

Figure 1-1:
Polite little
machines,
aren't they?

✔ **Don't unplug your Mac when it's turned on.** See my blurb in the preceding bullet.

✔ **Don't use your Mac when lightning is near.** Lightning strike = dead Mac. 'Nuff said. Oh, and don't place much faith in inexpensive surge protectors. A good jolt of lightning will fry the surge protector right along with your computer. There *are* surge protectors that can withstand most lightning strikes, but they're not the cheapies you buy at your local computer emporium. Unplugging your Mac from the wall during electrical storms is safer and less expensive. (Don't forget to unplug your modem as well — lightning can fry it, too.)

✔ **Don't jostle, bump, shake, kick, throw, dribble, or punt your Mac, especially while it's running.** Unless your Mac is ancient, it contains within it a hard disk drive that spins at 5,400+ rpm. A jolt to a hard disk while it's reading or writing a file can cause the head to crash into the disk, which can render many or all the files on it totally and irreversibly unrecoverable.

✔ **Turn off your Mac before plugging or unplugging any cables.** This advice may be overkill, as even Apple seems to say that you can safely plug cables into the serial ports — the modem or printer ports — while your Mac is turned on. But other cables, specifically SCSI cables and ADB cables, should never under any circumstances be plugged or unplugged without first shutting down your Mac.

Okay, that about does it for bad stuff that can happen. If something bad has already happened to you, see Chapter 18.

What You Should See After Turning the Power On

After a small bit of whirring, buzzing, and flashing (the System software is loading) you should see a cheerful little happy Mac in the middle of your screen like the one in Figure 1-2.

Figure 1-2:
The Mac
startup
icon. Cute
as puke,
isn't it?

Soon thereafter comes a soothing blue Mac OS logo, with the message "Welcome to Mac OS 8," followed by "Loading" and the infamous march of the icons across the bottom of the screen. Makes you feel kind of warm and fuzzy, doesn't it? These things indicate that Mac OS 8 is loading properly.

This might be a good time to take a moment to think good thoughts about whoever convinced you that you wanted a Mac. They were right.

A pop quiz on mousing

For those of you who need to hone your mousing skills, here's a little quiz.

1. How do you select an icon on the desktop?

    A. Stare at it intently for five seconds.

    B. Point to it with your finger, slap the side of your monitor, and say "That one, stupid!"

    C. Move the mouse pointer on top of the icon and click once.

2. When do you need to double-click?

    A. Whenever you find yourself saying, "There's no place like home."

    B. When you're using both hands to control the mouse.

    C. When you want to open a file or folder.

3. How do you select multiple items or blocks of text?

    A. Get several people to stare intently at the items you want to select.

    B. You need to attach multiple mice to your Mac.

    C. Slide the mouse on your desk, moving the on-screen pointer to the location where you want to begin selecting. Press and hold down the mouse button. Drag the pointer across the items or text that you want to select. Then let go of the mouse button.

4. How do you move a selected item?

    A. Call U-Haul.

    B. Pick up and tilt your monitor until the item slides to the proper location.

    C. Click the item and hold down the mouse button. With the mouse button still held down, drag the pointer to the new location and let go of the mouse button.

If you haven't figured it out by now, the correct answer to each of these questions is C. If any other answer sounded remotely plausible for you, sit down with your Mac and just play with it for a while. If you have kids at your disposal, watch them play with your Mac. They'll be showing you how to use it in no time.

Anyway, in a few more seconds, the familiar Macintosh desktop will materialize before your eyes. If you haven't customized, configured, or done any other tinkering, your desktop should look something like Figure 1-3. Don't worry if you don't see a desktop printer icon on your desktop (mine is named HP LaserJet 4ML); I cover desktop printers in Chapter 7. And don't worry if you don't see a little control strip hanging out near the bottom of your screen; I cover the ingenious control strip in Chapter 12.

In the unlikely event you didn't see the smiling Mac, soothing messages, and familiar desktop, read the next section — "What's Happening Here?" — very carefully. If this section doesn't set things right, skip to Chapter 18.

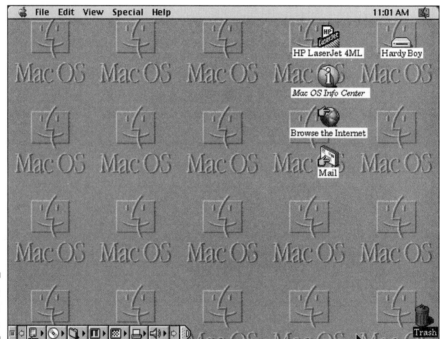

Figure 1-3:
The Mac desktop.

What's Happening Here? (The Startup Process Revealed)

When you turn on your Macintosh, you set in motion a sophisticated and complex series of events that culminates in the loading of Mac OS 8 and the appearance of the familiar Mac desktop. Fortunately, the mechanics of the process are unimportant. In brief, your Mac tests all your hardware — slots, ports, disks, memory (RAM), and so on. If everything passes, you hear a pleasing chord and see the happy Mac, the Mac OS logo, "Welcome to Mac OS 8," and "Loading" on your monitor as your Mac loads the System software it needs from disk to RAM.

You're not a failure

If any of your hardware fails when it is tested, you'll see a black screen with the dreaded Sad Mac icon (see Figure 1-4) and hear a far less pleasing musical chord known by Mac aficionados as the Chimes of Doom. The fact that something went wrong is no reflection on your prowess as a Macintosh user. Something inside your Mac is broken, and it probably needs to go in for repairs (usually to an Apple dealer). If it's under warranty, dial 1-800-SOS-APPL and they'll tell you what to do.

Before you do anything, though, skip ahead to Chapter 18. It's entirely possible that one of the suggestions there will get you back on track without your having to spend even a moment on hold.

Figure 1-4:
The Sad Mac icon: Look upon this face, ye mighty, and despair!

Question Mark and the Mysterians

Although it's unlikely that you'll see a sad Mac, all users eventually encounter the flashing question mark (shown in Figure 1-5) in place of the usual happy Mac at some time in their lives. Don't worry. This one is a breeze. This icon means that your Mac can't find a *startup disk:* a floppy disk, hard disk, or CD-ROM containing valid System software.

Figure 1-5:
Your Mac is
having an
identity
crisis if you
see this
icon.

When you turn on your Mac, the first thing it does (after the aforementioned hardware tests) is check the floppy disk drive for a startup disk (something with Mac OS 8 on it). If it doesn't find one there, it scans the SCSI bus. At this point, your Mac usually finds your hard disk, which contains a System Folder, and the startup process continues on its merry way with the happy Mac and all the rest.

Think of the flashing question mark as your Mac's way of saying, "Please provide me with a disk that contains some System software."

If Apple can figure out a way to put a flashing question mark on the screen, why the heck can't the software engineers find a way to put the words "Please insert a startup disk" on the screen as well. The curtness of the flashing question mark is one of my pet peeves about the Macintosh.

I know, you're clever and smart (you're reading *Mac OS 8 For Dummies*, aren't you?), so you know that a flashing question mark means that you should insert a startup disk. But what about everyone else?

Get with the program, Apple.

The ultimate startup disks

Chances are you have a copy of the ultimate startup floppy right there on your computer table. It's called Disk Tools, and it's one of the disks that you get with most versions of Mac OS. If you've got a flashing question mark, pop Disk Tools into your floppy drive and your Mac will boot, just like magic.

Or, if your Mac (or System software upgrade) didn't include floppy disks, it instead included a bootable CD-ROM disk. To boot from a CD-ROM you need to hold down the C key during startup on most Mac models. If that doesn't work, try holding down these four keys in the infamous four-finger salute: Delete-Option-Command-Shift.

The legend of the boot

Boot this. Boot that. "I booted my Mac and . . ." "Did it boot?" It seems nearly impossible to talk about computers for long without hearing the word.

But why boot? Why not shoe or shirt or even shazam?

It all began in the very olden days, maybe the 1970s or a little earlier, when starting up a computer required you to toggle little manual switches on the front panel, which began an internal process that loaded the operating system. The process became known as *boot-strapping* because if you toggled the right switches, the computer would "pull itself up by the bootstraps." It didn't take long for the phrase to transmogrify into *booting* and *boot*.

Over the years, booting has come to mean turning on almost any computer or even a peripheral device like a printer. Some people also use it to refer to launching an application: "I booted Excel."

So the next time one of your gearhead friends says the b-word, ask if he or she knows where the term comes from. Then dazzle your friend with the depth and breadth of your knowledge.

A good way to remember this keyboard combination — which is generally used to start up from a disk other than your internal hard drive, including a bootable CD-ROM — is to think of the mnemonic device DOCS (Delete-Option-Command-Shift).

Disk Tools or a bootable System software CD make the ultimate startup disks because, in addition to a System and Finder (the two files that must be present on a startup disk), they also have copies of Disk First Aid, Apple HD SC Setup, and Drive Setup, three programs that you may need if you see a flashing question mark. Disk First Aid can repair hidden damage to your hard disk; HD SC Setup or Drive Setup can install new hard disk drivers. Both Disk First Aid and Apple HD SC Setup/Drive Setup are described more completely in Chapter 18, and Apple HD SC Setup and Drive Setup are described in Appendix A.

Now what?

So you've gotten your Mac to boot from the Disk Tools disk or System Software CD-ROM but there's still this little problem. Like you'd prefer that your Mac boot from your (much faster) hard disk than that piddly little Disk Tools floppy or System software CD-ROM. Not to worry. All you need to do is reinstall Mac OS 8 (see Appendix A).

Those of you who are going to upgrade from System 7.*x* to Mac OS 8 may want to read Appendix A right about now. The rest of you, the ones whose Macs have already booted from a hard drive with Mac OS 8 installed, can breathe a sigh of relief and skip ahead to the next chapter.

How do you know which version of the Mac OS your computer has? Simple. Just pull down the Apple menu and choose About This Computer, the very first choice in the list. A window will pop up in the middle of your screen (see Figure 1-6). In the upper-right corner of this window you'll find the version number of your System software. As you can see, the About This Computer window not only tells you the version number of the Mac OS you're using, but also details your RAM usage. (You'll find out more about RAM usage and memory in Chapter 9.)

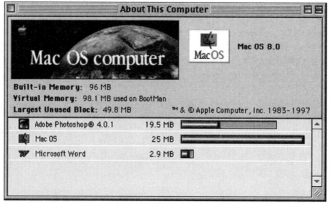

Figure 1-6:
I'm using
Mac OS
Version 8.0.
Look. It
says so
right there
in the
corner!

One Last Thing Before We Move On . . .

If the stuff on your hard disk means anything to you, you must back it up. Not maybe. You must. Which is why I recommend you read Appendix B right now instead of later. Unlike an earlier section in this chapter, Appendix B is a safety net for everyone. Before you do any significant work on your Mac (or even if your most important file is your last saved game of Marathon Infinity), you need to realize how important it is to back up.

Dr. Macintosh sez, "There are only two kinds of Mac users — those who have never lost data, and those who will." Which kind will you be?

I beg you: Please read Appendix B now, before something horrible happens to your valuable data.

Chapter 2
Meet the Desktop

. . . .

In This Chapter

▶ Using icons

▶ Using windows

▶ A treatise on folder management

. . . .

*T*his is where we get down to the nitty-gritty; this is the chapter about the
Macintosh desktop. Your desktop is the center of your Macintosh
universe. Just about everything you do on your Mac begins and ends with
the desktop. The desktop is where you manage files, store documents,
launch programs, adjust the way your Mac works, and much more. If you
ever expect to master your Mac, the first step is to master the desktop.

Once again, those of you who have been using Mac OS for a while may find
some of the information presented in this chapter repetitive; many of the
features discussed in this chapter are unchanged from earlier versions of
System 7. Still, you'd be foolish to skip it completely. If you do, I assure you
you'll miss sarcasm, clever wordplay, shortcuts, awesome techniques, a bad
pun or two, and lots of good advice on making the desktop an easier place
to be. If that's not enough to convince you, there's also a bunch of stuff
Apple didn't bother to tell you. (Like you read the manual anyway. . . .)

Tantalized? Let's rock.

I Think ICON, I Think ICON

Icons, those funny little pictures on your desktop and in your windows,
represent containers, and these containers hold things that you work with
on your Mac, like programs, documents, System software items, discarded
files (the Trash icon), and more. All icons appear on your screen as little
pictures with their names attached.

The first icon you should become familiar with is the icon for your hard disk. It's in the upper-right corner and is named Macintosh HD unless you've renamed it (see Figure 2-1). I've renamed mine Hardy Boy as a tribute to Frank and Joe.

Figure 2-1:
A plain vanilla hard disk icon.

The look you want to know better

Icons come in all shapes and sizes. After you've been around the Macintosh for a while, you get a kind of sixth sense about what an icon contains just by looking at it. For example, application (that is, program) icons are often diamond shaped. Unless, of course, they're rectangular or square or oddly shaped (see Figure 2-2).

Figure 2-2:
Application icons come in many different shapes.

Okay, so application icons are all over the place. Document icons, on the other hand, are almost always reminiscent of a piece of paper (as shown in Figure 2-3).

Figure 2-3:
Typical document icons.

See? You're already acquiring that sixth sense. Application icons are all over the place; document icons look like paper. Kind of.

Now let's talk about the four kinds of icons: application, document, folder, and System software.

(There are actually five kinds of icons. Aliases are an icon type in their own right. But I'm trying to keep things simple; I discuss these most excellent icons soon enough. Like in the very next chapter.)

Applications are programs, the software that you use to accomplish tasks on your Mac. Your word processor is an application. So are America Online and Prodigy. Titanic: Adventure Out of Time and Marathon are applications (they're also great games).

Documents are files created by applications. Letter to Mom, which you created in ClarisWorks, is a document. So are Bob's Calendar and Expense Report.

Folders are the Mac's organizational containers. You put icons, usually application or document icons, into folders. You can also put folders inside other folders. Folders look like, well, folders. Some folder icons have pictures; most don't (see Figure 2-4).

Figure 2-4:
Typical
folder
icons.

System software is the stuff in your System Folder — the System, the Finder, control panels, extensions, and almost everything else. The files that make up your System software have many purposes, most of which will be second nature to you by the end of this book. For now, I'll just talk about the icons, though.

System software icons usually have a distinctive look as well. For example, the System and Finder have distinctive, Mac-flavored icons (see Figure 2-5).

Figure 2-5:
The System
and Finder
icons.

Control panel icons usually have a slider bar at the bottom or on one side (as illustrated in Figure 2-6).

Figure 2-6:
Control
panel icons
generally
have a
slider bar.

Appearance   Control Strip   AppleTalk

Extension icons usually look like jigsaw puzzle parts (see Figure 2-7).

Figure 2-7:
Extension
icons
usually
display a
puzzled
look.

EM Extension   Apple CD-ROM   QuickTime™

But that's where the metaphor breaks down. The rest of your System software icons may look like just about anything (see Figure 2-8).

Figure 2-8:
Other
System
software
icons may
look like
almost
anything.

AppleShare   OpenTransportLib   Audio CD Access

There's lots more to be said about all of these kinds of icons, and I'll do so in upcoming chapters. But that's enough about what icons look like. I'm sure you're anxious to do something with icons already.

Open sesame

There are three ways to open any icon. (Okay, there are four ways, but, as I said, I'm saving aliases for later. You don't need to know just yet.) Anyway, here are the ways:

✔ Click the icon once to select it; then point to the File menu (it's the one that says File) and press the word File. Remember, a press is half a click. Don't release the mouse button yet. A menu drops down. Move the pointer downward until the word Open is highlighted (see Figure 2-9).

Figure 2-9:
Selecting
the Open
command.

(I probably could have saved a whole paragraph by simply saying "Choose File⇨Open." But you may have been pulling down a menu for the first time. I wanted to be safe.) The icon opens.

By the way, in case you hadn't noticed, I just showed you how to choose an item from a menu. Don't go hog-wild. There's lots more to know about menus, but it's in the next chapter. In fact, all of Chapter 3 is about menus.

✔ Double-click the icon by clicking it directly twice in rapid succession. If it doesn't open, you double-clicked too slowly.

✔ Select the icon and then use the keyboard shortcut Command-O. That means you press the Command key, the one with the pretzel and the apple on most keyboards, and then press the O key while continuing to hold down the Command key.

If you look at Figure 2-9, you'll see that the keyboard shortcut appears on the menu after the word Open. Pretzel-O. Any menu item with one of these pretzel-letter combinations after its name can be executed with that keyboard shortcut. Just press the pretzel (Command) key and the letter shown in the menu — Command and N for New Folder, Command and F for Find, and so on — and the appropriate command is executed.

It's never too soon to learn good habits, so I'll mention here that experienced Macintosh users use the keyboard shortcuts as often as possible. Keyboard shortcuts let you get things done without opening the menu, which means that you don't have to reach for the mouse, which means that you get more done in less time. It's a good idea to memorize shortcuts for menu items you use frequently.

Although the letters next to the Command-key symbol (I'm done calling it a pretzel now) in the Finder's menus are capital letters, you don't have to press the Shift key to use the keyboard shortcut. Command-P means hold down the Command key and press P. Some programs have keyboard combinations that require the use of Command-Shift, but these programs let you know by calling the key combination something like Command-Shift-S or Command-Shift-O. You don't have to worry about the capitalization of the letter.

The name game

Icon, icon, bo-bicon, banana fanna fo ficon. Bet that you can change the name of any old icon. Here are two ways:

  ✔ Click the icon's name directly. Don't forget to release the mouse button.

  ✔ Click the icon and then press the Return or Enter key on your keyboard once.

Either of these ways selects the icon's *name* and puts a box around it, waiting for you to type (see Figure 2-10).

Figure 2-10:
You can
change an
icon's name
by simply
typing a
new one;
when the
name is
highlighted,
as shown,
just start
typing.

In addition to selecting the name, the cursor changes from a pointer to a text-editing I-beam. An I-beam cursor is your Mac's way of telling you that it's okay to type now. At this point, if you click the I-beam cursor anywhere within the name box, you can edit the icon's original name. If you don't click and just begin typing, the icon's original name is completely replaced by what you type.

If you've never changed an icon's name, give it a try.

And don't forget: If you click the icon itself, the icon will be selected and you won't be able to change its name. (Selecting the icon itself enables you to move, copy, print, or open it, but we're getting ahead of ourselves.) If you do this, press Return or Enter to edit the name of the icon.

Other various and sundry icons

Before I get off the subject of icons completely, and because this is the chapter where you meet your desktop, I'd be remiss if I didn't mention a couple of other icons that you'll probably find there. The most important of these is . . .

The Trash

The Trash is a special container where you put the icons you no longer want on your hard or floppy disk. Got four copies of SimpleText on your hard disk? Drag three of them to the Trash. Old letters that you don't want to keep? Drag them to the Trash as well. To put an icon in the Trash, drag it on top of the Trash icon. When the tip (cool people call it the *hot spot*) of the pointer is directly over the Trash icon, the icon inverts (as shown in Figure 2-11).

Figure 2-11:
Takin'
out the
garbage.

When the Trash inverts, release the mouse button and, voilà, whatever you dragged to the Trash is trashed. But it's not gone forever until . . .

. . . you choose Special⇨Empty Trash. You know how the garbage in the can in your kitchen sits there until the sanitation engineers come by and pick it up each Thursday? The Mac OS Trash works the same. When you put something in the Trash, it sits there until you choose the Special⇨Empty Trash command.

You can also use Mac OS 8's new contextual menu⇨Empty Trash command by putting your cursor directly over the Trash icon and holding down the Control key on your keyboard as you click. You should see a menu like the one shown in Figure 2-12.

Figure 2-12:
Emptying the
Trash the
contextual
menu way
(hold
down the
Control key
when you
click the
Trash icon).

Think twice before you invoke Empty Trash. Once the Trash has been emptied, the files it contained are gone forever. Figure 2-13 shows what a full and empty trash can looks like. (Of course, you read Appendix B and you've backed up your hard disk several times, right? So even though the files are gone forever from your hard disk, you can get them back if you like, right?)

Figure 2-13:
Empty trash
can on the
left; full
and bulging
trash can
on the right.

There are utility programs available that let you retrieve a trashed file after you empty the Trash. Norton Utilities and the recently discontinued MacTools are the two most popular. They don't have a 100-percent success rate, so you should still consider the Empty Trash command fatal to files.

What the heck's the Finder, anyway?

You may have noticed that I use the words *Finder* and *desktop* interchangeably. As you probably know, the Finder is one of the files in your System Folder. The Finder is super-program. Among other things, it creates the desktop metaphor — the icons, windows, and menus that make up the Macintosh desktop. Unlike with ordinary programs, you can never quit the Finder. Like Katz's Deli, the Finder never closes. And unlike with ordinary programs, you don't have to open the Finder to use it. The Finder is always open; it opens automatically when you turn on your Mac.

Because the Finder is, among other things, responsible for creating the desktop and its menus, many people, myself included, use the words *Finder* and *desktop* interchangeably. You can too.

The only time it gets confusing is when you are talking about the Finder icon in your System Folder. Just say "the Finder icon" instead of "the Finder" and you'll sound like a pro. It can also be confusing when you're talking about the background you see on your screen (mine is Mac OS wallpaper), which is also called the desktop.

As with all icons, you can open the Trash (you know at least three ways to open an icon) to see what's in there. You can tell there's something in the Trash because the Trash icon bulges when it's full (as shown in Figure 2-13).

If you drag an icon that's *locked* to the Trash, you'll see a message telling you to hold down the Option key when you choose Special⇨Empty Trash to delete locked items. (To unlock locked icons, select the icon and then choose File⇨Get Info or its keyboard shortcut, Command-I, and then click the little box marked "locked.")

Close encounters of the icon kind

If you've used System 7.5, Mac OS 7.6, or Mac OS 8 for very long, you've probably encountered a couple of other icons. You've probably got an icon for a desktop printer on your desktop, which you can see in Figure 2-14.

Each Desktop Printer icon represents one printer available to your Mac or one set of printer-specific settings (scale, tile, crop, and so on). You may even have more than one Desktop Printer icon. If you don't have even one, don't fret. You'll make one soon (in Chapter 7).

If you performed a full install of Mac OS 8, you will see three other icons on your desktop: Mac OS Info Center, Browse the Internet, and Mail (see Figure 2-14).

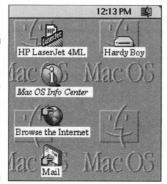

Figure 2-14:
Mac OS 8's
three new
desktop
icons with
my desktop
printer icon
above them.

Mac OS Info Center is worth exploring. If you haven't checked it out yet, I highly recommend it. Opening the Mac OS Info Center icon launches the included Web browser, Netscape Navigator, and also provides detailed information about the things you can do with Mac OS (see Figure 2-15). The Info Center also helps you solve problems and helps you explore the Internet if you have an Internet connection.

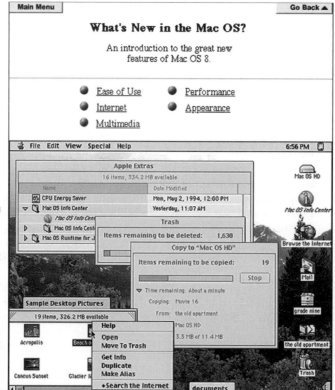

Figure 2-15:
You can
learn a lot
about Mac
OS 8 by
exploring
Mac OS
Info Center.
So what
are you
waiting for?

I cover Mac OS 8's amazing Internet capabilities as well as more about the Browse the Internet and Mail icons in Chapter 15, "InterNetWorking."

If you have any other icons on your desktop, ignore them for now. They probably won't hurt anything.

Windows (Definitely Not the Microsoft Kind)

Windows are such a fundamental part of the Macintosh experience that Microsoft blatantly ripped off the name for their operating system add-on.

Do your friends a favor. Before they buy a personal computer, make sure they know that Windows is not a Mac, regardless of what the lousy salesperson at the computer store says.

If you're relatively new to the Mac, you might want to read this section while sitting at your computer, trying the techniques as you read them. I've always found it easier to remember something that I read if I actually do it. If you've been abusing your Mac for a while, you've probably figured out how windows work by now, but there's still some stuff in here you may not have tried. Your mileage may vary.

Doin' windows

Windows are a ubiquitous part of Macintosh computing. Windows on the desktop show you the contents of disk and folder icons; windows in applications usually show you the contents of your documents.

You've already learned three different ways to open an icon, so you know how to open a window. When you open a window, its icon turns fuzzy gray (see Figure 2-16), which is your Mac's way of letting you know that that icon's window is open. Clever, eh?

Figure 2-16: A fuzzy gray (that is, open) icon.

Zooming right along . . .

Notice how the Macintosh HD window in Figure 2-17 says "9 Items" near the top, but only one item seems to be showing. That's easily remedied. To make a window larger, click the *zoom box,* one of the two boxes in the upper-right corner of most windows (circled in Figure 2-18). This action will cause the window to grow, which should reveal the rest of its contents.

Figure 2-17:
This window says that it contains nine items, but you only see one. What gives?

Figure 2-18:
When you click the zoom box in the upper-right corner of the window (circled at left), the window expands to show all the items it contains (right).

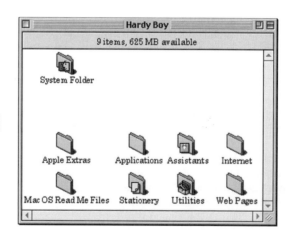

I say "should" because if a window contains more icons than the window can display, it will grow as large as it can and still leave room for your disk and Trash icons on the right side of the screen when you click the zoom box.

Click the zoom box again to return the window to its original size.

That shady window feeling . . .

If you want to collapse the window so just its title bar shows (Figure 2-19), either double-click in the title bar or click the windowshade box (circled in Figure 2-19).

Figure 2-19:
Clicking the window-
shade box
shrinks the
window so
just its title
bar shows.

Click the windowshade box again to return the window to its original size.

This little trick required a control panel known as WindowShade in earlier versions of the Mac OS. It's now integrated into Mac OS 8.

Cutting windows down to size

Another way to see more of what's in a window is by using the *sizer* in the lower-right corner. It's shown in Figure 2-20 on the left. Click the sizer and drag downward and to the right to make the window larger, as shown on the right in Figure 2-20. You use the sizer to make a window whatever size you like.

Figure 2-20:
Click and
drag the
sizer
(detailed at
left) and
then drag
down and
to the right
to make a
window
larger (as
shown on
the right).

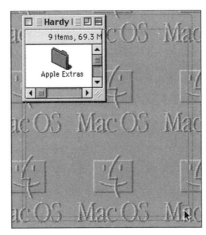

Notice the faint white lines when you drag; they're there to show you the size the window will be when you release the mouse button. Go ahead and give it a try; it's fun, it's easy, and it's free.

A scroll new world

Yet another way to see more of what is in a window is to *scroll*. You scroll using *scroll bars*, which appear on the bottom and right sides of any window that contains more icons than those that you can see in the window (see Figure 2-21).

There are four ways to scroll:

Way #1: Click a *scroll box* and drag, as shown in Figure 2-22.

Way #2: Click a *scroll arrow,* as shown in Figure 2-23.

Way #3: Click in the gray *scroll bar* area, as shown in Figure 2-24.

If the scroll bar is white, then there are no items to scroll to — everything that the window contains is visible.

Clicking the gray scroll *bar* scrolls the window a lot; clicking a scroll *arrow* scrolls the window a little; and pressing and dragging the scroll *box* scrolls the window an amount that corresponds to how far you drag it.

Way #4: Use the keyboard. Select an icon in the window first and then use the arrow keys to move up, down, left, or right. Using an arrow key selects the next icon in that direction and automatically scrolls the window if necessary.

You can also press the Tab key on the keyboard to select the next icon alphabetically. So if I clicked SimpleText and then pressed the Tab key, the System Folder (the icon that comes next alphabetically) would be selected. If the System Folder wasn't showing when I selected SimpleText, the Hardy Boy window would scroll automatically to reveal the System Folder after I pressed the Tab key.

For what it's worth, the Page Up and Page Down keys on extended key-boards function the same as clicking the gray scroll bar area (the vertical scroll bar only) in the Finder and many applications. But these keys don't work at all in some programs, so don't get too dependent on them.

Figure 2-21:
Scroll bars.

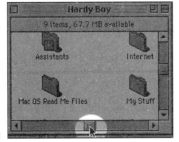

Figure 2-22:
You can
scroll by
clicking and
dragging a
scroll box.

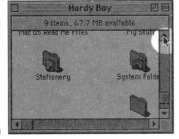

Figure 2-23:
You can
also scroll
by pressing
a scroll
arrow.

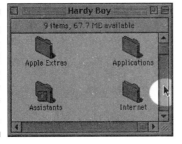

Figure 2-24:
You can
also scroll
by clicking
in the gray
scroll bar
area.

Transportable windows

To move a window, click anywhere in the *title bar* (shown in Figure 2-25) and drag the window to its new location. Figure 2-26 shows an example of moving a window by dragging its title bar. The title bar is the striped bar at the top of the active window. It contains the window's name, as well as the close box and the zoom box.

Figure 2-25:
A title bar.

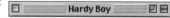

The window moves to its new position as soon as you release the mouse button.

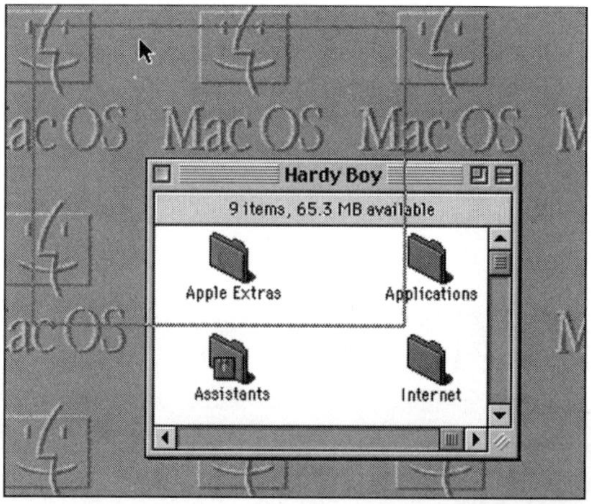

Figure 2-26:
Click and drag the title bar to move a window to a new location.

Now with Mac OS 8, you can also move a window by clicking on any side of it. Figure 2-27 shows all the places you can click and drag to move a window.

Just below the title bar is the window's *status line,* which tells you the number of items the window contains (9), and the amount of space available on this hard disk (65.3MB).

Figure 2-27:
Click and
drag any
edge of a
window, or
its title bar,
to move it
to a new
location.

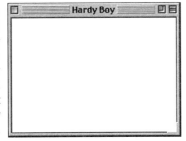

Ladies and gentlemen, activate your windows

In order to work with a window, the window must be active. Only one window at a time may be the *active window*. To make a window active, click it anywhere — in the middle, on the title bar, on a scroll bar. It doesn't matter where.

The active window is always the frontmost window, and inactive windows always appear behind the active window. The active window's title bar has black lines; its size, zoom, and close boxes are defined, as are its scroll bars. Inactive windows show the window's name but none of those other distinctive window features. See Figure 2-28 for an illustration of active and inactive windows.

Figure 2-28:
An active
window in
front of an
inactive
window;
notice how
the active
window's
features —
scroll bars
and boxes,
close box,
title bar,
and so
on — are
clearly
defined.

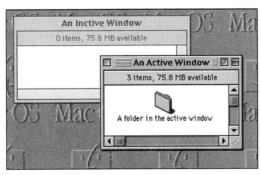

Shutting yo' windows

Now that you know just about all there is to know about windows, I suppose I ought to tell you how to close them. Here we go again with the ways. There are four ways to close an active window:

Way #1: Click the *close box* in the upper left corner of the title bar (see Figure 2-29).

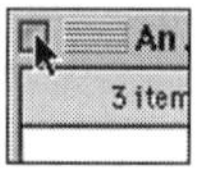

Figure 2-29:
You can click the close box to close a window.

Way #2: Choose File⇨Close Window (see Figure 2-30).

Figure 2-30:
You can use the Close Window command in the File menu to close an active window.

Way #3: Use the keyboard shortcut Command-W. Note that in Figure 2-30, the Close Window command in the File menu has this keyboard shortcut listed next to it.

If you're like me, by the end of the day, you've got windows open all over your desktop, sometimes a dozen or more. Wouldn't it be nice if there were a way to close them all at once with a single "close all windows" command? But you don't see a Close All command in the menus, do you?

You will in a second. There is one, but Apple, in its infinite wisdom, has hidden it from mere mortals. To make this useful command come out and play, merely hold down the Option key as you close the active window using Way #1, Way #2, or Way #3. In other words, hold down the Option key when you click the active window's close box, hold down the Option key when you choose File⇨Close Window, or hold down the Option key and the Command key while you press the W key (Command-Option-W).

Apple didn't hide the Close All command very well. As Figure 2-31 illustrates, if you press the Option key before pulling down the File menu, Close Window is magically transformed into Close All.

Figure 2-31:
Hold down the Option key while pulling down the File menu and you'll see the Close All command instead of the Close Window command.

Way #4: Use the contextual menu shortcut as shown in Figure 2-32. Just hold down the Control key on your keyboard when you click any window to get the contextual menu.

Figure 2-32:
Hold down the Control key when clicking a window to pop up the contextual menu.

Congrats: You now do windows

That retires the side. You now possess a massive, all-encompassing, thoroughly pervasive knowledge of windows and how they work. You can do windows with the best of them.

And I have good news for you: Windows in 99 percent of all applications (programs) that you will ever encounter work the same as windows in the Finder. Just about every application has active and inactive windows with title bars, close boxes, zoom boxes, scroll bars, scroll arrows, and scroll boxes.

Windows are windows, for the most part. As you use different programs, you'll probably notice that some of them (Microsoft Word, for example) take liberties with windows by adding features such as page counters and style indicators to the scroll bar area. Don't worry. You know how to do windows. That stuff is just window dressing (pun intended).

Disk Could Be the Start of a Beautiful Friendship

Groan. I apologize but assure you that you don't want to hear the alternatives. While I don't think there's such a thing as a good pun, in retrospect, this one *is* particularly odious. Sorry.

For all the lowdown on what floppy disks are and where they came from, you ought to see Poguerama's *Macs For Dummies* (published by IDG Books Worldwide, Inc.). I'm going to limit my discussion to stuff you do with disks when they're on the desktop.

You should think of the disk icons that appear on your desktop as if they were folders. When you double-click them, their windows open. You can drag stuff in and out of a disk's window, and you can manipulate the disk's window in all the usual ways.

Initialization and erasure

Brand new disks usually need to be *initialized* — prepared to receive Macintosh files — before they can be used. I say "usually" because you can buy new disks that are *preformatted* and are already initialized. It only takes a couple of minutes to initialize a disk, so don't pay a whole lot more for preformatted disks unless you really believe that time is money.

When you pop an uninitialized disk into your Mac, it will walk you through all the steps necessary to initialize it. If you need extra help, see *Macs For Dummies.*

Surprise: PC disks work as well!

One of Mac OS 8's most excellent features (if you have friends unfortunate enough not to own Macs and you want to share files with them) is the fact that it reads both Mac and DOS floppy disks without any user intervention. DOS disks are formatted for use with personal computers running DOS or Windows. If a friend has a Windows computer, you can now read his or her disks by just sticking them in your floppy drive. Your unfortunate friend, on the other hand, can't do diddly squat with your Mac-formatted disks — yet another reason why Macs are better.

When you insert a disk formatted for DOS, you'll see a distinctive PC disk icon like the one in Figure 2-33.

There are two other disk formats that you might run into: ProDOS is the Apple II format, rarely used anymore, and Macintosh HFS Interchange Format is a weirdo format nobody I know uses for anything.

Figure 2-33:
A PC-
formatted
disk on
your Mac
desktop.

Getting disks out of your Mac

You know about everything there is to know about disks except one important thing: how to eject a disk. Piece of cake, actually.

And, of course, there are four ways.

Way #1: Click the disk's icon to select it. Then choose Special⇨Eject or use the keyboard shortcut Command-E.

Way #2: Drag the disk's icon to the Trash.

This drives me nuts. Anything else you drag into the Trash dies (or at least it does when you Empty Trash). Why does dragging a disk to the Trash eject it?

Way #3: Select the disk and then choose File⇨Put Away (or use its Command-key shortcut, Command-Y).

Way #4: Click the disk while holding down the Control key; then use the contextual menu's Eject command.

Way #5: Use the keyboard shortcut Command-Shift-1. Notice how even though the disk has been ejected and is probably in your right hand, its icon still appears on the desktop, albeit with an unusual ghostly gray pattern (see Figure 2-34).

Figure 2-34:
The icon
of a disk
ejected
with
Command-
Shift-1.

The ghostly gray indicates that the disk is not currently mounted (inserted). Note that a dismounted disk's icon is not the same as that of a disk with its window open. The icon of a mounted disk with its window open is shown in Figure 2-35.

Figure 2-35:
The icon of
a mounted
disk with
its window
open.
See the
difference?

Why would you want the icon for an ejected disk on your desktop? So you can copy files from one floppy disk to another even though you have only one floppy disk drive. There's a whole section on copying files coming up in a few pages.

If you use the Eject command, drag a disk's icon to the Trash or use the Put Away command, the disk's ghost icon is *not* left on the desktop. If you used Way #1 or Way #2 to eject your disk, you can get rid of its ghost image by dragging the ghost icon to the Trash or selecting it and choosing File⇨Put Away. Unless you plan to copy files from one floppy to another, you don't want floppy disk icons on your desktop after you eject the disks. Ways #3 and #4 are the most commonly used methods of ejecting a disk.

If you insist on leaving ghost icons of long-ago-ejected disks on your desktop, it's only a matter of time before your Mac presents you with the dreaded "Please insert the disk" dialog box, which is shown in Figure 2-36.

Figure 2-36:
When you leave ghosted disk icons on the desktop, your Mac may ask for them back.

Please insert the disk:
MacsRBetter

Notice that there is no OK or Cancel button in the dialog box in Figure 2-36. There's no way out but to insert the disk your Mac is asking for.

Okay, I lied. There is a way out. Press Command-period. This keyboard shortcut cancels the dialog box and lets you drag the ghost disk icon to the Trash. Command-period is a good shortcut to remember. In most dialog boxes, Command-period is the same as clicking the Cancel button.

The dreaded "Please insert the disk" dialog box usually appears if you try to open the icon for an unmounted disk or try to open any of the files in the unmounted disk's window.

Get in the habit of dragging disks to the Trash or using the Put Away or Eject commands to get disks off your desktop. These techniques eject the disk and get rid of its pesky ghost icon. Unless you plan to copy files from one floppy to another, which you don't do all that often, avoid the Command-Shift-1 method of ejecting disks.

Up the Organization: Copying and Moving Files and Folders

Now that you know icons and windows and disks, it's time to get serious and learn something useful, like how to work with folders and how to move and copy icons from folder to folder and from disk to disk.

Know when to hold 'er, know when to folder

If your hard disk is a filing cabinet, folders are its folders. Duh. You use folders to organize your icons.

Makin' folders

To create a new folder, first decide which window you want the new folder to appear in. Make that window active by clicking it. Now either choose File⇨New Folder or use the shortcut Command-N. A new, untitled folder appears in the active window with its name box already highlighted and ready for you to type a new name for it (see Figure 2-37).

Figure 2-37:
A brand
new,
untitled
folder.

Name your folders with relevant names. Folders entitled sfdghb or Stuff — or worst of all, names like Untitled — won't make it any easier to find something six months from now.

Usin' 'em

Folders are icons; icons are containers. Folder icons (like disk icons) can contain just about any other icon.

You use folders to organize your stuff. There's no limit to how many folders you can have, so don't be afraid to create new ones and put stuff in them.

At the very least, you should have a System Folder (if you don't, go back and read Chapter 1 again). Until you get a *lot* of stuff, may I suggest that you start out with Application and Document folders, at the very least. You can even have the Mac create these two folders automatically by using the General Controls control panel (more about that in Chapter 12).

Later, when you get more files, you can subdivide the Documents folder into meaningful subfolders like those shown in Figure 2-38.

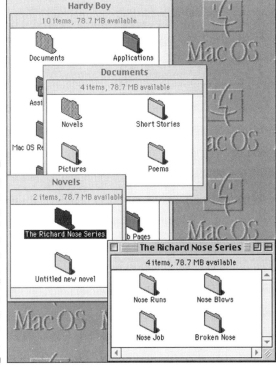

Figure 2-38:
The Documents folder contains numerous subfolders, each of which contains sub-subfolders.

As your subfolders get fuller, create subfolders within them. The idea is to have enough folders so that no one folder ever has hundreds of items in it, while simultaneously avoiding folders with only one or two items in them. Strive for balance. And try not to go deeper than four or five levels. If you find yourself creating subfolders that you have to open eight folders to get to, consider reorganizing the stuff in levels five through eight so that your folder hierarchy is no more than five levels deep. Trust me, you'll save a lot of time if you don't stash stuff ten folders deep.

Moving and copying and folders

You can move icons around within windows to your heart's content. Just click and drag within the window.

Now let's look at how you move an item into a folder. For example, let's see how you move One Folder into Another. As you might expect from me, the King of Ways, there are two ways to do it.

✔ As shown in Figure 2-39, drag the icon for One Folder onto the icon for Another and release when Another folder is highlighted. This technique works regardless of whether Another folder's window is open. If its window is open, you can use the second way.

✔ Drag the icon for One Folder into the open window for Another folder (or disk), as shown in Figure 2-40.

Figure 2-39:
Placing one
folder into
another.

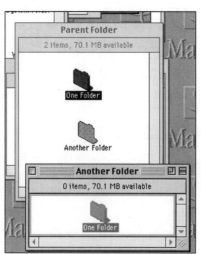

Figure 2-40:
You can
also move a
folder by
dragging its
icon into
the open
window of
another
folder, as
shown.

Notice the little gray border that appears around Another folder's window in Figure 2-40. This is your Mac telling you that if you release the mouse button right this second, the One Folder icon will be moved into Another folder. If you move the pointer out of the Another folder window, the gray border will disappear.

You use these two techniques to move any icon — folder, document, System software, or program icons — into folders or disks.

Before you read the next section, you should know that if you try to move an item from one disk to another disk, it will be copied, not moved. Always. Without exception. If you want to *move* a file or folder from one disk to another, you'll have to trash the original manually after the copying is complete.

But what if you don't want to move something from one place to another on your hard disk? What if instead you want to copy it, leaving the icon in its original location and an identical copy in the destination window?

You might be thinking, why would I want to do that? Trust me, someday you will. Say you've got a file called Long Letter to Mom in a folder called 1987 Correspondence. You figure Mom's forgotten it by now, so you want to send the letter again. But before you do, you want to change the date and delete the reference to Clarence, her pit bull, who passed away last year. So you want a copy of Long Letter to Mom in your 1997 Correspondence folder.

There are three ways to copy, but the first two are the same as you saw in the One Folder and Another example, with one small difference — you must hold down the Option key during the dragging portion of the move. In the Finder, Option-dragging an icon to any folder icon or window copies it instead of moving it. So you Option-drag the Letter to Mom icon onto either a folder icon or an open window to deposit a copy.

Now you have two copies of the file Long Letter to Mom, one in the 1987 Correspondence folder and another copy in the 1997 Correspondence folder. Open the one in the 1997 folder and make your changes. Don't forget to Save. (There's more about saving in Chapter 5.)

If I were you, I'd change the name of the 1997 copy, as it's not a good idea to have more than one file on your hard disk with the same name, even if the files are in different folders. Trust me, having 10 files called Expense Report or 15 files named Randall's Invoice can be confusing, no matter how well organized your folder structure is. Add something distinguishing to file and folder names so they're Expense Report 10/95 or Randall's Invoice 10/30/95. You'll be glad you did.

The third way to copy a file is to use the Duplicate command in either the File or the contextual menu, covered in depth in the very next chapter.

Moving and copying and disks

Moving an icon from one disk to another works the same as moving folders in the previous example. Because you're moving the icons from one disk to another disk, the copy part is automatic; you don't need the Option key. As I mentioned before, when you move a file from one disk to another, you're automatically making a copy of it. The original is left untouched and un-moved. If you want to move a file from one disk to another, copy it. You can then delete the original by dragging it to the Trash.

Copying the entire contents of a floppy disk to your hard disk works a little differently. To do this task, select the floppy disk's icon and drag it onto your hard disk's icon or onto your hard disk's open window, or onto any other folder icon or open folder window.

When the copy is completed, a folder bearing the same name as the floppy disk will appear on your hard disk. The folder on your hard disk now contains each and every file that was on the floppy disk of the same name.

Be careful copying disks containing System Folders to your hard disk. You never want to use the preceding technique to copy a floppy to your hard disk if the floppy has a System Folder. One hard and fast rule of the Mac is that there should never be more than one System Folder on your hard disk.

If a floppy disk contains a System Folder and you want to copy everything else to your hard disk, do the following: Create a new folder on your hard disk. Then select every icon in the floppy disk's window *except* the System Folder and drag all the selected icons onto the new folder's icon or window.

To select more than one icon, click once and drag. You'll see an outline of a box around the icons as you drag, and icons within or touching the box will highlight (see Figure 2-41).

Figure 2-41:
To select more than one item, click and drag with the mouse.

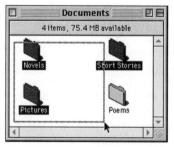

Another way to select multiple icons is to click one and then hold down the Shift key as you click others. As long as you hold down the Shift key, each new icon you click is added to the selection. To deselect an icon, click it a second time while still holding the Shift key down.

Be careful with multiple selections, especially when you drag icons to the Trash. It's easy to accidentally select more than one icon, so it's possible to put an icon in the Trash by accident if you're not paying close attention. So pay close attention.

Meet the desktop

Earlier I said that the terms *Finder* and *desktop* were used interchangeably, referring to the total Macintosh environment you see — icons, windows, menus, and all the other cool stuff. Well, just to make things confusing, the background you see on your screen, the gray or patterned backdrop behind your hard disk icon and open windows, is also called the desktop.

Any icon can reside on the desktop. Just move icons to the desktop from any window. It's not a window, but it acts like one. You can move any icon there if you like; the desktop is a great place for things you use a lot, like folders, applications, or documents that you use every day.

It's even better to use aliases of things you use often so that you can keep the originals tucked away in one of your perfectly organized folders. But I'm not going to talk about aliases until Chapter 3, so for now, just tuck that little tidbit away in the back of your mind.

In Figure 2-42, you see three icons on my desktop that you haven't seen before: Documents (folder icon), MS Word (application icon), and MOS8FD.Ch02.doc (document icon).

Disk icons always appear on the desktop, as does the Trash icon. The desktop printer, Browse the Internet, Mac OS Info Center, and Mail icons are created when you install Mac OS 8.

The other icons — a document, a folder, and an application — were moved from the root level of Macintosh HD to the desktop by me to make them easier to use.

Items on the desktop behave the same as they would in a window. You move them and copy them in the same way as you would an icon in a window — except that they're not in a window; they're on the desktop, which makes them more convenient to use.

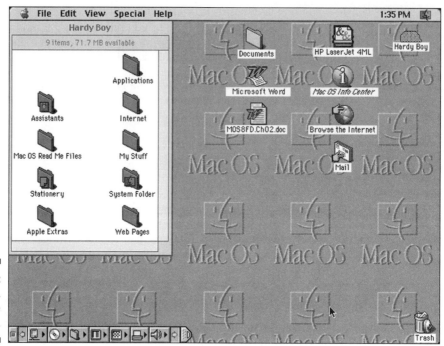

Figure 2-42:
My desktop,
with some
stuff on it.

Got it? It's convenient. It's fast. Put stuff there.

But not too much. If you keep putting stuff on the desktop, eventually it gets very cluttered. That's the time to put infrequently used icons on the desktop back in the folder or disk window they came from. Fortunately, your Mac makes this task easy, even if you've forgotten which folder they were in. Select the icon or icons that you want moved back to where they came from and then choose File⇨Put Away. The icon is magically transported back into the folder or disk icon from which it came and will no longer appear on the desktop. Neat, eh?

Many users cover their desktops with icons, sometimes dozens or more. That's because the desktop is the most convenient place for things that you use often. You save time and effort because you don't have to open any windows to open an icon on the desktop.

One Last Thing . . .

I'd be remiss (again?) if I didn't at least mention here that you can change the background pattern of your desktop. Though it's covered in full and loving detail in Chapter 12, if you're sick of the Mac OS desktop pattern seen in almost every screen shot so far, you can either of the following:

- ✔ Choose Apple menu⇨Control Panels⇨Desktop Pictures.
- ✔ Hold down the Control key, click anywhere on the desktop, and choose the Change Desktop Background menu item.

Either one will lead you to the Desktop Pictures control panel, where you can choose from 48 desktop patterns or 4 included pictures.

I am particularly fond of the new Desktop Pictures feature. I use the Cancun Sunset as my everyday background (see Figure 2-43).

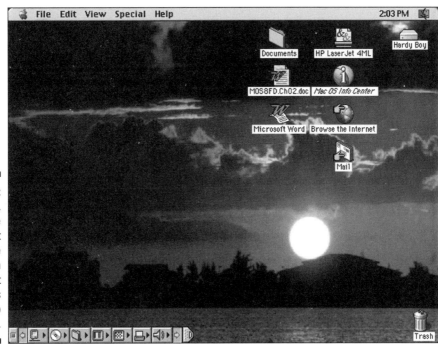

Figure 2-43: My desktop, with some stuff on it and the Cancun Sunset picture as my desktop background.

Chapter 3
A Bevy of Delectable Menus

. . . .

. . . .

*L*ike icons and windows, menus are a quintessential part of the Macintosh experience. In this chapter, I take a brief look at each and every Finder menu item.

I'm trying to provide an appropriate level of detail based on the menu item's importance. Trust me here. In earlier editions of this book, I said that Mac OS 7.*x*'s Label menu was dumb; apparently Apple agrees because that menu is gone from Mac OS 8. (The old Label menu's functions are available from either the File menu or contextual menus in Mac OS 8.)

Anyway, I'll start with a few menu basics and then move on to the menus in almost the order they appear on your screen: File, Edit, View, Special, Help, and Application. Last, but not least, I look at the context-sensitive contextual menus. Because the Apple menu is so long and so important, I'm going to give it its own chapter, the very next one after this one.

Menu Basics

Mac menus are often referred to as pull-down menus. That's because to use them, you click their names to make the menus appear and then pull (drag) down to select an item. Piece of cake, eh?

There's something new in Mac OS 8 — the menus now stay down when you click their names. They stay down until you either select an item or click outside the menu's boundaries.

Command performance

As noted previously, many menu items have Command-key shortcuts after their names. These key combinations indicate that you can activate the menu items without using the mouse by pressing the Command (notice I refrained from calling it a pretzel) key and then pressing another key without releasing the Command key. And, as I've said before and will say again, it pays to memorize the shortcuts you use often.

It's elliptical

Another feature of Mac menus is the ellipsis after a menu item's name. Ellipses, in case your English teacher forgot to mention them, are the three little dots (...) that appear after certain menu items' names. According to the Bible (actually, the *Chicago Manual of Style,* but for writers, it might as well be the Bible), "Any omission of a word or phrase, line or paragraph . . . must be indicated by ellipsis points (dots). . . ."

Apple is true to this definition. Ellipsis points in a menu item mean that choosing the item will bring up a dialog box where you can make further choices. Choosing a menu item with an ellipsis never actually makes anything happen other than opening a dialog box, where you make further choices and then click a button to make things happen.

Dialog box featurettes

Dialog boxes may contain a number of standard Macintosh features such as *radio buttons, pop-up menus, text entry boxes,* and *check boxes.* You'll see these features again and again, in dialog boxes, control panels, and elsewhere. So let's take a moment to look at each of these featurettes, and I'll demonstrate how they're used.

Radio, radio (buttons)

Radio buttons are called radio buttons because, like the buttons on your car radio, only one can be pushed at a time. Radio buttons always appear in groups of two or more; when you push one, all the others are automatically unpushed. I think eggheads call this setup "mutually exclusive." Take a look at Figure 3-1 for an example of radio buttons.

Figure 3-1:
A group of radio buttons. Only one radio button in each group may be selected at a time.

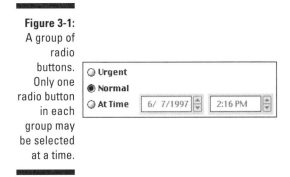

In Figure 3-1, Normal is currently selected. If you click the radio button for Urgent or At Time, Normal will be deactivated.

Menus redux: pop-up style

Pop-up menus are called pop-up menus because that's what they do — they pop up when you press them. You can always tell a pop-up menu because it appears in a rectangle with a shadow and a down-pointing arrow. Figure 3-2 shows a pop-up menu before you click it; Figure 3-3 shows the same menu after you click it and hold the mouse button down.

Figure 3-2:
Pop-up menus have a distinctive look, with a shadow and a down-pointing arrow.

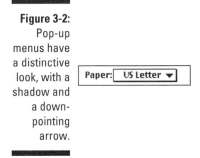

Figure 3-3:
To pop a
pop-up
menu up
(try saying
that three
times fast),
click the
shadowed
rectangle
and hold
down the
mouse
button.

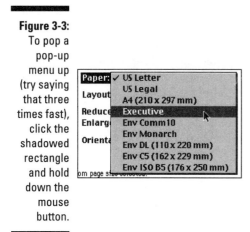

Okay, so now you've looked at two features, radio buttons and pop-up menus, and they both do the exact same thing: allow you to make a single selection from a group of options. Sometimes a radio button is associated with a text entry box, which happens to be the feature I cover next.

Championship boxing: text entry style

Text entry boxes let you enter text (including numbers) from the keyboard. When a text entry box appears in conjunction with a radio button, the text entry box or boxes only matter if the associated radio button is pressed. Take a look at Figure 3-4. You can enter text in the two text entry boxes next to the From radio button, but if you click the All radio button, your text disappears. Conversely, if you click in one of the text entry boxes and type, the From radio button automatically becomes selected.

Figure 3-4:
Type letters
or numbers
into text
entry boxes
such as
these.

Had Apple chosen to use a pop-up menu instead of radio buttons in the Figure 3-4 example, the menu would have taken up more valuable screen real estate. So that's the reason for two featurettes that do the same thing.

And now you know how to use both.

Checkmate

The last featurette you'll see frequently is the check box. Check boxes are used to choose items that are not mutually exclusive. In a group of check boxes, you can turn each one on or off individually. Check boxes are on when they contain a check mark and off when they're empty. Figure 3-5 shows four check boxes, three of which are on.

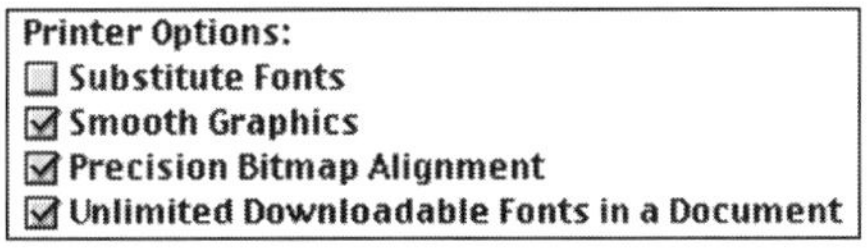

Figure 3-5:
In this example, three out of four boxes are checked.

> **Printer Options:**
> ☐ Substitute Fonts
> ☑ Smooth Graphics
> ☑ Precision Bitmap Alignment
> ☑ Unlimited Downloadable Fonts in a Document

Unlike radio buttons, which force you to choose one and only one item, check boxes are independent. Each one can either be on or off.

Here's a nifty and undocumented shortcut: Check boxes and radio buttons can usually be activated by clicking their names (instead of clicking the buttons or boxes). Didn't know that, did you?

File Management and More: Meet the File Menu

The File menu (shown in Figure 3-6) contains commands that let you manipulate your files and folders.

Menu items that can be used to act upon the item or items selected (the Documents folder in Figure 3-6) in the active window (or on the desktop) appear in black and are currently available; menu items not available at the current time are displayed in gray. You cannot select a gray menu item.

In this example, only three items are disabled — Print, Put Away, and Show Original. That's because you can only print documents, not folders, and the selected item in the active window is a folder (Documents). The Put Away command is dimmed because you can only put away items that reside outside of windows on the desktop itself. The Show Original command is dimmed because it only works when the selected item is an alias. (I know you don't know what an alias is yet, but you will soon.) The rest of the commands appear in black and are valid selections at this time.

Figure 3-6:
The File
menu.

New Folder (Command-N)

I talked about this command in the last chapter, but just for the record, New Folder creates a new, untitled folder in the active window. If no window is active, it creates a new folder on the desktop.

You'll probably do a lot of new-folder making, so it might be a good idea to memorize this command's keyboard shortcut, Command-N. It'll come in handy later, as most software uses the shortcut Command-N to create a new document, another thing you'll do a lot of.

If your memory is bad, use this mnemonic device — N is for New.

Most menu items, or at least most common ones, have keyboard shortcuts that have a mnemonic relationship to their names. For example, New is Command-N, Open is Command-O, Get Info is Command-I, Make Alias is Command-M (which is good news because in earlier versions of the Mac OS, there was no keyboard shortcut for Make Alias), and so on.

Open (Command-O)

This command opens the selected item. Not much more to say, except to remind you that in addition to the menu command and its shortcut Command-O, a double-click also opens this icon.

Print (Command-P)

This command, which prints the selected item, is only active if the selected icon is a document. Furthermore, it only works if you have the application that created the document on your hard disk. If you try to print (or open) a document when you don't have the application that created it, you'll see a dialog box like the one shown in Figure 3-7.

Figure 3-7:
Try to print
or open a
document
when you
don't have
the program
that created
it and you
may see
this dialog
box.

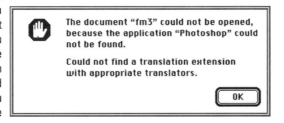

> The document "fm3" could not be opened, because the application "Photoshop" could not be found.
>
> Could not find a translation extension with appropriate translators.
>
> OK

I'll talk about what translators are when I discuss Macintosh Easy Open in Chapter 12. For now, let's leave it at this: If you select a document icon and then use the Open or Print command, the command will only work if you have the application that created the document or another application that is capable of opening that type of document.

That's where the translator part comes in (refer to Figure 3-7 again). Many programs can open files created by another program, but only if the proper *translator* is available. I'll save the details for later.

Move to Trash (Command-Backspace)

This command, new to Mac OS 8 and long needed, moves the selected icon to the Trash. Don't forget that the icon (that is, the item the icon represents) is not deleted from your hard disk until you choose the Empty Trash command from either the Special or contextual menu.

Close Window (Command-W)

This command closes the active window. Duh. Don't forget, if you hold down the Option key before you click the File menu, this command changes to Close All.

I talked about this command in Chapter 2, so I'll just move on.

Get Info (Command-I)

When you select any icon and choose the Get Info command (or use its keyboard shortcut Command-I), a Get Info window opens (see Figure 3-8).

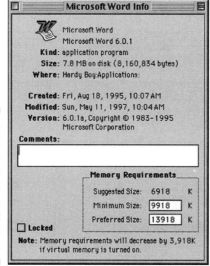

Figure 3-8:
A typical
Get Info
window
for an
application
(Microsoft
Word, in
this case).

The top portion of the Get Info window provides details about the icon, such as what it is (application, document, disk, folder, and so on), how big it is (7.8 megabytes, which equals 8,160,834 bytes), where it is on your disk (the Applications folder on the Hardy Boy disk), when it was created (Friday, August 18, 1995, 10:07 AM), when it was last modified (Sunday, May 11, 1997, 10:04 AM), and its version number (6.0.1a).

The middle section is called the Comments box because that's where you type your comments about the icon. In earlier versions of the Mac OS, these comments would disappear whenever you rebuilt your desktop or restored from a backup; and, as I discuss in Appendix B, you should rebuild your desktop and back up your hard disk on a regular basis.

Since Mac OS 7.6, an icon's comments *do* survive rebuilding the desktop. They don't always survive restoration from backup, so use them at your own risk.

The bottom section of an application's Get Info box deals with its memory requirements. This stuff gets a little complicated, so I won't go into it here. (If you just can't wait, skip ahead to my dandy and easy-to-understand explanation in Chapter 9.)

The last item in an application's Get Info box is the Locked check box. When an application is locked, its name can't be changed, and it can't be emptied from the Trash. (I mentioned locked files and the Trash briefly in Chapter 2, as you may remember.)

If you try to empty the Trash when there's a locked item in it, you'll see a message telling you to hold down the Option key before you choose Special⇨Empty Trash. Holding down the Option key when you choose Empty Trash empties the Trash even if there are locked items in it.

While I'm on the subject, do you hate the dialog box you see each time you try to empty the Trash (you know, the one that says: "The Trash contains X items. It uses X K of disk space. Are you sure you want to permanently remove it?")? If you never want to see this pain-in-the-bottom dialog box again, select the Trash icon, invoke the Get Info command (Command-I), and uncheck the Warn before emptying check box.

Documents, folders, and disks each have slightly different Get Info boxes. Folders and disks can't be locked; documents and applications can.

Sharing (sorry, it has no keyboard shortcut)

The Sharing command lets you decide who can share your files. There's so much to say about Macintosh File Sharing that I could write an entire chapter about it. And in fact, I have. If you're interested, take a look at Chapter 8.

Label (sorry, no keyboard shortcut either)

Maybe it's just me, but I've never really gone much for the Label feature. And I hardly know anyone who uses it diligently, which is the only way it's useful. Anyway, the Label submenu, which looks a lot neater in color than it does in Figure 3-9, lets you organize your files yet another way — by label.

Artistic icons

The Get Info box serves another more frivolous but fundamentally fun function — it lets you change any icon's icon to anything you like.

Don't like the Mac's folder icon? Give it a new one. Here's how. Find an icon you like — let's say it's an armadillo (hey, I'm a Texan). Select it and select the Get Info command. Now select the folder that you want to give the 'dillo icon to (we'll call it untitled folder for convenience) and bring up the Get Info window. In the upper-left corner of the 'dillo's Get Info box, you'll see the 'dillo (see below, left).

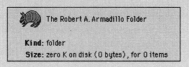

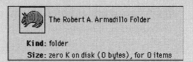

Click the 'dillo in its Get Info box. A box appears around the 'dillo icon indicating that it's now selected (see above, right). Choose Edit⇨Copy, as shown in the following figure.

Now click the untitled folder icon in its Get Info window and choose Edit⇨Paste. The results of this last step are shown below.

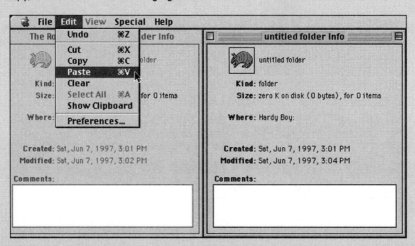

There you go! This technique works on any icon — disk, folder, application, or document. And if you can't find an icon you like, you can create a picture in any graphics program, select it, choose Edit⇨Copy, and then paste it into the Get Info box of any icon. Furthermore, online services like CompuServe and America Online, as well as Macintosh user groups and the Internet, offer humongous collections of icons for your pasting pleasure.

To apply a label to an icon, select it and then choose the appropriate label from the Label submenu as shown in Figure 3-9. Again, labels are more useful on a color screen, as they tint the icon the appropriate color.

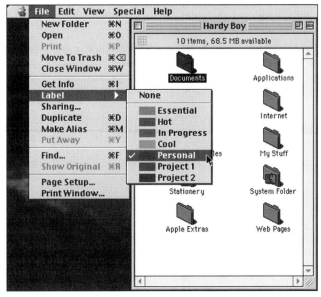

Figure 3-9:
Use the
Label
submenu
to assign
labels to
icons as
shown.

Because the Find command can search by label, you have reason to use labels. Still, unless you're very organized and remember to label every file (which, unfortunately, has to be done in the Finder, not when you save from within an application, when it might actually be useful), labels won't be much use.

The Dilemma: On one hand, several users (well, actually just two) took the time to write me and say they found labels useful. On the other hand, thousands of people didn't.

On the *other* other hand, severely obsessive, compulsive, or anal-retentive Mac users will have hours of pleasure assigning those pretty labels to their icons.

So labels: Yea or Nay? It's your call.

You can change the names and colors of your labels in the aptly named Labels control panel, which is discussed in Chapter 12.

Duplicate (Command-D)

Duplicate duplicates the selected icon. More precisely, it makes an exact copy of the selected icon, adds the word *copy* to its name, and places the copy in the same window as the original icon. Figure 3-10 shows the results of using the Duplicate command.

The Duplicate command can be used on any icon except a disk icon.

Figure 3-10:
The
Duplicate
command
in action.

Make Alias (Command-M)

Aliases are a wonderful, fabulous organizational tool introduced with System 7. An *alias* is a tiny file that automatically opens its *parent* file. To create an alias for any icon, select the icon (the parent) and then choose File⇨Make Alias or press Command-M.

When you open an alias, the parent opens.

An alias is different from a duplicated file. For example, my word processor, Microsoft Word 6.0.1, uses 7.8 megabytes of disk space. If I duplicated it, I would have two files, each using almost 8 megabytes of disk space. An alias of Microsoft Word, on the other hand, uses a mere 32K.

Due to a variety of complicated and unimportant reasons having to do with sector size and hard disk size, your mileage may vary depending on the size of your hard disk. In general, the smaller the disk, the smaller the aliases will be.

When you make an alias, it has the same icon as its parent, but its name appears in *italic* type and the suffix *alias* is tacked onto its name. Figure 3-11 shows an alias and its parent icon.

You can put aliases in convenient places like the desktop or the Apple Menu Items folder (so that they appear in your Apple menu).

Figure 3-11:
An alias
icon looks
identical to
its parent
'cept for the
italics.

There must be at least a dozen ways aliases can help organize your
Macintosh existence, and I'll talk about all of them in Chapter 6.

Put Away (Command-Y)

Choose Put Away to move the selected icon from your desktop to the
window it was in before you moved it to the desktop. This command even
works if it's been years since the icon was moved to the desktop and you
don't remember which folder it came out of.

The Put Away command is only active when an icon on the desktop is
selected; it is dimmed whenever any icon in a window is selected. Put Away
is also dimmed when the Trash icon is selected.

And, as mentioned previously, the Put Away command will eject a floppy
disk and remove its ghost icon from the desktop. In other words, Put Away
has the same effect on a floppy disk as dragging its icon to the Trash does.

Find (Command-F)

Use this command when you need to find an icon on your hard disk and you
can't remember where you put it. This is a Mac OS 8 feature that really kicks
earlier versions' butts.

There are three different ways to invoke the Find dialog box (here I go again
with the ways).

   ✔ Choose File⇨Find.

   ✔ Use the keyboard shortcut Command-F.

   ✔ Choose Find File from the Apple menu.

Whichever way you choose, the next thing you'll see is the Find File dialog box (shown in Figure 3-12).

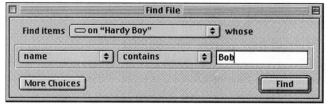

Just type in the name of the file that you're looking for and then click the Find button or press the Return key. In a flash (Mac OS 8's Find is even faster than earlier incarnations), you'll see the Items Found window (see Figure 3-13) showing every file on the disk you searched that matches the word you typed in the text entry box.

In Figure 3-13, 28 items on my hard disk (Hardy Boy) contain the word *Bob*.

Once I found all these files, I selected the one I wanted — Bob Bungees.sit. At this point there are three ways to open the file:

✔ Choose File⇨Open Item.

✔ Use the keyboard shortcut Command-O.

✔ Double-click the file in the top or bottom part of the Find File Results window.

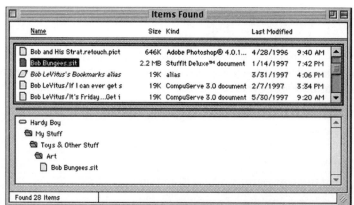

If you prefer to open the folder that contains the item, there are three ways to do that:

- Choose File⇨Open Enclosing Folder.
- Use the keyboard shortcut Command-E.
- Double-click the folder in the bottom part of the Items Found window.

If searching by name alone finds too many files, you can narrow your search by clicking the More Choices button in the Find dialog box and adding one or more additional criteria for the search. These criteria include the following:

- Size of file
- Kind of file (application, alias, and so on)
- Label (see the Label menu section later in this chapter)
- Creation Date (date the file was created)
- Modification Date (date the file was last saved)
- Version Number (is or is not)
- Lock Attribute (file is locked or is not)
- Folder Attribute (empty, shared, or mounted)
- File Type code
- Creator Type code

Figure 3-14 shows what the Find dialog box looks like after you click the More Choices button.

Show Original (Command-R)

Show Original only works on aliases. Select any alias icon and then choose this command to reveal the parent file of the selected alias.

Page Setup (no keyboard shortcut)

Choosing Page Setup brings up the Page Setup dialog box, which is where you specify the type of paper in your printer (letter, legal, envelope, and so on), page orientation (longways or wideways), and scaling (100% = full size).

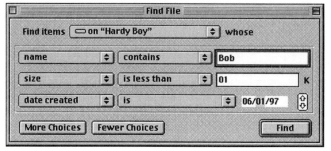

In addition to the one here in the Finder, you'll find a Page Setup command in almost every program that you use. There's a whole chapter on printing coming up in a little while (Chapter 7, to be exact), so I'll leave this topic alone for now. (That's also why I didn't waste space here on a screen shot.)

Print Desktop/Print Window (no keyboard shortcut)

This command is a little tricky. If no windows are open, the command is called Print Desktop. If a window is open, the command's name changes to Print Window.

If you choose Print Desktop, your Mac will print a picture of your desktop, with its icons and Trash (but not the menu bar), exactly as you see them on the screen. This image will generally require two or more pieces of paper.

If you choose Print Window, your Mac will print a picture of the active window, showing all the icons it contains, even if you would have to scroll to see the icons on the screen. If the window contains a lot of icons, printing this document may require more than one sheet of paper.

And if a document is selected when you choose the Print command, the application that created the document will launch automatically, and you'll see a Print dialog box. (Printing is covered in full and loving detail in Chapter 7, which is why there's no screen shot of this one either.)

The Edit Menu (Which Shoulda Been Called the Clipboard Menu)

In contrast to the File menu, which has commands that mostly deal with file management and are exclusive to the Finder, the Edit menu's commands and functions are available in almost every Macintosh program ever made (see Figure 3-15).

Figure 3-15:
The Edit menu. Memorize these five keyboard shortcuts even if you never memorize anything else.

Because almost every program has an Edit menu, and because almost every program uses the same keyboard shortcuts on its Edit menu, it will behoove you to learn these keyboard shortcuts by heart, even if you learn no others.

The Edit menu should probably have been called the Clipboard menu, because most of its commands deal with the Macintosh Clipboard.

If you read the little sidebar about the Clipboard, you'll find out 75 percent of what you need to know about the Edit menu. Still, because IDG's paying me to be thorough, and because the Finder's Edit menu has a couple of commands that aren't Clipboard-related, I'll go through the Edit menu's commands one by one.

The Clipboard

Essential to your understanding of the Mac and essential to your understanding of the Edit menu is an understanding of the concept of the Macintosh Clipboard. In one sentence: The Clipboard is a holding area for the last thing that you cut or copied. A thing can be text, a picture, a portion of a picture, an object in a drawing program, a column of numbers in a spreadsheet, or just about anything that can be selected. In other words, the Clipboard is the Mac's temporary storage area.

As a storage area, the Clipboard is ephemeral, which means that its contents are temporary. Very temporary. When you cut or copy an item, that item remains on the Clipboard only until you cut or copy something else. Then the Clipboard's contents are replaced by the new item, which remains on the Clipboard until you cut or copy something else. And so it goes.

To place the item that's on the Clipboard somewhere else, click where you want the item to go and then paste. Pasting does not remove the item from the Clipboard; the item remains there until another item is cut or copied.

Almost all programs have an Edit menu and use the Macintosh clipboard properly, which means that you can usually cut or copy something in a document in one program and paste it into a document from another program. Usually.

The Clipboard commands in the Edit menu are relatively intelligent. If the currently selected item *can* be cut or copied, then the Cut and Copy commands in the Edit menu will be enabled; if the item can't be cut or copied, the commands will be unavailable and grayed out. And when nothing at all is selected, the Cut, Copy, Paste, and Clear commands are grayed out.

The contents of the Clipboard don't survive a restart, a shut down, or a system error or crash. The Clipboard is ephemeral in the sense that any of these events purges its contents, so when your Mac comes back to life, the Clipboard will be empty.

Undo (Command-Z)

This is a great command! You're gonna love it. Undo undoes the last thing you did. Try it.

1. Create a new folder in any window or on the desktop. (It will be called Untitled Folder.)

2. Change the name Untitled Folder to Undo Me.

3. Without clicking anywhere else or doing anything else, choose Edit⇨Undo or use the keyboard shortcut Command-Z.

The folder's name should magically undo itself and change back to Untitled Folder.

Neat, huh? Don't forget about this command 'cause it can be a lifesaver. Almost every program has it.

Now for the bad news: The Undo command is ephemeral, like the Clipboard. It only undoes your last action, and as soon as you do something else, you lose the ability to undo the original action. To see what I mean, repeat the exercise and change Untitled Folder to Undo Me. But this time, click another icon before you undo. What's that, you say? The Undo command is grayed out and not available any more? I told you. When you clicked the other icon, you forfeited your chance to use Undo.

Unfortunately, Undo doesn't work with things like moving icons or copying files. In fact, as you learn more about using your Mac, you'll discover lots of actions that can't be undone. Still, Undo is a great command when it's available, and I urge you to get in the habit of trying it often.

Incidentally, the Undo command *toggles* (that is, switches back and forth) between the new and old states as long as you don't do anything else. So in the first example, if you chose Edit⇨Undo again without clicking anywhere else, the name would transform back to Undo Me. And if you chose Edit⇨ Undo again, it would change back to Untitled Folder. You can continue to undo and redo until you click somewhere else.

Cut (Command-X)

The Cut command removes the selected item and places it on the Clipboard. Let's see this command in action:

1. Create an untitled folder.

2. Select only the word *untitled* (*untitled* should be black or colored with white letters; *folder* should be white with black letters).

3. Choose Edit⇨Cut, or use the keyboard shortcut Command-X.

The word *untitled* disappears from the folder's name. Where did it go? You cut it! It's removed from the folder and is now waiting on the Clipboard.

(You could, of course, use the Undo command at this point to make *untitled* reappear, as long as you haven't clicked anything else.)

Show Clipboard (no keyboard shortcut)

I know I'm not covering the commands in the order that they appear on the Edit menu, but there's a method to my madness. If you don't believe that the word *untitled,* which you cut in the previous section, is on the Clipboard, choose Edit⇨Show Clipboard. A window will appear, telling you the type of item (text, picture, sound, and so on) on the Clipboard and displaying it if it can be displayed (see Figure 3-16).

Figure 3-16:
The Show
Clipboard
command
displays the
current
contents
of the
Clipboard.

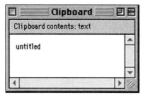

There is another way to display the Clipboard's contents — open the Clipboard icon in your System Folder. Because some programs don't have a Show Clipboard command, it's convenient to make an alias of the Clipboard file and put the alias in your Apple Menu Items folder so that it appears in your Apple menu. (Don't panic. I'm going to talk about the Apple menu in the very next chapter.) Then, even if you're in a program that doesn't have a Show Clipboard command, you can select the Clipboard alias from the Apple menu. This technique saves you two steps; without it you'd have to first go back to the Finder and then choose Edit⇨Show Clipboard. Choosing the Clipboard alias from the Apple menu does both steps automatically.

Copy (Command-C)

Copy makes a copy of the selected item and places it on the Clipboard. The original is not removed, as it is when you cut. Try it. Select your System Folder and choose Edit⇨Copy or use the keyboard shortcut Command-C. Now choose Edit⇨Show Clipboard. The Clipboard contains the text "System Folder."

It's that simple.

Paste (Command-V)

We've been cutting and copying but not doing much with the stuff on the Clipboard except looking at it to make sure it's really there. Now, let's use what we've cut or copied. Do this:

1. Create a new folder.

2. Change the folder's name to Elvis Costello.

3. Copy the word *Elvis* to the Clipboard. (C'mon, you know how.)

4. Create another new folder and select its name, which should be "untitled folder" if you've been following my instructions.

5. Choose Edit➪Paste.

The new folder is now called Elvis. Pasting doesn't purge the contents of the Clipboard. Don't believe me? Choose Edit➪Show Clipboard to confirm that Elvis is still alive and well and on the Clipboard.

Which is where he'll stay until you cut, copy, crash (the three Cs of Macintosh computing), or restart or shut down.

Clear (no keyboard shortcut)

Clear deletes the selected item without involving the Clipboard. It works the same as pressing the Delete key on your keyboard. Use it when you want to make something disappear forever.

Clear can be undone as long as you haven't done anything else like click, type, save, or use a menu.

Select All (Command-A)

Select All selects all. If a window is active, Select All selects every icon in the window, regardless of whether you can see them. If no window is active, Select All selects every icon on the desktop.

Go ahead and try it a couple of times. I'll wait.

Select All has nothing whatsoever to do with the Clipboard. So why is it on the Edit menu? Who knows? It just is and always has been.

Preferences . . . (no keyboard shortcut)

The Preferences item in the Edit menu combines a bunch of items (shown in Figure 3-17) formerly found in the Views and Labels control panels, both of which are discontinued in Mac OS 8, plus a couple of nifty new features that you'll meet in a second.

```
┌──────────────────────────────────────────────┐
│ □              Preferences                   ▤ │
│                                                │
│  Font for views:  [ Palatino      ◆ ] [12 ◆]  │
│  □ Simple Finder                               │
│      Provides only the essential features and commands │
│                                                │
│  ☑ Spring-loaded folders  ━━━━━━━━━▭━━━━        │
│      Delay before opening   Short   Medium   Long │
│                                                │
│  Grid Spacing: ▯ ▯ ▯ ▯  ● Tight (more items)   │
│                ▯  ▯  ▯   ○ Wide (neater arrangement) │
│                                                │
│  Labels: [▨] [Essential          ]             │
│          [▨] [Hot                ]             │
│          [▨] [In Progress        ]             │
│          [▨] [Cool               ]             │
│          [▨] [Personal           ]             │
│          [▨] [Project 1          ]             │
│      [?] [▨] [Project 2          ]             │
└──────────────────────────────────────────────┘
```

Figure 3-17: The Finder's preferences.

Here's a quick tutorial in the Finder Preferences window:

Font for views

The pop-up Font for views menu lets you select the font you see in Finder windows and on the desktop. The little triangles next to the *12* in Figure 3-17 let you choose the font size.

Simple Finder

The Simple Finder check box emasculates your Mac and makes it harder to use by removing a lot of useful commands from its menus (see Figure 3-18).

Simple Finder is only recommended for absolute rank novices. As you can see in Figure 3-18, Simple Finder hides many useful menu items — such as Move To Trash, Make Alias, and so on — and thereby (at least in my humble

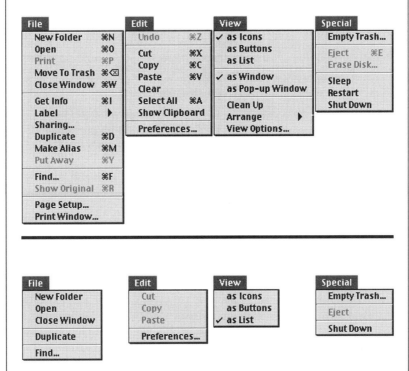

Figure 3-18:
Regular
Finder
menus (top)
and Simple
Finder
menus
(bottom).

opinion) reduces the usefulness of your Mac. If you have young children or old parents, this setting may be useful, but if your gray matter functions normally, just say No to the Simple Finder choice. In other words, unless you're computerphobic, don't bother with the Simple Finder for yourself.

Spring-loaded folders

The new option for spring-loaded folders is turned on or off with a check box. Spring-loaded folders are a nifty new feature that pops folders open when you hold an icon over them. They are opened only until you release the mouse button. Then they close automatically.

It's easier to demonstrate than write about, so follow along with this tutorial if you want to see a neat new Finder feature in action.

1. Check the Spring-loaded folders check box.

2. Set the Delay before opening slider to Short.

3. Close the Preferences window.

4. In the Finder, click any icon and drag it on top of any folder that contains at least two subfolders. Do not release the mouse button yet.

   The folder you've dragged the icon onto should spring open.

5. Move the icon over one of the subfolders inside the original folder. Do not release the mouse button yet.

   That folder springs open. If you were to release the mouse button right now, the original icon you clicked would be deposited in this subfolder.

6. Move the icon so it's not over any windows or folder icons.

   Folders that have sprung open will spring closed when you move the icon away from them.

In other words, spring-loaded folders let you move or copy an item deep into your folder hierarchy by automatically opening and closing folders for you with absolutely no double-clicking. Play around with this feature for a while and you'll wonder how you ever got along without it.

Grid Spacing

Grid Spacing deals with an invisible grid that the Finder maintains for your convenience. The invisible grid is only available in Icon views (which I cover in the very next section). Here in the Finder Preferences window you can only choose from Tight or Wide spacing.

The invisible grid can be turned on or off using the View Options window (also explained in the next section). Furthermore, if you have the grid turned off in View Options, hold down the Command key when you drag any item to have it snap to the invisible grid; alternately, if you have the grid turned on in View Options, hold down the Command key to temporarily disable the invisible grid and move the icon anywhere you like.

In the next section, I'll have you play more with the grid.

Labels

The Labels item in Finder Preferences lets you change the names and colors of the labels in the File menu's Label submenu.

To change the name associated with a label, double-click its name in the Finder Preferences window and type in a new one. To change a label's color, click directly on the color itself and a Color Picker window appears (see Figure 3-19).

I know that all the colors in the Color Picker look gray in the picture, but on a color monitor, they are in color, I promise. To select a new color, just click in the color wheel or change the Hue Angle, Saturation, and/or Lightness settings.

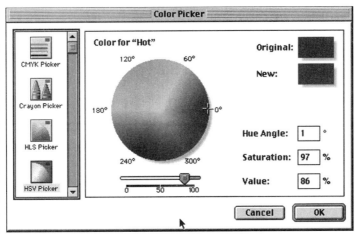

Figure 3-19:
A Color
Picker
window
appears
when you
click a
color in
the Finder
Preferences
window.

Color Pickers are a little hard to explain, but basically, they're just different windows that let you pick a color. The left side of the Color Picker window lets you choose from six different kinds of Color Pickers. I generally use the HSV (hue, saturation, value) Picker shown in Figure 3-19, mostly because I consider it the easiest to use. But Apple now provides many other ways for you to pick colors. So I recommend you play with all of them just a little. Just click a Color Picker — Crayon Picker, CMYK Picker, and so on — on the left side of the window and then play with the resulting controls on the right side of the window to pick a color.

Whee!

A View from a Window: The View Menu

The View menu governs the way icons look in a window or on your desktop. The View menu affects the icons in the active window or, if no window is active, it affects the icons on the desktop.

The first two parts of the View menu have to do with what the icons and windows look like; the third part of the View menu has to do with how icons and windows are arranged and/or sorted.

The first part: as Icons, as Buttons, or as List

Viewing by icon is the "Macintosh" view, the one most closely associated with the Macintosh experience. It's also, in my humble opinion, one of the two least useful views, as those big horsey icons take up far too much valuable screen real estate. And, as you'll see in a minute, list view offers a nifty navigational extra and saves space as well.

The window in Figure 3-20 uses the icon view.

Figure 3-20:
My hard disk window viewed as icons. Pretty and very Mac-like, but a total waste of perfectly good screen real estate.

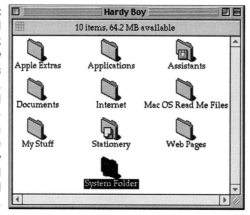

In all fairness I must say that there are many perfectly happy Macintosh users who love the icon view and refuse to even consider anything else. Fine. But as the number of files on your hard disk increases (as it does for every Mac user), screen real estate becomes more and more valuable.

By the way, if you like the icon view, they now make monitors as big as 21 inches.

The button view (shown in Figure 3-21) is no better and wastes just as much screen space as those blocky big icons.

The only thing the icon and button views have over the list view is the ability to arrange the icons anywhere you like within the window. Big deal.

Finally, the view I love and use most, the list view (shown in Figure 3-22).

Figure 3-21:
The same
window
viewed as
buttons.

	Name	Date Modified	Size	Kind
▷	Apple Extras	Sun, Jun 1, 1997, 10:04 AM	—	folder
▷	Applications	Yesterday, 2:51 PM	—	folder
▷	Assistants	Sun, Jun 1, 1997, 9:53 AM	—	folder
▷	Documents	Sun, Jun 1, 1997, 12:53 PM	—	folder
▷	Internet	Sun, Jun 1, 1997, 10:01 AM	—	folder
▷	Mac OS Read Me Files	Yesterday, 3:29 PM	—	folder
▷	My Stuff	Yesterday, 2:32 PM	—	folder
▷	Stationery	Sun, Jun 1, 1997, 9:57 AM	—	folder
▷	System Folder	Yesterday, 3:55 PM	—	folder
▷	Web Pages	Sun, Jun 1, 1997, 9:56 AM	—	folder

Hardy Boy — 10 items, 63.9 MB available

Figure 3-22:
The same
window
viewed as a
list.

The triangles

In list view, folder icons have a little triangle to the left of their names. This
is the outline metaphor, and it's only available in the list view. You click the
triangle to reveal the folder's contents right there in the same window.

In my humble opinion, this is a much better way to get to an icon buried
three or four folders deep than clicking through the folders themselves.
Figure 3-23 shows the slow and tedious way of getting to the icon named
Ch.01-Nose Runs. Figure 3-24 shows the cool, savvy, and efficient way of
getting to the same icon.

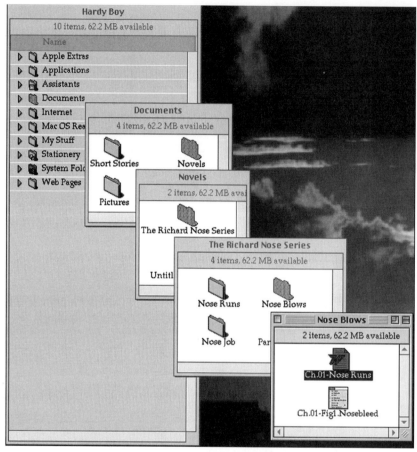

Figure 3-23:
Getting
to the
document
Ch.01-Nose
Runs the
usual way,
by opening
windows.

In Figure 3-23, I had to double-click four folders to get to Ch.01-Nose Runs. When I got to it, I had four windows open on the desktop.

In Figure 3-24, I had to single-click four triangles to get to Ch.01-Nose Runs. When I got to it, only one window was open, keeping my desktop neat and tidy.

There are other advantages to the triangles-outline metaphor. First and foremost, you can copy or move items from separate folders in one move, as Figure 3-25 illustrates.

Figure 3-24:
Getting
to the
document
Ch.01-Nose
Runs the
fast way,
using the
outline
triangles.

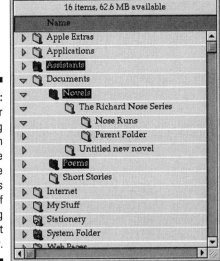

Figure 3-25:
Moving or
copying
files from
two or more
separate
folders is
easy if
you're using
the list
view.

In the list view, you can copy or move items from different folders with a single motion, without opening multiple windows. In either of the icon views, on the other hand, moving files from two or more different folders requires opening several windows and two separate drags.

Another feature of the triangles appears when you hold down the Option key and click a triangle. This action reveals *all* subfolders to the deepest level (see Figures 3-26 and 3-27).

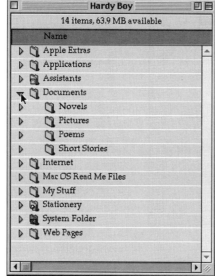

Figure 3-26:
A regular click on the Documents triangle reveals only the next level of folders.

The bottom line is that I have almost all of my windows displayed in the list view by name. Finally, I almost always use the triangles to reveal the contents of folders and rarely have more than a couple of windows open at a time.

The View Options command, which I'll talk about in a moment, offers additional controls and lets you choose stuff like the size of the icons and which columns appear in list view. If you feel adventurous, go ahead and play with it a little now.

You can also move among icons using the keyboard. If a window is active, make sure that no icons are selected and then type the first letter of a file's name. Regardless of which view you chose, the first icon that starts with that letter will be selected. To move to the next icon alphabetically, press the Tab key. To move to the previous icon alphabetically, press the Shift and Tab keys at the same time.

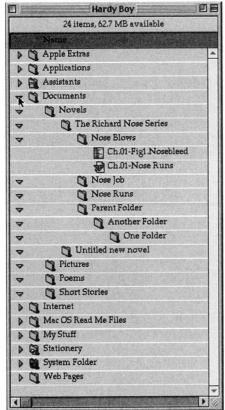

Figure 3-27:
An Option-
click on the
Documents
triangle
expands
all of its
subfolders.

If no window is active, typing a letter selects the first icon on the desktop that starts with that letter. The Tab and Shift-Tab commands work the same with desktop icons as they do with icons in a window.

If you have many icons that start with the same letter, you can type more than one letter (that is, type "sys" to select the System Folder, even if you've got folders called Stuff and Slime in the same window).

The second part: as Window or as Pop-up Window

The second part of the View menu lets you choose between regular old windows and nifty new pop-up windows, which let you arrange frequently used windows at the bottom of your screen for quick access (see Figure 3-28).

Figure 3-28:
I have three pop-up windows: Hardy Boy (open), Documents, and My Stuff.

To open a pop-up window, click its name at the bottom of your screen; to shrink it back down, click its name again. When you open one pop-up window, any other open pop-up window closes automatically (but regular windows remain open).

You can drag any icon onto the name of a pop-up window at the bottom of your screen; the pop-up window will scroll down, revealing its contents.

Pop-up windows are a nifty new feature of Mac OS 8. I recommend you play with them a little now and decide whether they suit your work style. (I still haven't decided; I fluctuate between using them and not.)

The third part: Clean Up, Arrange, and View Options

These last few commands on the View menu help you keep your stuff in order.

Clean Up

The Clean Up command aligns icons to the invisible grid; it is used to keep your windows and desktop neat and tidy. (If you like this invisible grid, don't forget that you can turn it on or off for the desktop and/or individual windows using View Options.)

Clean Up is only available in icon views or when no windows are active. If no windows are active, the command instead cleans up your desktop.

If you're like me, you have taken great pains to place icons carefully in specific places on your desktop. Cleaning up your desktop will destroy all your beautiful work and move all your perfectly arranged icons around.

Arrange

The command beneath Clean Up says Arrange (see Figure 3-29) if you're viewing icons, or Sort List (see Figure 3-30) if you're viewing a list.

Figure 3-29:
The View menu's Arrange menu item is only available when the active item (a window or the desktop) contains icons or buttons.

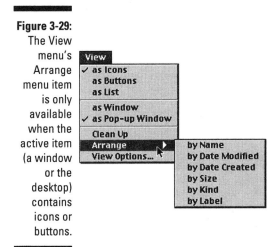

Let's talk about Arrange first. Choosing Arrange by Name causes icons in the active window (or on the desktop if no windows are open or active) to magically rearrange themselves into alphabetical order.

Choosing Arrange by Date Modified causes icons in the active window (or on the desktop if no windows are open or active) to magically rearrange themselves, with the most recently modified icon at top left and the icon modified longest ago at bottom right.

Use this view for folders with lots of documents in them. That way, the ones you used most recently will be listed first. If that gets confusing, you can easily switch to the list view for a second to find things alphabetically.

Choosing Arrange by Date Created causes icons in the active window (or on the desktop if no windows are open or active) to magically rearrange themselves, with the most recently created icon at top left and the icon created longest ago at bottom right.

Choosing Arrange by Size causes icons in the active window (or on the desktop if no windows are open or active) to magically rearrange themselves in descending order by size, with the largest item at top left and the smallest item at bottom right.

Choosing Arrange by Kind causes icons in the active window (or on the desktop if no windows are open or active) to magically rearrange themselves in this order from top left to bottom right: applications in alphabetical order, documents in alphabetical order, and then folders in alphabetical order.

Choosing Arrange by Label causes icons in the active window (or on the desktop if no windows are open or active) to magically rearrange themselves in the order in which labels appear in the File menu's Labels submenu, with icons in each label group arranged alphabetically.

Sort List

If you're viewing a window containing a list, the command beneath Clean Up says Sort List (see Figure 3-30).

Figure 3-30:
If the active window contains a list (instead of icons or buttons), you see the Sort List command instead of Arrange.

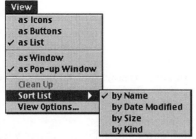

As you might expect, these items sort the contents of the active window.

Here's a shortcut for changing between sorting orders in list views: Notice how the appropriate column title is highlighted in Figure 3-31 — how Name is dark and Date Modified, Size, and Kind are not. This highlight tells you which list view is in use.

Now for the shortcut: You don't need to use the Sort List submenu to switch between list views. Instead, just click directly on the column title, and the window's view changes. Go ahead, give it a try. The only proviso is that you must be in a list view in the first place (the column titles don't appear in icon views). In Figure 3-32, I've clicked the Date Modified column; the window is now sorted with the most recently modified items on top.

In other words, clicking the title of the column is the same as using the Sort List submenu, only faster and easier.

View Options

The View Options command applies to the active window. If no window is active, it applies to the desktop. If icons or buttons are active when you choose View Options, you see a window like the one in Figure 3-33. If a window using list view is active, you instead see a window like Figure 3-34.

Figure 3-31:
This window is sorted by name, as evidenced by the word *Name* highlighted at the top of the window.

Hardy Boy			
10 items, 64 MB available			
Name	Date Modified	Size	Kind
▷ 🗀 Apple Extras	Sun, Jun 1, 1997, 10:04 AM	—	folder
▷ 🗀 Applications	Today, 1:05 PM	—	folder
▷ 🗀 Assistants	Sun, Jun 1, 1997, 9:53 AM	—	folder
▷ 🗀 Documents	Today, 12:40 PM	—	folder
▷ 🗀 Internet	Sun, Jun 1, 1997, 10:01 AM	—	folder
▷ 🗀 Mac OS Read Me Files	Today, 12:31 PM	—	folder
▷ 🗀 My Stuff	Yesterday, 2:32 PM	—	folder
▷ 🗀 Stationery	Sun, Jun 1, 1997, 9:57 AM	—	folder
▷ 🗀 System Folder	Yesterday, 3:55 PM	—	folder
▷ 🗀 Web Pages	Sun, Jun 1, 1997, 9:56 AM	—	folder

Figure 3-32:
I've clicked
Date
Modified at
the top of
the window;
as a result,
this window
is now
sorted with
the most
recently
modified
items at the
top of
the list.

	Name	Date Modified	Size	Kind
▷ 📁	Applications	Today, 1:05 PM	9 MB	folder
▷ 📁	Documents	Today, 12:40 PM	76K	folder
▷ 📁	Mac OS Read Me Files	Today, 12:31 PM	342K	folder
▷ 📁	System Folder	Yesterday, 3:55 PM	88.3 MB	folder
▷ 📁	My Stuff	Yesterday, 2:32 PM	989.7 MB	folder
▷ 📁	Apple Extras	Sun, Jun 1, 1997, 10:04 AM	23.9 MB	folder
▷ 📁	Internet	Sun, Jun 1, 1997, 10:01 AM	20.1 MB	folder
▷ 📁	Stationery	Sun, Jun 1, 1997, 9:57 AM	76K	folder
▷ 📁	Web Pages	Sun, Jun 1, 1997, 9:56 AM	798K	folder
▷ 📁	Assistants	Sun, Jun 1, 1997, 9:53 AM	475K	folder

Hardy Boy — 10 items, 62.1 MB available

Figure 3-33:
View
Options for
icon or
button
views.

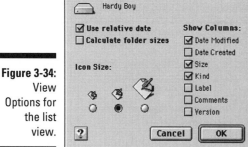

Figure 3-34:
View
Options for
the list
view.

In View Options for icons and buttons (Figure 3-33), choosing None for your icon arrangement turns off the invisible grid, choosing Always snap to grid turns it on, and choosing Keep arranged forces the Finder to constantly clean up the window according to the criteria you choose from the pop-up menu (by Name in Figure 3-33).

The Icon Size control lets you choose between small and large icons.

View Options for lists (Figure 3-34) has different controls. The Use relative date option intelligently substitutes "yesterday" and "today" for numerical dates. Calculate folder sizes does just what its name implies — it lets you see how much stuff is in each folder when you look at it in list view. The Show Columns check boxes govern which columns appear in the active window.

Finally, the Icon Size control lets you choose between small, medium, and large icons in your lists. For what it's worth, I think the smallest ones make windows appear noticeably faster; your mileage may vary.

If you have the Calculate folder sizes option turned on in View Options, the icons in the active window, including folder icons, will be sorted in descending order from biggest to smallest when you sort by size.

If you don't have Calculate folder sizes turned on, icons other than folders will be sorted by size, with all folders — regardless of their size — appearing at the bottom of the list.

Though sorting by folder size may seem convenient, I recommend that you keep this option turned off, as I believe that Calculate folder sizes makes the Finder feel a bit sluggish. If you really need to know how big a folder is, select it and use the File⇨Get Info command (keyboard shortcut Command-I).

Something Special in the Menu Bar: The Special Menu

The Special menu is a repository for a group of unrelated functions that don't really fit in any of the other menus: cleaning up (rearranging) icons; emptying trash; erasing and ejecting disks; and the Restart, Shut Down, and Sleep commands, to be precise.

Interestingly, only the Eject Disk command has a keyboard shortcut. One explanation might be that you wouldn't want to accidentally erase a disk, or restart or shut down your Mac, with something as easy to do as pressing the wrong key combination.

Empty Trash

I've already talked about the Trash (just last chapter, as a matter of fact). And I talked about it earlier in this chapter when I showed you the Get Info box.

I've said it before and I'll say it again: Use this command with a modicum of caution. Once a file is trashed and emptied, it's gone. (Okay, maybe Norton Utilities can bring it back, but don't bet the farm on it.)

Eject Disk and Erase Disk

See Chapter 2 for more information than you need on ejecting and erasing disks.

Sleep

Sleep puts your Mac and monitor into a state of suspended animation complete with lower power consumption. Waking up from sleep mode is much faster than restarting. You can control when your Mac goes to sleep automatically with the Energy Saver control panel, discussed in Chapter 12.

Restart

The Restart command shuts down your Mac briefly and then starts it back up. Why do you need such a thing? Every so often, your Mac will act wonky. By wonky, I mean things don't seem to work right. You can't launch a program that used to launch fine. You can't rename an icon. You can't use the keyboard. Or something. That's when to use Restart.

You see, computer problems often disappear when you clear the computer's memory, which is one of the things that occurs when you restart.

One of the best pieces of advice I give people when they call me in a panic is to restart their Macs and try it again. At least half the time the problem goes away and never comes back after restarting. I'm a little paranoid about things going wrong, so I often restart my computer in the middle of the day, just in case something is *about* to go wrong. It couldn't hurt.

Sometimes when your Mac gets really wonky, you may be unable to choose Special⇨Restart for one reason or another. If you can't, because the cursor won't move, or for any other reason, try pressing the Command and Option keys while you press the Escape (Esc) key. If things aren't too messed up, you should see a dialog box asking if you're sure you want to force the current application to quit. You do. Your Mac is so wonked that you had to resort to the Command-Option-Escape technique, so click the Force Quit button. If it works, the current application (or the Finder) will quit. If you're in the Finder, it will relaunch itself automatically. You'll lose any unsaved changes in the application that you quit, but you may regain the use of your Mac. If you do, immediately save any documents you have open in other applications and restart. *The Force Quit command leaves your Mac in an unstable state, and you should always restart as soon as possible after using it.* After, of course, saving any unsaved documents.

If that trick doesn't work, try pressing both the Command and Control (Ctrl) keys while you press the Power-On key (the one with the little left-pointing triangle on it). This technique forces your Mac to restart. Unfortunately, it doesn't work all the time or on all Macintosh models. But it usually does.

If Command-Control-Power-On doesn't work for you, look for the reset and interrupt switches on the front or side of your Mac and press the reset switch, which is the one with a triangle. This technique will also force your Mac to restart. Unfortunately, not all Macs have these switches.

If you're still having problems and still can't choose Special⇨Restart, turn the power off using the power switch and leave your Mac off for at least ten seconds before you try to start up again.

Shut Down

Shutting down is the last thing you do at the end of every session at your Mac. When you're all done using the machine, choose Special⇨Shut Down.

Because I ragged on endlessly in Chapter 1 about how important the Shut Down command is, I'm not going to do it again.

Use it or lose it.

Not Just a Beatles Movie: Help and the Help Menu

One of System 7.5's niftiest new features was its built-in interactive assistance system, Apple Guide. It's back and it's even better now. Faster, too. You'll find it in the Help menu, which is, for the first time, titled *Help*.

For what it's worth, Balloon Help is still available, but Mac OS Help goes it one (actually, a few) better.

About Help (no keyboard shortcut)

Choose the About Help command to read about the Help menu. You probably never need to do so because you're reading *Mac OS 8 For Dummies,* and my text is usually better than theirs.

If you insist, you'll see a single little screen that doesn't say much.

Show Balloons (no keyboard shortcut)

The Show Balloons command turns on Balloon Help. When Balloon Help is on, pointing at almost any item on the screen causes a little help balloon to pop up and explain it (as illustrated in Figure 3-35).

Figure 3-35:
Balloon
Help in
action.

After you choose Show Balloons, the command in the Help menu changes to Hide Balloons until you choose it again, at which time the command changes back to Show Balloons. And so on.

I rarely use Balloon Help myself, but if you're relatively new to the Mac, you may find it helpful. Most applications include Balloon Help, so don't forget that you can turn balloons on in programs as well as in the Finder.

Help (Command-?)

In the beginning, there wasn't much help built into your Mac. In fact, before System 7, there was none. System 7 introduced Balloon Help, and it was good. Well, actually, it was kind of lame, and not that many developers implemented it at first, but it was better than nothing.

Once most software did start including Balloon Help, Apple raised the bar in System 7.5 with Apple Guide, an interactive step-by-step guidance system for accomplishing tasks on your Mac. It's hot. Apple calls it an electronic assistant, and for once I don't think it's oversell. It was dubbed Mac OS Guide in Mac OS 7.6, and its new Mac OS 8 name is Mac OS Help.

It's like having a consultant at your side. But there's nothing to open your eyes like a demonstration, so here's how to have your new assistant, Mac OS Help, answer a question for you.

1. Choose Help from the Help menu (or use the keyboard shortcut Command-?).

2. When the Mac OS Help window appears (see Figure 3-36), click the Topics button at the top of the window. Then click "application programs" in the topic list on the left, and in the list on the right, click "switch between programs?" and then click OK.

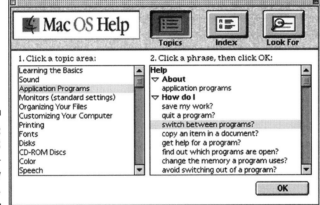

Figure 3-36:
Mac OS
Help —
your new
assistant.

3. Glance at the arrow in the upper-right corner of your screen directing you to the Application menu. Read what Mac OS Help has to say in this first screen and then click the right-arrow button at the bottom right of the *windoid* (as this type of window is called) to receive further instructions.

4. When windoid 2 appears (look between the arrows to see the windoid number), your assistant tells you what to do and points to where you should do it with a red arrow (see Figure 3-37).

5. That's it. You're done. Close Mac OS Help.

Mac OS Help has circles, arrows, and a whole arsenal of other visual cues to help you figure out how to do things on your Mac. There's even a Huh? button in case you don't understand (unfortunately, it's not active in all screens). Mac OS Help is an excellent resource, especially for those of you who are new to the Mac. I urge you to explore it further at your leisure.

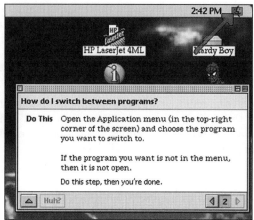

Figure 3-37:
Your faithful
assistant
shows you
where to
click next
with a
bright red
arrow.

Incidentally, the Mac OS Help engine is built into the System software. That means your word processor, spreadsheet, or graphics program can use it as easily as Apple uses it in the Finder. Although it may be a while before third-party developers (that is, the folks who publish application software) implement Mac OS Help in their programs, look for "Includes Mac OS Help" (or its old name, Mac OS Guide) on the box and in advertisements as a selling point. I know I'd rather buy a program that has it than buy one that doesn't.

Apply Yourself: The Application Menu

Last but not least (at least for menus in the menu bar; I talk about contextual menus in a moment) is the Application menu. It's the one in the upper-right corner. Because all of this menu's functions are related, I'm going to skip describing its commands one at a time and try to convey the gestalt of the Application menu instead.

If the Finder is the active application, the Application menu displays a little Mac OS icon like the one shown in Figure 3-38.

Figure 3-38:
The
Application
menu as it
appears
when I'm in
the Finder.

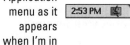

If another application is currently active, a little version of that application's icon represents the Application menu instead (see Figure 3-39).

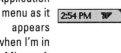

The Application menu lets you choose which program you want to use. As with windows, only one application is active at a time. Because Mac OS 8 allows you to open more than one application at a time (if you have enough RAM), the Application menu is one of the ways to switch between all currently running applications and the Finder (I discuss the other methods near the end of this section).

If a program is running, its name appears in the Application menu; the Finder's name always appears in it. In Figure 3-40, I have two programs running in addition to the Finder: Microsoft Word and Adobe Photoshop.

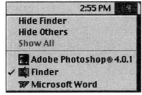

Figure 3-40:
The Application menu itself.

If the Finder is currently active and you want to switch to Microsoft Word, choose its name in the Application menu. Microsoft Word's menus appear in the menu bar, and if there's a document open (or an untitled new document), its window becomes the active window.

To switch back to the Finder, you choose Finder in the Application menu. Piece of cake, right?

Wrong. When you switch back to the Finder, Microsoft Word's document window may obscure items on the desktop. Finder windows aren't a problem — they float to the front. But icons on the desktop may be covered.

This is where the Hide and Show commands come into play. You could switch back to Microsoft Word and quit that program, but there's an easier way to free up desktop real estate. Choose Hide Others from the Application menu, and the Microsoft Word windows and toolbars will be hidden from view. Microsoft Word is still running, but its window or windows and toolbars are hidden from view.

To make Microsoft Word visible again, choose Show All from the Application menu.

Open any application and play around with the Hide and Show commands on the Application menu. They're easier to understand after you play with them a little.

They're Sooo Sensitive: Contextual Menus

Context-sensitive menus are a neat new Mac OS 8 feature. A contextual menu lists commands that apply to the item the cursor is over. Contextual menus appear in windows, on icons, and most places on the desktop when you hold down the Control key and click (see Figure 3-41).

Figure 3-41:
The contextual menu when you Control-click a document icon; notice that only actions that apply to a document icon appear.

If you click inside a window but not on any icon, the contextual menu contains actions you perform on a window (Figure 3-42).

Figure 3-42:
The
contextual
menu when
you Control-
click a
window;
notice that
only actions
that apply
to a window
icon
appear.

Notice how a contextual menu for a document (Figure 3-41) differs from the
contextual menu for a window (Figure 3-42). That's why they call 'em contextual. Actions appear in contextual menus only when they make sense for
the item you Control-click.

Don't believe me? Control-click the desktop (that is, click somewhere that's
not in any window and not on any icon) and you'll see a contextual menu
with different commands (Figure 3-43).

Figure 3-43:
The
contextual
menu for
the desktop.

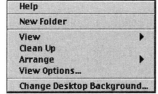

Contextual menus are perhaps the niftiest new Finder feature. Get in the
habit of Control-clicking items. Before you know it, using contextual menus
will be second nature to you.

Chapter 4
Polishing the Apple (Menu)

● ●

In This Chapter

▶ About This Computer (yours)

▶ Desk accessories

▶ Those interestingly named folders in the Apple menu

▶ Customizing your Apple menu

▶ A deep, dark secret

● ●

*T*he Apple menu is beneath the little Apple logo, an apple with a bite taken out of it, that graces the upper-left corner of your screen. It gets its own chapter because, unlike the menus I discussed previously, it's entirely configurable by you, the user. This is one of the finest features of the Mac — the ability to create your own customized file-launching and folder-accessing environment.

System 7.5's Apple menu broke new ground. It's still wonderful in Mac OS 8. Most significant was the addition of hierarchical submenus, which power users have loved in the form of Now Software's NowMenus and other similar programs for years. Finally everyone else can see what the power-user elite have been raving about for so long. Submenus in the Apple menu are fantastic!

So I'll show you the basics of configuring *your* Apple menu in this chapter, but I'm telling you in advance: I'm saving the really cool tricks for Chapter 11.

Before I talk about how to customize your Apple menu, I'll describe the stuff that's already in it: *desk accessories,* the little miniprograms (Jigsaw Puzzle, Calculator, and so on) that Apple thoughtfully stuck in your Apple menu along with several special folders. In all fairness, I'll also show you how to use the essential and useful desk accessories such as the Scrapbook and the Chooser, so don't that think all desk accessories are lame. Only most of them are.

Oh, and one last thing: At the end of this chapter, I'll let you in on a deep, dark secret that you probably figured out already.

About This Computer (Yours)

Before we do anything, let me tell you a bit about the Apple menu's only permanent item, About This Computer.

The first item on every Apple menu (at least if the Finder is the active application) is the About This Computer command. Take a peek at it from time to time — it lets you know how much of your memory (RAM) is currently being used, how much of it is real RAM and how much of it is virtual memory, which programs are using it, and how much is left for programs yet to be launched. Those are good things to know. It also tells you what version of the System software is running.

In Figure 4-1 you can see that my System software is using 11.1MB of RAM (random access memory).

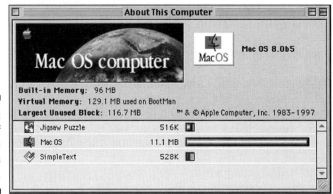

Figure 4-1:
A wealth of information about this computer.

11.1MB of RAM is a lot for System software. But I'm running all the options Mac OS 8 has to offer — QuickDraw 3D, QuickDraw GX, QuickTime VR, File Sharing, AppleScript — the whole shebang. In Chapter 14, I'll show you how to turn this stuff off (or get rid of it completely), as well as give you advice on when it's safe for you to do so. For now, let's just say that your System software will probably use somewhat less RAM than mine.

In Figure 4-1, the Jigsaw Puzzle application is using 516K, and SimpleText is using 528K. The bars to the right of the programs' names and numbers are especially meaningful. The right part of each bar reflects the amount of memory the program has grabbed (and corresponds to the number just to the left of the bar). The highlighted part of the bar shows how much of that memory the program is actually using at the moment. My System software looks like it's using almost all of its allocation; SimpleText looks like it's using about a third of its. Jigsaw Puzzle seems to be using about two thirds.

What? You aren't willing to accept "about two thirds" as an answer? Sigh. Okay. To find out *exactly* how much RAM Jigsaw Puzzle is using, choose Help⇨Show Balloons and then point at the bar for Jigsaw Puzzle. What you ought to see is shown in Figure 4-2.

Figure 4-2:
Jigsaw
Puzzle is
using
exactly
324K of the
516K it
requested
when I
opened it.

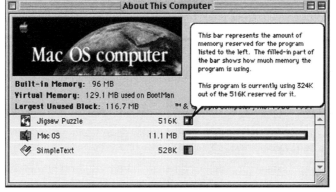

Why is the information in the About This Computer window important? I'll tell you why. First, you can see how much RAM is left (the Largest Unused Block) for launching additional programs. I have approximately 117 megabytes (wow!), but I have a lot of RAM (96MB of real RAM, plus 32 additional megabytes of virtual memory). If you try to launch a program that requires more RAM than the Largest Unused Block at any given time, your Mac will politely inform you that there's not enough memory to launch this program.

The other thing that's important is that I can see that SimpleText gobbled up 512K when I launched it, but it's only using 128K of its allocation at this time. (I found that out using the Balloon Help tip.) So it's grabbing about 400K of precious RAM and not using it.

What can I do about it? Well, I can tell SimpleText to grab less RAM next time I launch it. Here's how:

Oops. Almost forgot. If SimpleText is open, quit before performing the following procedure. An application cannot be running when you adjust its Preferred Memory Size.

1. Select the SimpleText icon.

2. Choose File⇨Get Info or use the keyboard shortcut Command-I.

   The SimpleText Info window appears (as shown in Figure 4-3).

3. In the lower portion of the SimpleText Info window, change the Preferred Size from 512K to a smaller number, somewhere between the Minimum and Suggested Size.

4. Close the Get Info window.

The change doesn't take effect until the Get Info window is closed.

Figure 4-3:
Reduce the Preferred Size from 512K to a lower number (but not lower than the Minimum Size above it).

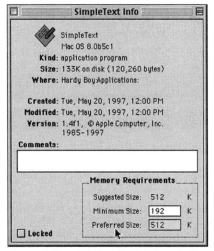

When I say "a smaller number," it's not because I don't want to tell you what number to use. But it's not a precise science. I don't know how big the documents you open with SimpleText are, and that's what determines how much RAM it needs. Try 256K. If you someday discover that you can't open a document due to low memory (your Mac will tell you so), increase this number a bit — to 384K or even 450K. It still saves you a little over the old setting of 512K.

Don't perform the preceding procedure haphazardly. Most programs run better with their Preferred memory set *higher* than the suggested size. But (and it's a big but) if you're short on RAM for other programs and you can see that a program is only using a fraction of the RAM that it requests, you can probably reduce its Preferred size at least a little and maybe a lot.

From the Desk (Accessories) of . . .

You use items in the Apple menu the same way that you use any menu item — click the Apple and drag down to the item. When you release the mouse button, the item opens. If the item is a folder, it will have a submenu; you can see its contents by dragging down until the folder is highlighted and stopping. Don't release the mouse button, or the folder will pop open. To choose an item in the submenu, drag to the right.

If you haven't modified your Apple menu, it probably looks something like Figure 4-4.

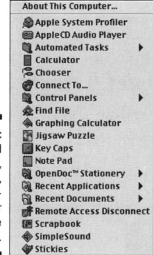

Figure 4-4:
A standard issue, unconfigured, fresh-from-the-installer Apple menu.

Ignoring the folders for now (I'll talk about them after I ridicule a few desk accessories), let's take a look at each desk accessory in turn.

Technically, only a few of the items in the Apple menu are desk accessories (known affectionately as DAs), special types of miniprograms that are a little different from regular applications and are a holdover from System 6 and earlier. The rest are regular old applications. Even so, most people refer to the programs Apple sticks under the Apple menu as desk accessories, and so will I. Desk accessories are basically miniapplications, and they're discussed further along with control panels and extensions in Chapter 14.

Profile THIS: Apple System Profiler

Apple System Profiler was new in Mac OS 7.6. It's a little program that gives you information about your Mac. What a concept. If you're curious about things like what processor your Mac has, or what devices are on its SCSI bus, give it a try. Poke around the Select menu and check it out if you like; this little puppy is benign and won't hurt anything.

If you ever have occasion to call for technical support for your Mac, software, or peripherals, you will probably be asked to provide information from Apple System Profiler. So don't get rid of it just because *you* don't care about this kind of stuff.

So? Apple finally provides a useful tool and then stupidly leaves out the most useful features: the ability to save your profile as a text file (to e-mail to technical support???) and the ability to print (to fax to technical support???). Sigh. I guess it's better than nothing.

Sounds good to me: AppleCD Audio Player

Next on the Apple menu is the AppleCD Audio Player. It's a little program you use to play regular old stereo CDs on your CD-ROM drive (see Figure 4-5). Just pop your *Elvis & Steve* CD into the CD-ROM drive, select AppleCD Audio Player from the Apple menu, and then click the Play button. Your room will be filled with the mellow tones of Elvis Costello and Steve Nieve.

Figure 4-5:
AppleCD Audio Player is a slick remote control program for playing audio CDs in your CD-ROM drive.

TIP

You may have to plug a pair of amplified stereo speakers into the stereo output jacks on some external CD-ROM drives. If you have an internal CD-ROM drive, you may need to select Internal CD from the Sound Input pop-up menu in the Monitors & Sound control panel before you hear music through your Mac's built-in speaker. Finally, you must have the Audio CD Access extension in the Extensions folder within your System Folder for the AppleCD Audio Player to function.

Because the internal speakers in most Macs suck, a good pair of multimedia speakers is a good investment; then you'll be able to rattle the walls when you slap that Elvis CD in your drive.

There's a whole chapter (Chapter 14) about every item in your System Folder and whether you need it. It also explains what an extension is, in case you're wondering. In any event, it should be obvious to you even now that this program isn't much use if you don't have a CD-ROM drive.

A calculated risk: Calculator

The Calculator has been in the Apple menu as long as I can remember, and it hasn't changed one iota since it was introduced. (All right, it got a spiffy new icon when System 7 first arrived, but that's the extent of it.) Figure 4-6 shows what the ol' Calculator (still) looks like.

Figure 4-6:
The
ancient-yet-
venerable
Calculator
DA.

The Calculator DA is the *pixel* (for picture element, the little dots that make up your screen) equivalent of the cheesy calculators that cheap companies give away — or the kind you see at the grocery store for $1.99. The Apple Calculator does have one feature that makes it different from all those Taiwan specials — cheap calculators don't require a four-figure investment in computer equipment.

I'm kidding, of course. Even though it's looking a little long in the tooth (Hey, Apple — how about a facelift for the old fellow? Maybe some pastel colors? More graceful-looking buttons? A paper tape? And a Clear Entry button instead of only Clear All?), it still comes in handy more often than you might expect. For example, my wife used it to balance our checkbook for years (till she got hooked on Quicken).

The Calculator DA works just like a real calculator. Use the numeric keypad on your keyboard; the keys correlate to their on-screen counterparts.

Unfortunately, the Calculator lacks all but the most basic features. As noted, it doesn't have a paper tape, a Clear Entry key, or even a single memory recall. There are shareware and commercial calculators galore, with features galore. If you need a calculator DA, almost anything you can buy or download will be better than the Calculator DA that comes with Mac OS 8.

Be choosy: Be a Chooser user

The Chooser is a desk accessory that lets you choose at least two things: which printer to use and which computer(s) to share files with.

If you click a printer icon on the left side of the window, all the printers available on the network appear in a list on the right side of the window (see Figure 4-7).

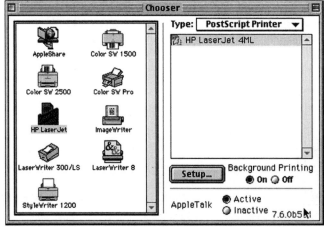

Figure 4-7:
The
Chooser.

The Chooser is also where you choose other Macs to share files with. If you click the AppleShare icon on the left side of the Chooser, every Mac on your network that has file sharing turned on will appear in the list on the right.

Finally, the Chooser is also where you create desktop printer icons, but because there's an entire chapter on printing and yet another one about file sharing. I think you know enough about the Chooser to hold you till you get to them.

Connect To

The Connect To Apple menu item, new in Mac OS 8, brings up a dialog box where you can type an Internet address (URL). Click the Connect button, and Connect To launches Netscape Navigator and displays the Web page you typed into the dialog box.

Sure you could launch Netscape, type Command-L (Open Location), type a URL, and then press Return or Enter and get the same effect. But Connect To is easier.

Finder of lost files: Find File (again)

Choosing Find File from the Apple menu is the same as choosing File⇨Find in the Finder (try saying that fast three times). The only advantage this DA has is that, because it is in the Apple menu, you can choose it even if the Finder isn't currently the active application. If you've forgotten how Find File works, read Chapter 3.

Fakin' it with Graphing Calculator (Power Macs only)

I still have no idea what this thing is really supposed to do. I do enjoy running its demos for my friends and pretending I do, though. If Graphing Calculator appears in your Apple menu, here's how to fake it. Choose 3D Surfaces from the Demo menu. You should see something like Figure 4-8.

Click the Stop button and then use your mouse to spin the graph. Mumble something half-intelligibly about "PowerPC processors and real-time 3D surface mapping capabilities." I guarantee you'll impress your friends.

Better than puzzles of old, it's Jigsaw Puzzle

Better than the old 15-numbers-in-16-squares puzzle of System software of old, the Jigsaw Puzzle is only a little less lame. It's a jigsaw puzzle. Click the pieces to move them around (see Figure 4-9).

One cool thing is that you can paste another picture onto the puzzle and that picture becomes the jigsaw puzzle. It's kind of fun. Here's how to do it:

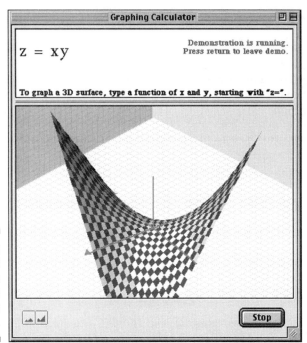

Figure 4-8:
The 3D
Surfaces
demo in
Graphing
Calculator.

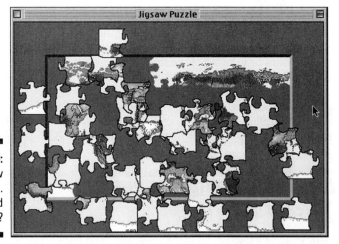

Figure 4-9:
It's a jigsaw
puzzle.
What did
you expect?

1. Select any picture in a graphics program, word processor, or
   SimpleText (what I used).

2. Choose Edit⇨Copy.

3. Choose Apple menu⇨Jigsaw Puzzle.

4. Choose Edit⇨Paste.

In Figure 4-10, I've pasted my own picture into Jigsaw Puzzle.

Figure 4-10:
Paste
a new
picture, get
a new
puzzle.

And there you have it — a new puzzle for you to solve. This technique works with any picture you can copy to the Clipboard, and also with icons (see the preceding chapter for information on copying and pasting).

The key to all your fonts: It's Key Caps

Want to know what every character in a font looks like? Or where the funny optional characters like ™, ®, ©, ¢, and • are hidden on your keyboard? Sounds like a job for Key Caps, a modest little desk accessory that shows you a lot about your installed fonts.

If you're not sure what a font is, choose Apple menu⇨Key Caps. You'll see something like Figure 4-11.

The items in the Key Caps menu are your fonts. When you pull down the Key Caps menu you see a list of your installed fonts. To see what a particular font looks like, choose it in the Key Caps menu and type a few words. They appear in the white text entry box at the top of the Key Caps window. If you want to see what those words look like in another font, choose that font from the Key Caps menu.

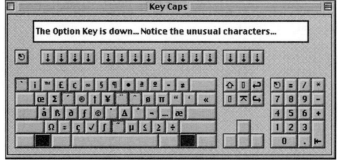

Figure 4-11:
The Key
Caps DA
shows you
all the cute
characters
in your
fonts.

Of course, you could do the same thing in any program that has a font menu. In fact, you can do more because Key Caps only displays the font in a single size, 12 points; other programs let you change the size as well as the font, and you can also apply character styles such as bold, italic, and outline.

So what good is Key Caps? It's the easiest way to find special symbols like ™, ®, ©, ¢, and •, or ß, √, £, °, and ¿. Just open Key Caps, choose a font, and hold down the Option key. Key Caps displays the special symbols and characters on the keyboard. For example, to type ™ in your document, hold down the Option key and press the 2 key on your keyboard. Instant ™.

What Key Caps doesn't show you is how to create diacritical marks such as acute accents and umlauts. To type them, follow these instructions:

✔ To type a grave accent (`), type Option-` and then type the character. So to accent an *e,* you type **Option-`** and then type **e**. It will come out looking like this: è. (The ` key is usually in the top row to the left of the 1 key.)

✔ To type an acute accent (´), type Option-e and then type the character. So to accent an *e,* you type **Option-e** and then type **e**. It will come out looking like this: é.

✔ To type a circumflex (^), type Option-i and then type the character. So to put a circumflex over an *i,* you type **Option-i** and then type **i**. It will come out looking like this: î.

✔ To type a tilde (~), type Option-n and then type the character. So to put a tilde over an *n,* you type **Option-n** and then type **n**. It will come out looking like this: ñ. I'm pretty sure that the *n* is the only character you can put a tilde over; I tried to put it over other characters, but they came out looking like this: ~b.

✔ To type an umlaut (¨), type Option-u and then type the character. So to put an umlaut over a *u,* you type **Option-u** and then type **u**. It will come out looking like this: ü, as in Motley Crüe.

Take note of the Note Pad

Note Pad is a handy, dandy little note-taking utility that lets you store gobs of unrelated text items without saving a zillion different files all over your hard disk. Everything that you type into Note Pad is automatically saved in the Note Pad File, which is in your System Folder. Figure 4-12 shows Note Pad in action.

Figure 4-12: Note Pad is a handy little program for jotting random thoughts and phone numbers.

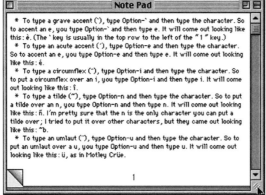

Note Pad uses a page metaphor. Click the dog-ear corner at bottom left to change the page or choose File⇨Go to Note and type in the page number of the note that you want to go to.

The Note Pad in Mac OS 8 has several improvements over Note Pads of old. Most welcome is the Find command. And its window is resizable and has scroll bars. (Can you believe it took Apple until System 7.5 to add scroll bars and make its window resizable?) Finally, the pages seem to hold a lot more text than older versions. Oh, and you can choose a font in the Preferences dialog box; the older Note Pads gave a choice of Geneva or Geneva.

You can print notes, and Note Pad (like almost every Mac application ever made) includes full support of Cut, Copy, or Paste, so you can easily get text in and out of Note Pad by using the Clipboard.

Some people prefer Note Pad to Stickies (you'll hear about Stickies in a second), some people use both, some people use neither. For a freebie, Note Pad is relatively well equipped. If you have a lot of random thoughts that you'd like to type, you might want to leave it open all day (it only uses a little RAM). It's also a good spot for frequently dialed phone numbers.

Remote Access Disconnect

A component of ARA (Apple Remote Access). See Chapter 8.

The not-so-scrappy Scrapbook

The Scrapbook is like the Note Pad, but you use it to store graphics, text, and sounds. Instead of pages, the Scrapbook uses an item metaphor. You move from item to item by using the scroll bar in the lower part of the Scrapbook window (see Figure 4-13).

Figure 4-13:
The Scrapbook is a storage repository for graphics, sounds, and text; you control it with the Cut, Copy, Paste, and Clear commands.

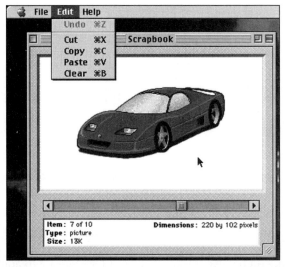

To put something into the Scrapbook, copy it to the Clipboard; then open the Scrapbook and choose Edit⇨Paste or use the keyboard shortcut Command-V. The pasted item will become the item before the current item. So if you're looking at item 1 when you paste, the pasted item becomes item 1, and the former item 1 becomes item 2, and so on.

Here are the various ways to use the Scrapbook:

✔ To remove an item from the Scrapbook and use it elsewhere, choose Edit⇨Cut or use the keyboard shortcut Command-X. This action removes the current item from the Scrapbook and places it on the Clipboard for pasting into another document.

✔ To use a Scrapbook item in another document without deleting it, choose Edit⇨Copy or the keyboard shortcut Command-C. Then open a document and choose Edit⇨Paste.

✔ To delete a Scrapbook item forever, choose Edit⇨Clear or use the keyboard shortcut Command-B. Doing so deletes the item from the Scrapbook without placing it on the Clipboard.

You can't always paste a picture or sound into a document. The determining factor is the kind of document that you're trying to paste into. For example, you can't paste a picture into cells in spreadsheets or most fields in databases. And you can't usually paste a sound into a graphics file.

If you try to paste an inappropriate item into a document, your Mac will either beep at you or do nothing. If nothing happens when you paste, assume that the document can't accept the picture or sound you're trying to paste.

You can paste text into the Scrapbook, but it's probably easier to paste it into the Note Pad where you can select only a portion of it or edit it. After text is pasted into the Scrapbook, it can't be selected or edited, so if you want to change it, you'll have to copy and paste the entire chunk of text into an application that supports text editing (such as Note Pad, SimpleText, or a word processor).

If you want to replace the old version of an item in the Scrapbook with a changed version, you'll have to copy the new version to the Clipboard and then paste it into the Scrapbook. Don't forget to delete the old version by scrolling until it appears and choosing Edit⇨Clear (Command-B) to delete it.

SimpleSound

A simple little DA for recording your own alert sounds. You have to have a proper microphone; contact your nearest Apple or clone dealer for details. Just open SimpleSound, click the Add button, the Record button, and then the Save button, and just like that you'll have a new beep sound.

SimpleSound has one other feature: its Sound menu lets you choose between CD Quality, Music Quality, Speech Quality, and Phone Quality sound. Frankly, I can't tell the difference, even using excellent amplified speakers.

Don't be stuck up: Use Stickies

Stickies, which were new in System 7.5, are electronic Post-it® Notes for your Mac. They are akin to the Note Pad; they're a slightly different but no less convenient place to jot notes or phone numbers. Stickies are shown in Figure 4-14.

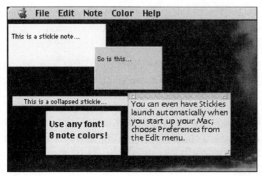

Figure 4-14: Stickies are the electronic equivalent of Post-it® Notes.

Stickies are nothing if not flexible. They can be moved around on-screen (just drag 'em by the title bar). They can display text in any font you desire. They can be collapsed by Option-clicking their grow boxes. They can be any color you like (if you have a color monitor, of course). You can import and export text files. And, of course, you can print Stickies.

As with the Note Pad, anything that you type on a Sticky is saved automatically as long as you keep that note open. But when you close a note (by clicking its close box, choosing File⇨Close, or using the keyboard shortcut Command-W), you lose its contents forever. Fortunately, Stickies gives you a warning and a second chance to save the note in a separate file on your hard disk.

If you like to live dangerously, you can turn the warning off by choosing Edit⇨Preferences and unchecking the Confirm Window-Closing option. In the Preferences dialog box, you can also tell Stickies to save all notes every time you switch to another application (safer), set the zoom box so that it collapses the window without the Option key, and set whether Stickies should launch automatically at startup (if you check this item, Stickies creates an alias of itself and puts it in your Startup Items folder).

Those interestingly named folders in the Apple Menu

There are a handful of folders in your Apple menu spread out amongst the desk accessories. You may see little triangles to the right of their names (if you don't, I'll show you how to turn them on in a minute). The triangles indicate that these folders have hierarchical submenus and will reveal their contents when you pull down the Apple menu and drag the cursor onto them. Submenus are a newish feature, introduced with System 7.5, though commercial programs like NowMenus and shareware programs like MenuChoice have provided this functionality since the early days of System 7.

To select an item in the submenu, drag to the right and highlight it, as shown in Figure 4-15.

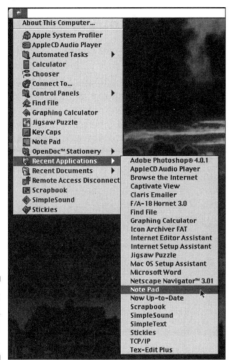

Figure 4-15:
A
hierarchical
submenu.

To choose Note Pad in the Recent Applications folder (see Figure 4-15), click the Apple, drag down until the Recent Applications folder is highlighted, drag to the right and down until Note Pad is highlighted, and then release the mouse button.

If you don't see the little triangles to the right of your folders, here's how to turn them on:

1. Choose Apple menu⇨Control Panels.

2. Open the Apple Menu Options control panel.

3. Click the On radio button, as shown in Figure 4-16.

What is a control panel, anyway?

Control panels are little programs that you use to adjust and configure your Mac. Each one has one or two specific functions — set the Mac clock (Date & Time), change menu blinking (General Controls), configure memory (Memory), adjust the mouse (Mouse) and keyboard (Keyboard), and so on.

Control panels go in the Control Panels folder inside your System Folder. The Installer automatically creates an alias of the Control Panels folder and puts it in your Apple menu for you when you install Mac OS 8.

If you get a new control panel (many screen savers and other utilities are control panels), simply drag it onto the System Folder icon, and Mac OS 8 automatically puts it in its proper place, the Control Panels folder. (Incidentally, Mac OS 8 is smart about extensions, fonts, and sounds as well. If you drag an extension, font, or sound onto the System Folder icon, Mac OS 8 puts it in its proper place automatically.)

There's a whole chapter on control panels and how to configure them (Chapter 12), so I'll leave it at that for now.

Figure 4-16:
Turning
on the
hierarchical
submenus
in the Apple
Menu
Options
control
panel.

Now that you know how submenus work, let's talk about the five or six folders you may see in your Apple menu.

The Control Panels folder

As previously noted, the Installer creates an alias of the Control Panels folder and puts it in your Apple menu that so you always have access to your control panels, even when you're using an application other than the Finder. Before submenus were introduced (1994), you had to choose the

Control Panels folder from the Apple menu. That action would automatically switch you to the Finder (if you were in another application) and open the Control Panels folder's window. Then you had to open the icon for the control panel manually. Ugh. Mac OS 8, with its marvelous submenus, is much nicer.

Recent Applications, Recent Documents, and Recent Servers

I'll discuss these three Apple menu items together because they're related and work the same way.

If you don't see them in your Apple menu, open the Apple Menu Options control panel (choose Apple menu⇨Control Panels⇨Apple Menu Options) and check the Remember recently used items check box (see Figure 4-16). This action will create the folders in your Apple Menu Items folder as soon as you open an application, document, or server. If you never open a server (access another Macintosh over a network), the Recent Servers folder will never be created.

Even if you do see these items in your Apple menu, you may want to use the Apple Menu Options control panel to change the number of applications, documents, and servers that the folders will remember. I find that 30 is a good number on my big 20-inch monitor— enough to ensure that the application or document (I rarely use the server folder) that I am looking for is still there, but not so many that the submenu scrolls off the screen.

These three folders track the last *x-many* applications, documents, and servers that you opened. Each time you open one of these three types of icons, the System makes a mental note of it and then creates an alias of that application, document, or server and pops it into the appropriate folder in your Apple Menu Items folder. The System also limits the number of items in each folder based on the Apple Menu Options control panel's settings. So when you open your 31st application, the oldest application alias in the Recent Applications folder disappears.

Why are these folders useful? Often the document or application that you're looking for is one you had open earlier in the day or yesterday. These special folders in the Apple menu keep recently used items handy. Chances are, if you used it recently, you'll want to use it again soon. If so, look in one of these folders. (Hint: Use the submenu — it's faster.)

Automated Tasks

The Automated Tasks folder contains a collection of useful AppleScript scripts. AppleScript is the Mac's internal scripting language. Scripts can perform many Macintosh tasks that would take several steps to perform manually, such as turning File Sharing on and off, changing the number of colors that you see on your monitor, and adjusting the speaker's volume. Many people refer to what a script does as a *macro*.

AppleScript is kind of neat, and it's included with Mac OS 8 at absolutely no charge. If you're the kind of person who likes to climb under the hood and get your fingers dirty, there's a whole chapter (Chapter 13) about AppleScript, the scriptable Finder, and tips on creating your own scripts. Don't miss it.

OpenDoc Stationery

The OpenDoc Stationery folder (if you installed OpenDoc) is where you store stationery files for OpenDoc applications such as CyberDog. See the "What's Open, Doc?" sidebar in Chapter 15 for info on OpenDoc.

Roll Your Own: Customizing Your Apple Menu

Do you remember Figure 4-4, way back there at the beginning of the chapter? Can you say "Boooorrrring"?

The Apple menu is fully configurable. Whatever is in the Apple Menu Items folder appears in the Apple menu. It's that simple.

So let's start to transform your Apple menu from a dull repository for barely useful software to a turbocharged powerhouse that lets you open any file in seconds. (You'll finish the transformation in Chapter 11.)

So open your Apple Menu Items folder (it's in your System Folder) and get ready to rock.

Before you do anything else, choose View⇨by Name. Now the Apple Menu Items folder's contents reflect the order that they appear in the Apple menu.

Doing the right thing with your desk accessories

As you've seen, most of the desk accessories are pretty lame. You probably won't use most of them very often. We're going to rearrange your Apple menu now so that desk accessories take up so much space while preserving your ability to open them quickly. Here's how:

1. Open the System Folder by double-clicking its icon (or by single-clicking its icon to select it and then choosing File⇨Open or pressing its keyboard shortcut Command-O).

2. Open the Apple Menu Items folder (it's in the System Folder) and create a new folder inside it. (To create a new folder, choose File⇨New Folder or press Command-N.) Name the new folder Desk Accessories.

3. Select all the icons in the window *except* the folders (see Figure 4-17). There are two ways to do this: the easy way and the hard way. Easy way first: Press Command-A (or drag a selection box around the entire contents of the window) to select all the icons; then hold down the Shift key and click each folder. Hard way: Click Apple System Profiler, hold down Shift key, click AppleCD Audio Player, hold down Shift key, click Calculator, hold down Shift key, and so on until all the non-folder icons are selected.

Figure 4-17:
Select all the icons except the folder and folder alias icons and drag them into the Desk Accessories folder.

	Apple Menu Items		
	20 items, 49.1 MB available		
Name	Date Modified	Size	Kind
AppleCD Audio Player	Sun, Jun 1, 1997, 9:47 AM	19K	alias
Automated Tasks	Sun, Jun 1, 1997, 9:47 AM	19K	alias
Control Panels	Sun, Jun 1, 1997, 9:47 AM	19K	alias
OpenDoc™ Stationery	Sun, Jun 1, 1997, 9:58 AM	19K	alias
Apple System Profiler	Thu, May 15, 1997, 12:00 PM	551K	application program
Connect To...	Fri, May 16, 1997, 12:00 PM	19K	application program
Find File	Fri, Mar 15, 1996, 12:00 PM	266K	application program
Graphing Calculator	Sat, Jan 8, 1994, 12:00 PM	532K	application program
Jigsaw Puzzle	Thu, Nov 17, 1994, 12:00 PM	114K	application program
Note Pad	Tue, Aug 2, 1994, 12:00 AM	76K	application program
Remote Access Disconnect	Fri, May 24, 1996, 12:00 PM	19K	application program
Scrapbook	Thu, Nov 21, 1996, 12:00 PM	57K	application program
SimpleSound	Thu, Jun 22, 1995, 12:00 PM	114K	application program
Stickies	Mon, Mar 31, 1997, 12:00 PM	114K	application program
Calculator	Yesterday, 4:27 PM	19K	desk accessory
Chooser	Yesterday, 4:31 PM	57K	desk accessory
Key Caps	Yesterday, 5:02 PM	19K	desk accessory
▷ Desk Accessories	Today, 2:38 PM	—	folder
▷ Recent Applications	Today, 2:31 PM	—	folder
▷ Recent Documents	Today, 2:35 PM	—	folder

This illustrates one of the Finder's finer points. You can extend or unextend your selection by using the Shift key. In other words, if you hold down the Shift key and then click an icon, it is added to or subtracted from the selection; if you don't hold down the Shift key when you click an icon, only that single icon is selected.

4. Drag these icons onto the Desk Accessories folder that you created in Step 2; when you release the mouse button, all the desk accessories, applications, and aliases that aren't folders move into the Desk Accessories folder.

5. Pull down your Apple menu and revel in your handiwork. It should look like Figure 4-18.

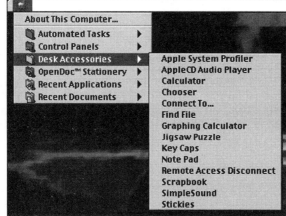

Figure 4-18:
Your Apple menu is now a lean, mean, file-launching machine.

Putting your stuff into the Apple menu

That last trick was pretty easy, wasn't it? Try one more thing before you move on. Why not add your favorite applications — the programs you use most often — to the Apple menu?

1. Find a favorite application on your hard disk, select it, and make an alias of it (File⇨Make Alias or Command-M).

2. Move the alias to the Apple Menu Items folder.

3. Repeat Steps 1 and 2 for any additional applications that you want to appear in your Apple menu.

If you have a lot of programs that you use often, you can create a folder called My Favorite Programs in the Apple Menu Items folder and put all the application aliases there instead, which keeps your Apple menu short and sweet (see Figure 4-19).

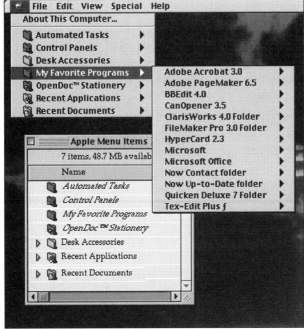

Figure 4-19:
My short
and sweet,
do-it-
yourself file
launcher.

My Deep, Dark Secret

I can't go on with this charade any longer. The figure caption for that last picture did it. "*My* short and sweet" my butt. I confess: The screen pictures you've been looking at aren't from my real hard disk at all. They're from a hard disk called Hardy Boy that I borrowed from Apple to create the screen shots for this book. When I start up using my real hard disk, my Mac looks *totally* different.

I'm a power user. I've got my Mac souped up and tricked out to the max. I've got strange icons in the menu bar. My menus are in Vintage Typewriter font. I've got a Trash alias behind the Apple menu (hidden in this shot). There's a slot machine in my control strip.

I didn't want to confuse you, so I wrote the book using the Hardy Boy hard disk, a disk that had nothing on it except Mac OS 8–related stuff. It makes for much cleaner screen shots and lets me avoid explaining every last difference between your Mac and mine. For the record, my Mac really looks like Figure 4-20.

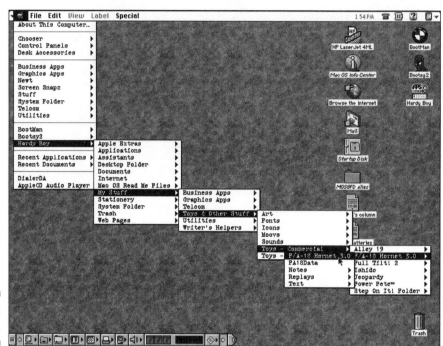

Figure 4-20:
My Mac.

I'll just point out a few highlights. First, I have a 20-inch Sony Trinitron monitor. The clock and telephone in the menu bar let me look at my appointments or phone book file without launching my calendar (Now Up-To-Date) or contact database (Now Contact) programs. The small font and all other nifty handiwork in my Apple menu — the divider lines, the lack of icons, and so on — are courtesy of another fine Now Software product, NowMenus. The CC icon next to the Help menu is for Conflict Catcher, a kind of Extensions Manager (see Chapter 12) on steroids from Casady & Greene. The slot machine in my control strip is shareware.

I have three hard disks — Bootman (internal) and Bootsy2 and Hardy Boy (both external).

There. I feel better having gotten that off my chest.

P.S.: By the time you read this, I'll be running the final released version of Mac OS 8 — in case you noticed that I wasn't in Figure 4-20.

Chapter 5

Save Yourself Heartache: Master the Save and Open Dialog Boxes

• •

In This Chapter

▶ Nested folders and paths

▶ Save your document before it's too late

▶ Save versus Save As

▶ The Open dialog box

• •

*M*ark my words, this may well be the most important chapter in this book. If you don't understand the Open and Save dialog boxes, the doohickeys that appear when you choose File⇨Open or File⇨Save in most programs, you'll never quite master your Macintosh. Yet mastering these essential techniques is perhaps the biggest problem many users have. I get more phone calls that begin, "Well, I saved the file, and now I don't know where it went."

This chapter is the cure. Just pay attention and it'll become crystal clear. And keep saying to yourself, *"The Save and Open dialog boxes are just another view of the Finder."* I'll explain in a moment.

The Open and Save dialog boxes are virtually unchanged from earlier versions of the operating system, which means that they're just as confusing and difficult to master now as they were before. Too bad. While Apple was souping up Mac OS 8, it could have made the Open and Save dialog boxes a little easier to use.

Never mind. They're not that bad. Even though they're still *modal* and can't be moved about on-screen, once you figure out how they work, you'll never forget. It will soon become second nature to you, and you'll cruise through Open and Save dialog boxes just like the pros, barely thinking about them as your fingers type and click at high speeds.

Nested Folders and Paths (It's Not as Bad as It Sounds)

Before we get started, I need to remind you that you work with Open and Save dialog boxes within applications. I assume that you know how to launch your favorite application and that you know how to create a new document.

For the rest of this chapter, I'm going to use SimpleText as the sample application. SimpleText comes with Mac OS 8, so you should have it too. In fact, you've probably already used SimpleText to read any Read Me files that came with Mac OS 8. (If you can't find a copy, Command-F gives you the Find dialog box. Search for Simple.)

So if you want to follow along, keystroke by keystroke, launch SimpleText and use File⇨New to create a new document. Type a few words in your document, like "All work and no play makes Jack a dull boy." Or something like that. (Forgive me, Stephen King.)

Switch from SimpleText to the Finder (you remember how). You may find the next part easier if you hide SimpleText (you know how to do that, too!) while you work in the Finder. If you've forgotten how to do either, pull down the Application menu, the one at the far right; everything you need is right there.

1. Open your hard disk's icon and create a new folder at root level (that is, in your hard disk's window). Name this folder Folder 1 to reflect the fact that it's one level deep on your hard disk.

2. Open Folder 1 and create a new folder in its window. Name this folder Folder 2 to reflect the fact that it's two levels deep on your hard disk.

3. Open Folder 2 and create a new folder in its window. Name this folder Folder 3 to reflect the fact that it's three levels deep on your hard disk.

You should now have a set of nested folders looking something like Figure 5-1.

Let me make this perfectly clear: Stuff *inside* Folder 3 is four levels deep. Folder 3 itself is three levels deep. Folder 2 itself is two levels deep, but stuff inside Folder 2, such as Folder 3, is three levels deep. And so on. Got it?

What's important here is that you are able to visualize the *path* to Folder 3. To get to Folder 3, you open Hardy Boy, open Folder 1, open Folder 2, and then open Folder 3. Remember this concept. You'll need it in a moment when you look at the Save dialog box.

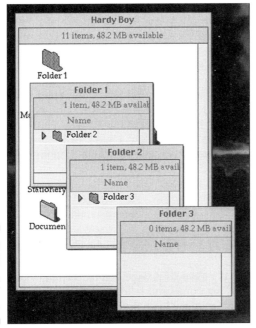

Figure 5-1:
Nested
folders,
going four
levels deep.

An easy way to see the path to any open folder is to Command-click its name in the title bar of its window (hold down the Command key before you press the mouse button). This action displays a drop-down path menu for that folder starting at the desktop level, as shown in Figure 5-2.

Figure 5-2:
The drop-
down path
menu for
Folder 3
appears
when you
press its
name in the
title bar
while
holding
down the
Command
key.

This path menu is live, which means that you can choose another folder from it by sliding the cursor to the folder's name and releasing the mouse button.

Try out this feature with Folder 3. Command-click its name in the title bar, move the cursor down until Folder 1 is highlighted, and then release the mouse button. Folder 1 pops to the front and becomes the active window. Try to remember this shortcut, as Command-clicking title bars can save you lots of time and effort.

Okay, our preparatory work in the Finder is through. Use any of the techniques you know to make SimpleText the active application. And don't forget what that path to Folder 3 looked like.

Save Your Document before It's Too Late

Okay, back in SimpleText, it's time to save your masterpiece. Choose File⇨Save (Command-S). This command brings up the Save dialog box (shown in Figure 5-3). Don't panic. These dialog boxes are easy as long as you remember that they're just another view of the folder structure in the Finder.

When the Save dialog box appears, the first thing I want you to do is click the Desktop button to view the icons on your desktop.

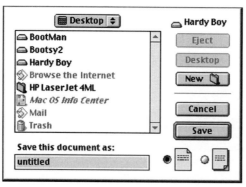

Figure 5-3:
The Save dialog box for SimpleText after clicking the Desktop button.

Let's talk about the Save dialog box for a moment. It contains that other view of your hard disk I talked about earlier. You're looking at the icons on your desktop right now. You know that they're the icons on your desktop because the active item is the desktop. Its name appears on the drop-down menu at the top and center.

In programs other than SimpleText, the Save dialog box may look slightly different because it contains additional options. Don't worry. The Save dialog box always *works* the same, no matter what options are offered. Once you can navigate with the SimpleText Save dialog box, you'll be able to navigate with any program's Save dialog box. So don't worry if the one you're used to seeing doesn't look exactly like Figure 5-3; just follow along and learn.

Click Hardy Boy (that is, your hard disk, whatever its name is) in the scrolling list (known as the *file list box*) and then click the Open button or press the Return or Enter key on your keyboard. (In all dialog boxes, the Return or Enter key activates the default button, which is the one with the heavy border around it.) Double-clicking Hardy Boy will open it as well.

Open Folder 1 the same way. Open Folder 2 the same way. Open Folder 3 the same way. Your Save dialog box should look like Figure 5-4.

Figure 5-4:
If you save now, the document will be saved into Folder 3 and named untitled.

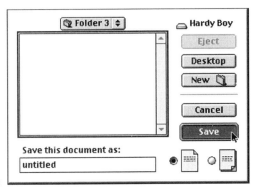

In other words, you navigate folders in the Save dialog box the same way you navigate folders in the Finder: by opening them to see their contents.

In the Save dialog box, the name at the top in the drop-down menu is the name of the active item (a folder, disk, or the desktop). Think of the active item in a Save dialog box as the active window in the Finder. That's where your file will be saved if you click the Save button. That's an important concept. The file is always saved in the active folder (or disk or the desktop) — the folder (or disk or the desktop) whose name appears at the top of the dialog box in the drop-down menu.

To make comprehension easier, think back to when I asked you to remember the path to Folder 3 in the Finder. Now look at the current path to Folder 3 in the Save dialog box by clicking the drop-down menu.

Like the drop-down path menu in the Finder (Command-click the window's name in the title bar), the drop-down menu in the Save dialog box is also live, so if you slide the cursor down to another folder (or Hardy Boy or the desktop), that item becomes the active item (see Figure 5-5).

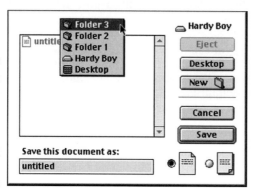

Figure 5-5:
The drop-
down menu
shows the
path to the
current
folder.

The Save (and Open) dialog boxes treat disk icons and the desktop the same as they treat folders. Though they're not really folders, you can save items to the desktop or root level (your hard disk's window).

You always move through the hierarchy in the same way. The desktop is the top level. When you're at the desktop level, you can see all mounted disks and any folders on the desktop. If you open a disk icon, you see its folder structure. You always navigate up and down the tree. Your most deeply nested folders are at the very bottom; the desktop is at the very top.

If you have more than one disk mounted, make sure that the disk name, which appears in the top right next to a little disk icon (hard disks have a hard disk icon; floppies have a floppy disk icon), is correct. If it's not, navigate back up to the desktop level and choose the correct disk.

Get into the habit of noticing the disk name in the Open and Save dialog box if you often have multiple disks mounted. Nothing is more frustrating than saving a file to the wrong disk and not being able to find it later.

Your file is saved to the active item in the drop-down menu when you click Save. In other words, when the desktop is the active item (as it is in Figure 5-3), your document will be saved on the desktop if you click the Save button. When Hardy Boy is the active item, your document will be saved in the Hardy Boy window if you click the Save button. When Folder 3 is the active item, your document will be saved in Folder 3 if you click the Save button.

1. In the Save dialog box, navigate to Folder 3; that is, make Folder 3 the active item.

2. When Folder 3 appears as the active item, select the words "untitled" and type in a more descriptive name. (I called mine Love Letter to Lisa.)

3. Click the Save button (or press the Return or Enter key).

That's it. If you switch to the Finder and open up Folder 3 (if it's not already open), you'll see that the file is saved right there in Folder 3.

Congrats. That's all there is to it. You now know how to navigate in a Save dialog box.

Remember the path I asked you to remember, the one you saw when you Command-clicked the name in the title bar of Folder 3's window? Just remember that the path in the Save dialog's drop-down menu (shown in Figure 5-5) is the same.

If that information makes sense to you, you're golden. If you're still a little shaky, go back and try the exercise again and keep trying to understand the relationship between the three folders that you created (one inside the other inside the other) and the drop-down path menus you see when you Command-click Folder 3's title bar or click its name in the drop-down menu in the Save dialog box. Keep reviewing the illustrations. Eventually it'll just click, and you'll slap yourself in the head and say, "*Now* I get it."

Don't read on until you get it. This idea of paths and navigating is crucial to your success as a Macintosh user.

There's a little more, but if you get it so far, you're home free.

The rest of what you should know about Save dialog boxes

One thing you need to know is that the file list box and the file name field are mutually exclusive. Only one can be active at a time. You're either navigating the folder hierarchy or you're naming a file. When a Save dialog box first appears, the file name field is active, ready for you to type a name (as shown on the right in Figure 5-6).

Notice the border around the file list box when it is active. Also notice how the bottom button changes from Open to Save when the file name field is active. You'll hear more about this phenomenon in a few pages.

Figure 5-6:
The file list
box is
active on
the left; the
file name
field is
active on
the right.

Active File List Box

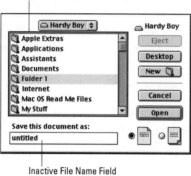

Inactive File Name Field

Inactive File List Box

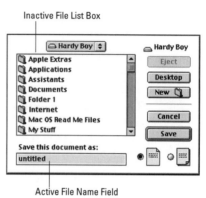

Active File Name Field

When you want to navigate, click anywhere in the file list box to make it active. In Figure 5-6, this box is beneath the active item (Hardy Boy), which contains several folders. When you click anywhere in the box, it becomes active and displays a double-line border around it. If you type something while the file list box is active, the list scrolls and selects the folder that most closely matches the letter(s) you typed. Go ahead and give it a try. It's easier to experience than explain.

For what it's worth, you can also type the first letter or two in any Finder window to select the icon closest alphabetically to the letter or letters you typed.

When the file list is active, the letters that you type do not appear in the file name field. If you want to type a file name, you have to activate the file name field again in order to type in it. Here's how:

Regardless of which is active at the time, when you press the Tab key on your keyboard, the other becomes active. So if the file name field is active, it becomes inactive when you press Tab, and the file list box becomes active. Press Tab again and they reverse — the file name field becomes active again.

If you don't feel like pressing the Tab key, you can achieve the same effect by clicking either the file list box or the file name field to activate them.

Try it yourself and notice how visual cues let you know which is active. When the file list is active, it displays a border; when the file name field is active, the file list has no border and the file name field is editable.

The buttons

There are five buttons in SimpleText's Save dialog box: Eject, Desktop, New Folder, Cancel, and Open/Save. The first four are straightforward and almost explain themselves, but the fifth requires a bit of concentration. I'll describe them all (except for the radio buttons, which are application-specific).

Ejector seat

The Eject button is only active when an ejectable disk is selected in the file list box. It's mostly used to save a file to a different floppy than the one currently in the drive. Use the Eject button to eject that floppy so that you can insert another. When you insert a floppy disk, it becomes the active item automatically. You can tell because its name appears in two places (see Figure 5-7):

✔ At the top right of the Save (or Open) dialog box above the buttons

✔ In the drop-down menu above the file list box

Figure 5-7:
The floppy disk automatically becomes the active item.

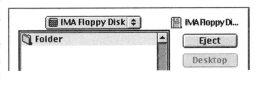

Do it on the desktop

The Desktop button takes you rocketing up the hierarchy of folders to the very top level, as high as you can go. When you click the Desktop button, the desktop becomes the active folder (I know that the desktop isn't really a folder, but play along) in the Save dialog box. From here, you can navigate your way down into any subfolder.

If you get lost in a Save (or Open) dialog box, the best thing to do is click the Desktop button and start from the top (the desktop), which should make it easy to find your way to the folder you desire. Just remember to navigate down through folders in the same order you would in the Finder.

Something new: the New Folder button

This button is a nice touch. If you click the New Folder button, a new folder is created inside the active folder in the Save dialog box. You can then save your document into it. Not every program has this button; in fact, many don't. So don't get too used to it.

What usually happens is that you don't think about needing a new folder until the Save dialog box is on-screen. And in most Save dialog boxes, there's not a thing you can do about it.

What I do in these cases is to save my file on the desktop. Later, when I'm back in the Finder, I create a new folder in the proper place on my hard disk and then move the file from the desktop to its folder.

That's an 86: Cancel

The Cancel button dismisses the Save dialog box without saving anything anywhere. In other words, the Cancel button returns things to the way they were before you brought up the Save dialog box.

The keyboard shortcut for Cancel is Command-period (the Esc key sometimes works too). I said it before and I'll say it again: Command-period is a good command to memorize. It cancels almost all dialog boxes, and it also cancels lots of other things. If something is going on (for example, your spreadsheet is calculating or your database is sorting or your graphics program is rotating) and it's taking too long, try Command-period. It works (usually).

The Open/Save button: the exception to the rule

If you've been paying extra-careful attention to the illustrations, you've no doubt noticed that the button near the bottom sometimes says Save and other times says Open. I even called your attention to it a few pages ago. So? What gives?

In particular, how do you save something when there's no Save button (see Figure 5-8)?

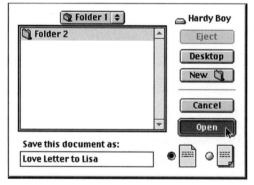

Figure 5-8:
How do you save when this is what you see?

Say I want to save the file Love Letter to Lisa in Folder 1. I navigate my way to Folder 1. I see it at the top in the drop-down menu. I'm ready to save it, but there's no Save button, as is the case in Figure 5-8.

That's because Folder 2 is selected in the file list box, and if a folder is selected in the file list box, the button says Open, not Save. To deselect Folder 2, click anywhere in the file list box except on Folder 2, or press the Tab key. When Folder 2 is no longer selected in the file list box, the Open button becomes the Save button, and you can now save (see Figure 5-9).

Figure 5-9:
The Open button changes to the Save button, which allows me to save Love Letter to Lisa in Folder 1.

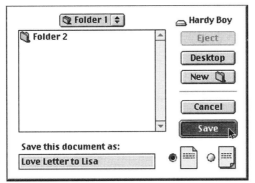

I know. It doesn't really make sense, but that's how it works. Try it a couple of times. It's not as straightforward as other parts of the Mac interface, but once you get it, you get it for life.

I could have just as easily pressed the Tab key instead of clicking. The net result would be exactly the same — the Open button would change to the Save button.

If this little section confuses you, look again at Figures 5-8 and 5-9. Folder 1 is where I want to save the file. But there's no Save button in Figure 5-8 because a folder, Folder 2, is currently selected. When I click anywhere in the file list box (anywhere except on Folder 2) or press the Tab key on my keyboard, Folder 2 is deselected, the Open button changes into the Save button, and I can save the file named Love Letter to Lisa in Folder 1.

If you still aren't sure what all this stuff means, try it. It's not particularly intuitive, but it's relatively easy to get the hang of.

1. Select Folder 2 in the file list box of the Save dialog box (Folder 1 is the active folder).

2. Click the file list box anywhere but on Folder 2. Notice the Open or Save button before and after you click.

3. Press the Tab key. Notice the Open or Save button before and after you press Tab.

When the button says Save and you click the button or press Return or Enter, the file is saved in Folder 1. When the button says Open (because Folder 2 is selected) and you click the button or press Return, you move down one level and Folder 2 becomes the active folder.

Got it?

It Looks Like Save, It Acts Like Save, So Why Is It Called Save As?

The Save As command, which you'll find in the File menu of almost every program ever made, lets you save a file that's already been saved and give it a different name.

Why might you want to do that? Let's say you have two sisters, Jodie and Zelda. You write Jodie a long, chatty letter. You save it as Letter to Jodie. Now you decide you want to send it to Zelda too, but you want to change a few things. So you change the part about your date last night (Zelda isn't as liberated as Jodie) and replace all references to Steve (Jodie's husband) with Zeke (Zelda's husband). Aren't computers grand?

Save early, save often = no heartache

This is as good a time as any to talk about developing good saving habits. Needless to say, it's a very good idea to save your work every few minutes.

Here's my advice:

✔ Always save before you switch to another program.

✔ Always save before you print a document.

✔ Always save before you stand up.

If you don't heed this advice and your Mac crashes while switching programs, printing, or sitting idle (which, not coincidentally, are the three most likely times for it to crash), you'll lose everything you've done since your last save.

Command-S is the keyboard shortcut for Save in almost every program I know. Memorize it. See it in your dreams. Train your finger muscles to do it unconsciously. Use it (the keyboard shortcut) or lose it (your unsaved work).

You've made those changes to Letter to Jodie, but you haven't saved again since you decided to make the changes. So now the document on your screen is actually a Letter to Zelda, but its file name is still Letter to Jodie. Think of what would happen if you were to save now.

I'll tell you: If you save now, the file named Letter to Jodie will reflect the changes you just made. The stuff in the letter that was meant for Jodie will be blown away and replaced by the stuff you said to Zelda. If you save now, the file name Letter to Jodie will be inaccurate.

That's what Save As is for. If you use Save As now (it's a different command from Save — look on the File menu and see), you get a Save dialog box where you can type in a *different* file name. You can also navigate to another folder, if you like, and save the newly named version of the file there.

Now you have two files on your hard disk — Letter to Jodie and Letter to Zelda. Both contain the stuff they should.

That's what Save As is for.

Open (Sesame)

You already know how to use the Open dialog box; you just don't know you know yet.

Using the Open dialog box

Guess what? If you can navigate using a Save dialog box, you can navigate using an Open dialog box. They work exactly the same except for a couple of very minor differences.

First, there's no file name field. Of course not. This dialog box is the one you see when you want to open a file! There's no need for the file name field 'cause you're not saving a file.

There's also no New Folder button. You don't need it when you're opening a file. (It sure comes in handy when you're saving a file though, doesn't it? Sure wish every program had one.)

Anyway, that's it. Those are the differences. Navigate the same way as you would in a Save dialog box. Don't forget your mantra, *"The Open and Save dialog boxes are just another view of the Finder."*

Figure 5-10 shows two different ways of viewing the same file. The Open dialog box, at top, has navigated to the file Love Letter to Lisa in Folder 3. I clicked the drop-down menu in the Open dialog box to show you the path to the file Love Letter to Lisa.

Below the Open dialog box is the Finder view of the path to the file Love Letter to Lisa.

If you aren't 100 percent comfortable with the relationship between the two views, please go back and try the hands-on exercises earlier in this chapter again. Please. Keep reviewing the pictures and instructions until you understand this concept. If you don't, your Mac will continue to confound and confuse you. Do yourself a favor — don't read any further until Open and Save dialog boxes feel like the most natural thing in the world to you.

A really big show — Show Preview

Okay, there's something else about the Open dialog box that's different. As you can see in Figure 5-10, the Open dialog box for SimpleText has a check box called Preview. What does this little box do? It lets you create little previews for PICT files, which are the type of files created by many popular graphics programs. Click the check box and then click the Create button when a PICT file is highlighted in the file list. After a moment, a little picture will appear (see Figure 5-11). From now on, every time that file is highlighted in an Open dialog box, its preview picture will automatically appear (as long as the Show Preview check box remains checked).

As you might guess, previews are a nice feature to have. Many graphics programs include previews in their Open dialog boxes. At least one, Adobe Photoshop, creates a custom icon for its documents that reflects their contents when it saves them.

Unfortunately, you have to be in the icon view, which you know I dislike, to see these icons. Still, they're pretty cute.

Weird folder or file names

Every so often, you'll see some weird folder names — such as Move & Rename, or Network Trash Folder, or Desktop DB or DF, or VM Storage — in the Open dialog box, but you don't see these folders when you look at the corresponding windows in the Finder. Don't worry. It's perfectly natural.

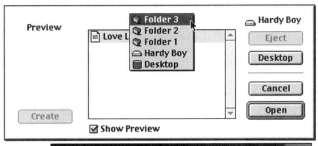

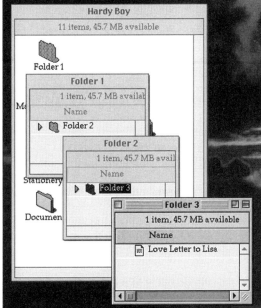

Figure 5-10:
The Open
dialog box,
like the
Save dialog
box, is just
a different
view of the
Finder.

Figure 5-11:
The
Preview
area in this
Open dialog
box shows
a small
picture
of what
the file
MOS8FD.
0511.pict
looks like.

Here's what's going on:

Move & Rename and VM Storage are invisible files. You aren't supposed to see them. The System uses them to keep track of stuff that you don't need (or want) to know about. They're invisible when you look in the Hardy Boy window, but they show up in some applications' Open dialog boxes. This anomaly is known as a *bug*. You shouldn't be able to see those files. Just ignore them, and they won't bother you. If you're lucky, you won't even see them on your Mac (many people don't).

The last thing you need to know

Selectively displaying certain items in Open dialog boxes is a feature of most applications. When you use a program's Open dialog box, only files that the program knows how to open appear in the file list. In other words, the program filters out files that it can't open, so you don't see them cluttering up the Open dialog box. Pretty neat, eh?

On the other hand, not seeing every item in an Open dialog box can be a little disconcerting when you're trying to envision the correlation between the Finder and the Open dialog box. Just remember this: Stuff you see in the Finder doesn't always appear in the Open dialog box. That's why I showed you the Save dialog box first. It always includes everything. In a Save dialog box, items that you can't select appear grayed out, but they do appear. Open dialog boxes usually show only files that you can select and open with the current application.

So . . . if you know something is in a particular folder but you can't see it in the Open dialog box . . . consider that possibly the program you're using isn't capable of opening that kind of document (not every program can open every document).

Mac OS Easy Open, a standard part of the Mac OS, can often allow one program to open documents created by another program. If you can't see the document in the Open dialog box, quit the current program and find the file in the Finder (that is, open the folders it's in). When you open the document in the Finder, Mac OS Easy Open will kick in and offer you a list of programs on your hard disk that can open that particular type of document.

In other words, just double-click most documents and the Mac OS will do the rest, finding and launching the appropriate application via Mac OS Easy Open. Neat, huh?

Part II
Making It Purr

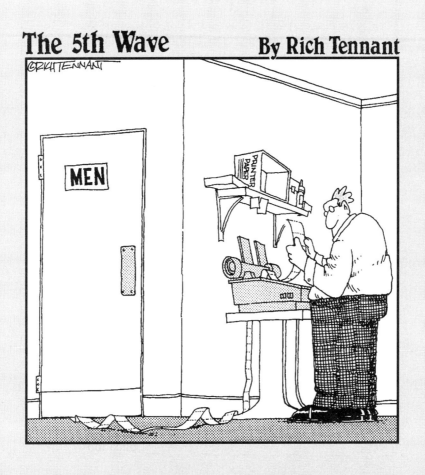

The 5th Wave   By Rich Tennant

In this part . . .

The chapters in this part show you how to perform important hands-on tasks. But don't get all worked up: This stuff is easy. In fact, I think of this part as "The Lazy Person's How-To Guide."

Chapter 6 deals with how to organize your Mac. You discover, among other things, how to do routine file-management and navigating tasks the easy way.

Next is the how-to-print chapter, Chapter 7. It includes info on how to decipher Print options and plenty of other hows and whys that will help you become a modern day Gutenberg.

In Chapter 8, you find out how to share. Files, that is. It's easy, it's convenient, it's free, and it beats the heck out of sneakernet.

Finally, there's a wonderful chapter (numbered, conveniently enough, 9) on how to manage memory (and other seemingly complicated arcana), an easy-to-understand, almost jargon-free primer on how the whole memory thing works.

Chapter 6
File Management Made Simple

● ●

In This Chapter

▶ Using Launcher (or not)

▶ Getting yourself organized (or something like it)

▶ Using aliases

▶ Working with spring-loaded folders

● ●

*I*n Chapters 1 through 5, I detail for you the basics about windows and icons and menus. In this chapter, you apply that knowledge as you begin a never-ending quest to discover the fastest, easiest, most trouble-free way to manage the files on your Mac.

I can help. I'm not a doctor, but I play one in books and magazines. I've been wrangling with the Macintosh interface for more than ten years now, and I've learned a lot about what works and what doesn't — at least what works for me. This chapter will spare you at least part of the ten-year learning curve.

Remember, we're talking about Mac OS here. And we're talking about developing your own personal style. There is no right way to organize your files, no right way to use aliases, no right way to use the Apple menu, and no right way to use drag and drop. The only thing for sure is that these features are useless if you don't use them.

Please take the time to understand these wonderful features. They make your Mac so much easier to use. I'll show you how, and it's *easy*. After absorbing that info, you'll have all the ammunition you need to create your own personal Macintosh experience, a Mac environment designed by you, for you.

Launcher (Or Not)

Launcher is a relatively new (unless you have a Performa — Apple included a similar Launcher with Performas for a while) control panel, introduced in System 7.5, that creates a window in the Finder with single-clickable icons that launch (open) frequently used files.

If you don't see Launcher, choose Apple menu⇨Control Panels⇨Launcher. If you want Launcher on all the time, choose Apple menu⇨Control Panels⇨General Controls and click the box marked Show Launcher at system startup.

The advantage of Launcher is that the icons in the Launcher window can represent items in many different folders on your hard disk (see Figure 6-1).

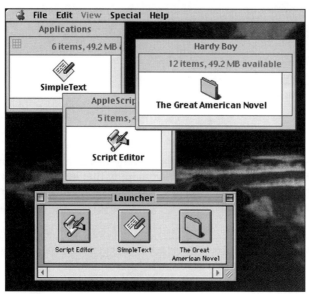

Figure 6-1: Launcher makes frequently used items available in a single, convenient window, even if the items are in different folders as shown.

So Launcher, at least in theory, saves you time by saving you from rooting through folders every time you need one of those items.

Launcher is easy to configure. Just drag anything you want to add to the Launcher window onto the Launcher window.

Here's what happens when you drag an icon onto the Launcher window: Your Mac creates an alias of that icon and places that alias in the Launcher Items folder, which you'll find in your System Folder (see Figure 6-2).

If you want something to appear in the Launcher window, put an alias of it in the Launcher Items folder or drag its icon onto the Launcher window. To remove an item, hold down the Option key and drag it to the Trash. That's it. The whole enchilada.

Figure 6-2:
If an item's alias is in the Launcher Items folder, the item appears in the Launcher window.

Well, almost the whole enchilada. There's one other feature I feel obligated to mention. You can create categories for Launcher by creating folders in the Launcher Items folder and starting their names with the bullet character (•, which you create by pressing Option-8). This creates categories with different buttons for different stuff as shown in Figure 6-3.

For what it's worth, I couldn't find anything about Launcher in my Apple manual, but I got a great demo of this trick by searching for *Launcher* in Mac OS Help. Yet another reason for you to check out Apple's cool new active assistance.

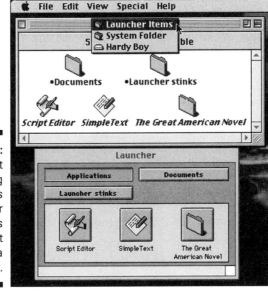

Figure 6-3:
The secret for creating categories in Launcher is folders that start with a bullet.

I think I've been objective up to this point. Now I'll tell you why I think Launcher stinks:

- ✔ It doesn't float in front of other Finder windows, so it's easy to lose behind other windows.
- ✔ It has only an icon view, so it wastes valuable screen real estate.
- ✔ It can't be chosen from the Application menu.
- ✔ It's no different from a regular window in View as Button mode except that . . .
- ✔ . . . It uses single clicks to open icons, a clear violation of *Macintosh Human Interface Guidelines,* the bible of Macintosh interface design.

Gasp. And this heresy has spread to windows viewed in the button mode as well in Mac OS 8! So why did Apple start including Launcher, first with Performas and now with System 7.5 and Mac OS 8? And why, after ten years of rabid insistence that double-click means *open,* did Apple change its mind?

My take on it is that Apple is afraid that new users are too stupid to grasp the concept of double-clicking to open a file. And too stupid to realize that you can do everything Launcher does and more by customizing your Apple menu (as you'll see later in this chapter).

I don't think you're that dumb. I say get rid of the lame-o Launcher. (See Chapter 14 for complete instructions on shuffling Launcher off this mortal coil.)

With what I present in this chapter, you'll instead be able to create your own customized environment, which I promise will let you find and launch items faster and more flexibly than Launcher, or the clunky button view.

On the other hand, if for some unfathomable reason you *like* Launcher or even the button view, by all means enjoy them. Launcher doesn't use all that much disk space or RAM, so there's no great advantage to trashing it.

No advantage, that is, besides never seeing Launcher again (which I consider a big advantage). If a single-click file launcher tickles your fancy, there are plenty of excellent commercial and shareware utilities that make Launcher seem even crummier.

Getting Yourself Organized (Or Something Like It)

I won't pretend to be able to do this task for you. Organizing your files is as personal as your taste in music. You develop your own style with the Mac. So in this section, I'll give you some food for thought, some ideas about how I do it, and some suggestions that should make organization easier for you, regardless of how you choose to do it yourself.

And it's root, root, root for the root level

Root level refers to the window you see when you open your hard disk's icon. It's the first level down in the hierarchy of folders. How you organize root level is a matter of taste, but let me try to give some guidance.

KISS: Keep It Simple, Stupid

I find that less is more when it comes to organizing files and folders. I try to use the simplest structure that meets my needs. For example, if I have more than a handful of icons at root level, I begin to look for ways to reorganize. I shoot for no more than ten items at root level; fewer is better.

At the very least . . .

Root level must contain the System Folder. It won't work properly if you put it somewhere else (like in another folder or on the desktop). Beyond that, what you place on the root level is up to you.

I think most people should start with two other folders, Applications and Documents, at the very least, but even these don't *have* to go at root level. The desktop is an equally good place for them, as you'll see in a later section.

A full install of Mac OS 8 leaves ten folders at root level in addition to your System Folder. To keep things tidy, create a new folder at root level called Mac OS 8 Stuff and put these folders inside it, as shown in Figure 6-4.

Documentary evidence: the Documents folder

Remember, you don't need to have a Documents folder, but if you do, here are some tips for organizing it:

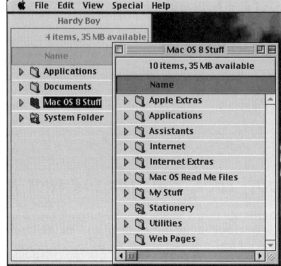

Figure 6-4:
Reducing
clutter on
your hard
disk with a
Mac OS 8
Stuff folder.

✔ Don't create subfolders (within the Documents folder) until you need them.

✔ Creating a bunch of empty folders because you think that you might need them someday is more work than creating them when you need them. You end up opening an empty folder when you're looking for something else — a complete waste of time.

✔ I recommend saving everything in the Documents folder for a week or two (or a month or two, depending on how many new documents you save each day). Once a decent-size group of documents has accumulated in the Documents folder, take a look at them and create logical subfolders to put them into.

✔ Let your work style decide file structure.

You should create the subfolders based on a system that makes sense to you. Here are some ideas for subfolders:

✔ By type of document: Word Processing Documents, Spreadsheet Documents, Graphics Documents

✔ By date: Documents May-June, Documents Spring '97

✔ By content: Memos, Outgoing Letters, Expense Reports

✔ By project: Project X, Project Y, Project Z

When things start to get messy, and you start noticing some folders bulging (that is, filled up with tons of files), subdivide them again and use a combination of the methods I just mentioned.

For example, if you start by subdividing your Documents folder into four subfolders — Memos, Expense Reports, Letters, and Other Documents (as shown in Figure 6-5) — a few months later, when those folders begin to get full, you might subdivide them in one or more of the ways, as shown in Figure 6-6.

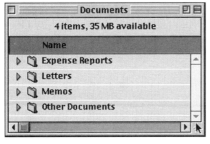

Figure 6-5:
A Documents folder containing four subfolders.

Figure 6-6:
The same Documents folder several months later, with new subfolders for three of the original four subfolders.

The folder called Other Documents hasn't required subdividing yet, as it only contains a dozen items.

The point is that your folder structure should be organic, growing as you need it to grow. Let it happen. Don't let any one folder get so full that it's a hassle to deal with. Create new subfolders when things start to get crowded.

How full is too full? That's impossible to say. If I find more than 15 or 20 files in a single folder, I begin thinking about ways to subdivide it. On the other hand, some of my subfolders that contain things I don't often need, such as my Correspondence 1992 folder, contain more than 100 files. Because I don't use the folder all that much (but want to keep it on my hard disk just in case), its overcrowded condition doesn't bother me. Your mileage may vary.

After almost ten years of growth, my Documents folder contains only about a dozen subfolders, most of which contain their own subfolders (see Figure 6-7). Being a nonconformist, I call my Documents folder Stuff.

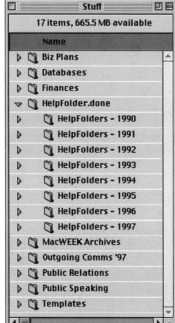

Figure 6-7:
My
Documents
folder
and its
subfolders.

Other folders at root level

You can follow this same philosophy for other folders at root level, subdividing them as needed. If you use a particular folder a great deal, move it from the Documents folder to root level or to the desktop (more about that in a few pages) to make it easier to use. For example, if you write a lot of letters, keep your Correspondence folder at root level or on the desktop. And so on.

The only thing I might caution you against is storing stuff in the System Folder that doesn't belong there. There's no harm in it, but the System Folder is already the repository for many files used by the System software and by applications. For most people, the System Folder is the most crowded folder on their disk, so sticking items that don't belong in it would only cause further clutter. Word processing documents and spreadsheets (and indeed almost all documents) don't belong in the System Folder. You know how the file system works. Create a folder somewhere else for your documents.

Other than that, the only rule is that there are no rules. Whatever works for you is the best way. And don't forget Find File if you lose something!

Apply here: the Applications folder

I recommend having an Applications folder for all your programs. The best place for this folder is either at root level or on the desktop. Your Applications folder can also be subdivided when the need arises. Given what I do for a living, I have a lot of programs, so mine has subfolders for business programs, graphics programs, writing tools, utilities, toys, and online (modem) stuff, as shown in Figure 6-8.

Figure 6-8:
My
Applications
folder
contains six
subfolders.

It'll probably be a while before you need so many subfolders — unless you're like me and try a lot of new software. Either way, organize your applications the same way you organized your documents — in a way that makes sense to you. Follow this advice, and I promise that you'll always be able to find what you're looking for.

The Greatest Thing Since Sliced Bread: Aliases

When System 7 first arrived several years ago, many of its features were heralded as breakthroughs. But of these features, none has proved to be more useful than the *alias*.

An alias, if you've forgotten, is a quick-opener for another file. With aliases, a file can be in two (or more) places at once. When you create an alias of a disk, file, or folder, opening its alias is the same as opening the item. And an alias takes up only the tiniest bit of disk space.

Why is this feature so great? First, it lets you put items in more than one place, which on many occasions is exactly what you want to do. For example, it's convenient to keep an alias of your word processor on your desktop and another in your Apple menu. You may even want a third alias of it in your Documents folder for quick access. Aliases let you open your word processor quickly and easily without navigating into the depths of your Applications folder each time you need it.

Here's another example: If you write a memo to Fred Smith about the Smythe Marketing Campaign to be executed in the fourth quarter, which folder does the document go in? Smith? Smythe? Marketing? Memos? 4th Quarter?

With aliases, it doesn't matter. You can put the actual file in any of the folders and then create aliases of the file and place them in all the other folders. So whichever folder you open, you'll be able to find the memo.

Finally, many programs need to remain in the same folder as their supporting files and folders. Some programs won't function properly unless they are in the same folder as their dictionaries, thesauruses, data files (for games), templates, and so on. Ergo, you can't put those programs on the desktop or in the Apple Menu Items folder without impairing their functionality.

Icons on the desktop

How about a little hands-on training? You'll create an alias for your favorite application and put it on the desktop, a very good place for it.

1. Find your favorite application — ClarisWorks, Microsoft Word, Titanic, whatever — and select its icon, not the folder that it's in. Be sure to select the program's icon.

2. Choose File⇨Make Alias, or press Command-M, as shown in Figure 6-9.

An alias of the application appears right next to the original. The alias's file name will be the same as the original's, except that it is in italics and has the word *alias* appended at the end.

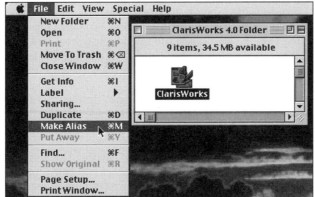

Figure 6-9:
Make an alias of your very favorite program.

3. Drag the alias onto the desktop and move it to a convenient place.

Next to the hard disk icon is one prime location (see Figure 6-10). Along the bottom of the screen is another.

Figure 6-10:
Next to the hard disk icon is an excellent place to put a frequently used alias.

There. You've just made it easier to use your favorite program. Next time you need your favorite program, just open its alias right there on your desktop instead of opening several folders and cluttering up your screen.

Frequently used folders or documents are good candidates for aliases-on-the-desktop. In fact, any icon you use more than a couple of times a day is a good candidate for an alias on the desktop.

Remember, aliases don't take up much disk space (a measly 3K or 4K each), so there's no penalty for making an alias and later deciding that you don't like it. Big deal. Drag it to the Trash.

The temporary alias theory

I use a lot of *temporary* aliases on my desktop. When I first create a file, I save it in its proper folder, inside my Documents folder somewhere. If it's a document that I plan to work on for more than a day or two, such as a magazine article, I make an alias of the document (or folder) and put it on the desktop. When the article is done and I've submitted it to my editor, I trash the alias. The original file is already stashed away in its proper folder.

With bigger projects like books, which have multiple subfolders of their own, I keep an alias of the parent folder on the desktop for easy access. When I submit the last chapter, the alias goes into the Trash.

Incidentally, a similar technique can be used without the aliases. Just save all your new documents on the desktop (click the Desktop button in the Save dialog box or use the shortcut Command-D). Later, when you're done with them, you can file them away in their proper folders.

My point is that the desktop is an excellent place for the things that you need most often. Whether you use aliases of documents or save the actual files on the desktop until you figure out where you want to store them, the desktop is a fine place for the things you use most. Keep frequently used programs on the desktop forever, and use the desktop as a temporary parking place for current projects.

Whatever you do, I encourage you to do it on the desktop.

What a drag it is not to drop

Macintosh drag and drop deals with dragging text and graphics from one place to another. But there's another angle to drag and drop, one that has to do with documents and icons.

You can use drag and drop to open a file using a program other than the one that would ordinarily launch when you open the document. This concept is easier to show than to tell, so follow along on your own computer:

1. Make a screen shot picture of your desktop by holding down the Command and Shift keys and pressing the 3 key. Command-Shift-3 takes a picture of your desktop.

2. You hear a cute snapshot sound, and a document called Picture 1 automatically appears in your hard disk's root level window. Open it.

3. Assuming that there's a copy of SimpleText on your hard disk, SimpleText will launch and display Picture 1.

   But you don't want to use SimpleText. SimpleText can open and display a picture file but can't make changes to it. You want to open the picture with a program that can edit it. What do you do? Use drag and drop.

4. Quit SimpleText.

5. Drag the icon for Picture 1 onto the alias of your favorite program that you created earlier. Figure 6-11 shows how I made changes to Picture 1.

Figure 6-11:
After dragging Picture 1 onto the Photoshop icon, I was able to make a few minor changes to it . . .

If the alias of your favorite program didn't highlight when you dragged Picture 1 on top of it, or if dragging Picture 1 onto the alias launched the program but didn't open Picture 1, then your favorite program isn't capable of opening picture files.

Your solution if your favorite program can't open Picture 1: Get a different favorite program. Just kidding. The solution is to try dragging Picture 1 onto other program icons (or aliases of program icons) until you find one that opens it. When you do, you might want to put an alias of that application on the desktop, too.

What happens if you don't have a copy of SimpleText on your hard disk when you try to open Picture 1? Mac OS Easy Open kicks in and offers you a choice of other programs that can open it (see Figure 6-12).

Figure 6-12:
Mac OS
Easy Open
lets you
choose
from
compatible
applications
if you try
to open a
document
created by
a program
you don't
have on
your hard
disk.

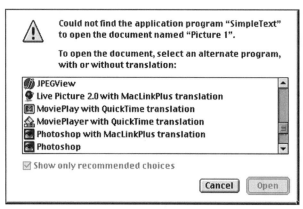

When I trashed SimpleText and tried to open Picture 1, Figure 6-12 is what I saw. In a more technical book, I'd go on to explain about file type and creator codes and how they have to do with which program gets launched when you open a document. But this is *Mac OS 8 For Dummies,* so I won't.

Suffice it to say that Mac OS 8 is smart enough to figure out which applications on your hard disk can open what documents and offer you a choice. Earlier versions weren't that smart.

Spring has sprung: Meet your nifty new spring-loaded folders

Speaking of dragging and dropping, Mac OS 8 adds a new wrinkle that makes dragging and dropping less of a drag: the useful and usable spring-loaded folders. Spring-loaded folders make folders spring open temporarily when you hold an item over them.

To turn on spring-loaded folders and give them a try:

1. Make the Finder the active application.

2. Choose Edit⇨Preferences.

3. Click the Spring-loaded folders check box.

4. Set the Delay Before Opening slider to Short (at least for this demo).

Now grab an icon in the Finder, any icon, and drag it onto the System Folder icon. Don't release the mouse button. There. See how the System Folder springs open automatically when you hold an icon on top of it? That's spring-loaded folders in action.

If you can stand more excitement, without releasing the mouse button, drag the icon you're holding onto the Preferences folder (or any other subfolder in the System Folder). That folder will spring open. Finally, without releasing the mouse button, drag the icon away from any windows or folder icons, or drag it into the menu bar. All sprung folders should magically spring shut.

I used to use a third-party utility (PopUp Folder) for this. While I wish spring-loaded folders worked with the pointer cursor alone (they only work when you're dragging an icon), they're still a big improvement. Nice going, Apple!

Smart Apple menu tricks

Remember when I called the Launcher lame? Here's something way better. I talked a bit about the Apple menu in Chapter 4; now I'll show you how to make it work for you.

First, make sure that you've turned the wonderful submenus on in the Apple Menu Options control panel. If you don't see little black triangles to the right of all the folders in the Apple menu, they're not turned on.

Now do something useful. Let's make a file launcher that enables you to open every file on your hard disk from a single Apple menu item.

The hard-disk-alias-in-the-Apple-menu trick

1. Select your hard disk icon and make an alias of it by selecting your hard drive and choosing File⇨Make alias or by using the shortcut Command-M.

2. Put the alias of your hard disk in the Apple Menu Items folder (which is in your System Folder).

3. Pull down the Apple menu and admire your handiwork.

If having your hard drive on the Apple menu is too overwhelming for you, consider putting an alias of your Documents folder or your Applications folder in the Apple menu. It's easy, it's fast, and it's convenient. Get in the habit of putting frequently used items (it's not just for desk accessories and folders anymore) in the Apple menu. You'll be glad you did.

A quick trick for adding an alias to the Apple menu

1. Select the icon of the item that you want to appear in the Apple menu.

2. Choose Apple menu⇨Automated Tasks⇨Add Alias to Apple Menu.

This script automatically creates an alias of the selected item and puts it in the Apple Menu Items folder.

The old alias-of-the-Apple-Menu-Items-folder-on-the-desktop trick

Are you growing fonder of your Apple menu? You should be. It's a great resource and it's easy to customize. If you find yourself customizing yours a lot, here's a tip to make it easier to use.

Make an alias of the Apple Menu Items folder and put it on your desktop for easy access.

If you make frequent changes to your Apple menu, this tip saves you at least one step. And here's another tip: You can also put an alias of the Apple Menu Items folder in the Apple menu so that you can select it even if a window is covering the alias on your desktop.

When you put an alias of the Apple Menu Items folder in your Apple menu, it won't have subfolders, which makes sense when you think about it. If it had subfolders, they would create an endless loop.

By the way, I reveal some more very cool Apple menu tricks in Chapter 11.

Chapter 7

Publish or Perish: The Fail-Safe Guide to Printing

. . . .

In This Chapter

▶ Choosing a printer

▶ Setting up your page with Page Setup

▶ Printing to most printers

▶ Using desktop printers

▶ The death of QuickDraw GX

▶ Font mania

. . . .

*P*rinting is like being. It just is. Or at least it should be. It should be as simple as typing Command-P and then pressing the Return or Enter key. And usually that's how it is. Except when it isn't, and printing turns into a raging nightmare.

You won't be having any nightmares. If you get your printer and printing software configured properly, printing is simple as can be. And that's pretty darn simple.

So this is a chapter about avoiding nightmares. We'll go through the entire process, as if you just unpacked a new printer and plugged it in. If you upgraded from an earlier version of System 7 and are able to print with Mac OS 8 already, you can probably skip some of the steps. The objective here is to familiarize yourself with the printing process from start to finish.

One thing I suggest is that you read the documentation that came with your specific printer. There are hundreds of different printer makes and models available for the Mac, so I may contradict something that your printer manual says. If you run into this discrepancy, try it the way the manual says first. If that doesn't work, try mine.

Another thing you need to know is that every application can use its own custom print and Page Setup dialog box. Though many will look like the ones in this chapter, others won't. For example, the Print and Page Setup dialog boxes for Microsoft Word include choices not covered in this chapter, such as Even or Odd Pages Only, Print Hidden Text, and Print Selection Only. If you see commands in your Print or Page Setup dialog boxes that aren't explained in this chapter, they're specific to that application and should be explained in its documentation. I'll be using Apple's SimpleText program for this demonstration.

Don't forget about Balloon Help and Mac OS Guide. Many programs support these excellent Apple technologies; they can be the fastest way to figure out a feature that has you stumped.

Let's get started then. Begin by connecting the printer to the Printer port on the back of your Mac (with both the Mac and the printer turned off, of course — but you knew that, didn't you?). If you don't have a cable (and many Apple printers don't come with cables), contact your printer manufacturer and ask where it is. Plug the printer into an outlet. Turn it on. If the printer came with software, install it on your hard disk, following the instructions that came with the printer. That's it.

Ready, set, print!

Ready: Choosing a Printer in (What Else?) the Chooser DA

The path to printing perfection begins with the humble Chooser DA. In earlier versions of the Mac OS, it was a necessary evil, but with Mac OS 8's desktop printers, you'll use it once to set up your printer, and under ordinary circumstances, you'll rarely use it again.

Note that this chapter describes Mac OS 8 without QuickDraw GX installed. There's a section near the end of the chapter that briefly describes QuickDraw GX and why you might want to install it. If you want to know more about the optional QuickDraw GX, check out Chapter 16. And if you want to install it, look in Appendix A for complete instructions.

Many of the steps involving the Chooser require that the printer be turned on and warmed up, so if yours isn't, it should be. Do that now so that you'll be able to choose a printer.

From the Apple menu, grab the Chooser. The Chooser desk accessory opens. If you have previously chosen a printer, its icon is selected when the Chooser opens; if you've never printed before, the Chooser appears with no printer icon selected.

The Chooser is also where you choose network connections. You will see an icon for AppleShare and may also see one for your fax modem. Don't mess with them yet. I'll talk about File Sharing in the next chapter.

If no icon is selected in your Chooser, click the printer icon that matches your printer. If you have an Apple printer, there should be an icon that matches it. If you have an Apple printer and there is no icon that matches your printer, try clicking the one that sounds most like your printer.

If you have a non-Apple printer, see its manual for instructions on installing printer drivers for your printer. Or try clicking one of the Apple printer drivers (if it's a laser printer, try LaserWriter 8; if it's an inkjet, try the StyleWriter 1200).

Most of the icons in the Chooser represent *printer drivers.* Printer drivers translate between your Mac applications and your printer, ensuring that what you see is what you print. Technically, a printer driver is a special piece of software called a Chooser extension. When you drag a printer driver onto your System Folder, Mac OS 8 automatically places it in the Extensions folder for you. As long as a printer driver is in the Extensions folder, you should see an icon for it in the Chooser.

If you have a printer made by someone other than Apple, you might want to contact the manufacturer about getting the latest, greatest driver. Many printer manufacturers are offering new drivers with enhanced functionality. If you have a modem, you may find new drivers for your printer on America Online, CompuServe, or the Internet. Check with your printer manufacturer for details

Apple printer drivers are installed automatically when you install the Mac OS. You remove them by dragging them from the Extensions folder to the Trash. It's perfectly safe to remove printer drivers for printers that you never intend to use. Removing unneeded printer drivers can free up more than a megabyte of hard disk space.

Now let's get down to business. The left side of the Chooser should be displaying a selection of printer icons; the right side of the Chooser should be displaying either your printer's name (see Figure 7-1) or a pair of icons (see Figure 7-2).

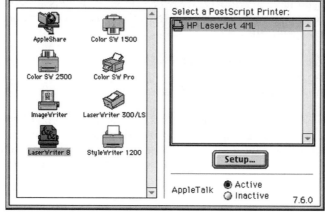

Figure 7-1:
The
Chooser DA
as it
appears
when you
select an
AppleTalk
printer.

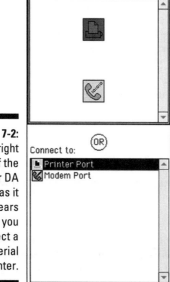

Figure 7-2:
The right
side of the
Chooser DA
as it
appears
when you
select a
serial
printer.

If you have an AppleTalk printer

If you have an AppleTalk printer, click your printer's name to select it —
even if only one name appears, as shown in Figure 7-1.

If you have a serial printer

If you have a serial printer, you'll see two icons on the right side of the Chooser instead of a printer name. Choose whichever port — Printer or Modem — the printer cable is connected to on the back of your Mac.

If you have a SCSI or server-based printer

If you have a SCSI or server-based printer, you're on your own. What you see on the right side of the Chooser depends on the SCSI printer's manufacturer or your server's setup. I couldn't beg or borrow one, so I don't know what you'll see. With luck, you'll figure it out.

My printer is a Hewlett Packard LaserJet 4ML, a compact, inexpensive 300-dots-per-inch PostScript AppleTalk laser printer. I've had the HP for more than a year and it has performed like a champ. At some point I plan to upgrade to a 600- or 800-dpi printer, but it's not mission critical as long as the faithful HP keeps chugging along.

The AppleTalk Active/Inactive radio buttons

Okay. Here's something I can help you with. Should AppleTalk be active or inactive? My answer: Inactive unless you need it.

How do you know if you need AppleTalk? Well, for starters, if you're on a network and use File Sharing, you need it. If your printer is an AppleTalk-only printer (many are), you need it. If you're in neither of these situations, you probably don't need AppleTalk. There's no reason to keep it turned on if you don't need it.

If in doubt, just give it a try. You'll know if your printer works with AppleTalk inactive if your printer spits out a page.

That's it for the Chooser. Go ahead and close it. A desktop printer will be created automatically on your desktop for the printer you chose. I'll talk much more about those desktop printers later in the chapter. For now, just know that if for some strange reason you hate it, you can trash it later. (But, much like the proverbial bad penny, it'll keep coming back every time you select a printer in the Chooser.)

Before you close the Chooser . . .

You're going to go through the rest of this exercise using my printer, an AppleTalk printer, as the example. If you have a different kind of printer — a serial, SCSI, or server — and you can print to your printer at this point (close the Chooser, open a document, and choose File⇨Print — if the document comes out of the printer, you can print to your printer), everything in the rest of the chapter should work the same for you.

Set: Setting Up Your Page with Page Setup

The hard part is done. Now you should be able to print a document quickly and easily. Right? Not so fast, bucko. Though you may not need it right this second, you need to know about the Page Setup dialog box.

Almost every program that can print a document has a Page Setup command on its File menu. Some programs call it Page Setup and others call it Print Setup. (Print Setup is the quaint, old-fashioned term, more popular in the System 6 era than today.) Either way, this dialog box lets you choose paper type, page orientation, scaling percent, page flipping, and page inverting.

The Page Setup dialog box should look like Figure 7-3.

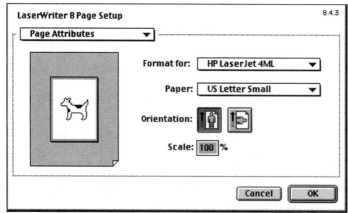

Figure 7-3:
The Page
Setup
dialog box.

Paper type

The objective here is to choose the type of paper currently in the paper tray of your printer, or choose the type of paper that you're about to feed manually.

To do that, click the Paper pop-up menu (see Figure 7-4) and choose the type of paper you plan to use for your next print job.

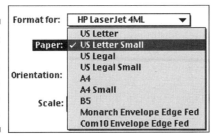

Figure 7-4:
Choosing a paper type in the Page Setup dialog box.

Page Setup dialog box settings remain in effect until you change them. So if you are printing an envelope this time, don't forget to change back to US Letter before trying to print to letter-size paper.

Page orientation

Page Orientation lets you tell the printer whether the page you're about to print is a portrait-oriented (letter, longways) or landscape-oriented (spreadsheet, sideways) page (see Figure 7-5).

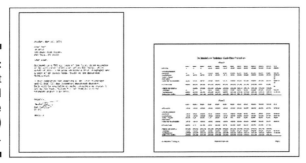

Figure 7-5:
Portrait (left) and landscape (right) pages.

The Page Setup dialog box offers a choice of portrait or landscape, as shown in Figure 7-6.

Figure 7-6:
Portrait
(left) and
landscape
(right)
orientation
buttons in
the Page
Setup
dialog box.

Scale

The Scale control (see Figure 7-7), lets you print pages bigger or smaller than their size on the screen.

Just type a new value into the text entry box, replacing the number 100 (200 in Figure 7-7). In old-style Page Setup dialog boxes, you can also use the arrow buttons on the screen to change the value.

The range of scaling is 25 percent to 400 percent. If you try to enter a higher or lower number, your Mac beeps at you and changes it automatically to the closest acceptable number. Nice touch.

Figure 7-7:
The Scale
control lets
you enlarge
or reduce
your image
for printing.
This setting
(200%) will
double the
size of my
printout
from
normal.

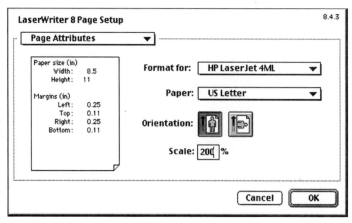

To see the statistics on the left in *your* Page Setup dialog box, just click the dog. Click again to see them in centimeters.

PostScript options

But wait, there's more. The Page Setup dialog box offers two additional sets of options if you choose PostScript Options from the pop-up menu (see Figure 7-8) — Visual Effects and Images & Text.

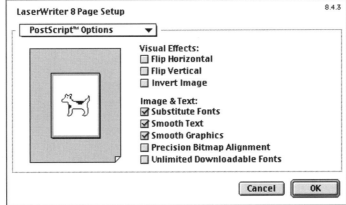

Figure 7-8:
PostScript
Options in
the Page
Setup
dialog box.

Visual Effects

Flipping the page vertically or horizontally merely requires that you check the appropriate check box. The dogcow on the miniature page reflects your choices (see Figure 7-9).

The tail of the dogcow

The dogcow has appeared in the Page Setup dialog box since time immemorial. He is a kind of unofficial Macintosh mascot. His name, they say, is Clarus. His bark, they say, is *Moof.*

As you can see in Figure 7-9, Clarus is more than just a mascot. He's an elegant way to give you visual feedback on your choices. Look at Figure 7-9. It works.

Figure 7-9:
The
miniature
page
featuring
Clarus the
Dogcow
(Moof!)
provides
visual
feedback
for your
choices of
Visual
Effects.

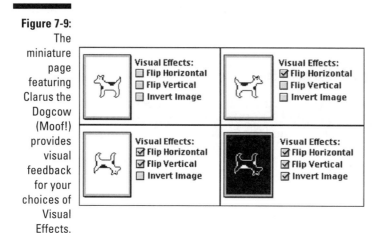

Checking the Invert Image option inverts your page, making light areas dark and dark areas light, like a photograph negative.

Note that this option will generally use a lot of toner or ink. And printing a large number of inverted pages could cause a laser printer to overheat or an inkjet printer to clog. So use this feature sparingly.

I suppose that the Invert Image option is useful for creating artsy effects or making negative images of documents that will be printed to film. I've never used it in the eleven years I've used a Mac.

Image & Text

These next five options are thrilling. I could spend two pages explaining them, but I'm going to invoke another weasel-out (see Chapter 1) and tell you to look at the Balloon Help to find out what they do.

To do that, while the Page Setup PostScript Options dialog box is on the screen, choose Show Balloons from the Help (question mark) menu and point at each of the five check boxes, as shown in Figure 7-10.

Figure 7-10:
Balloon
Help
explains
these five
check
boxes
almost as
well as I
could.
It'll save a
tree (part
of one, at
least), too.

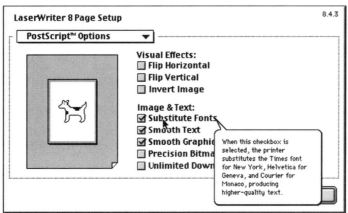

One last thing . . .

Most programs also offer their own Page Setup choices. To see them (if your program offers them, of course), choose the program from the pop-up menu below the words "LaserWriter 8 Page Setup." Photoshop and Microsoft Word have them (Figures 7-11 and 7-12); SimpleText doesn't.

LaserWriter 8 Page Setup			8.4.3
Adobe Photoshop® 4.0.1 ▼			

Screen... Border... ☐ Calibration Bars ☐ Labels
Transfer... Bleed... ☐ Registration Marks ☐ Negative
Background... ☐ Caption ☐ Corner Crop Marks ☐ Emulsion Down
  ☐ Center Crop Marks ☐ Interpolation

[Cancel] [OK]

Figure 7-11:
Photoshop's
Page Setup
choices.

```
LaserWriter 8 Page Setup                              8.4.3
  ┌ Microsoft Word          ▼ ┐
 ┌─────────────────────────────────────────────────────────┐
 │ [ Custom... ]  No custom page size selected.   [ Margins... ] │
 │                                                 [ Print... ]   │
 │ Apply Size and Orientation To:                  [ Word Help ]  │
 │ [ Whole Document         ▼ ]                    [ Default... ] │
 │                                                                │
 │                                                                │
 │                                                                │
 │                                      [ Cancel ]  [   OK   ]    │
 └─────────────────────────────────────────────────────────┘
```

Figure 7-12:
Microsoft
Word's
Page Setup
choices.

The Print Dialog Box: Printing to Most Printers

Now we come to the final step before that joyous moment when your printed page pops out of the printer. It's the Print dialog box, and it's the last thing standing between you and your output.

While most of you will see Print dialog boxes that look like the ones in this chapter, others won't. The features in the Print dialog box are strictly a function of the program with which you're printing. Many programs choose to use the standard-issue Apple dialog boxes as shown in this chapter, but others don't. If a feature isn't explained in this chapter, chances are it's a feature specific to the application that you're using and should be explained in that program's documentation.

Your printer is chosen in the Chooser. Your page is set up in Page Setup. If, up to this point, you haven't been working with a document that you want to print, find one now and open it because it's time to . . .

1. Choose File⇨Print (Command-P).

One of the best things about the Mac is that Apple has published a set of guidelines that all Mac programs should use. Consistency among programs is one of the Mac's finest features. Notice how 99 percent of all programs have Open, Close, Save, Save As, Page Setup, Print, and Quit commands in their File menus and Undo, Cut, Copy, and Paste commands in their Edit menus. That's the kind of thing *Macintosh Human Interface Guidelines* recommends.

According to Apple's guidelines, the Print command should always appear in the File menu, which is good. *Macintosh Human Interface Guidelines* also says that the keyboard shortcut Command-P should be reserved for plain text (the way Command-B is often used for bold or Command-I for italic). This is bad.

Fortunately, software developers listened to Apple about the first item and ignored Apple about the second, so Command-P is almost always the shortcut for the Print command in the File menu.

Every so often you come across a program that doesn't follow these conventions, but I'd say at least 90 percent of commercial Mac programs put the Print command in the File menu and use Command-P for its keyboard shortcut.

The point is that there is a slight chance that Step 1 won't work for you. If the Print command is on a different menu, if there is no Print command, or the keyboard shortcut is anything but Command-P, you'll have to wing it.

Then write the software company a brief note mentioning that they *could* make things easier on everyone by putting the Print command in the proper place and using the generally-agreed-upon keyboard shortcut.

Anyway, the Print dialog box appears. It looks like Figure 7-13 when it first appears.

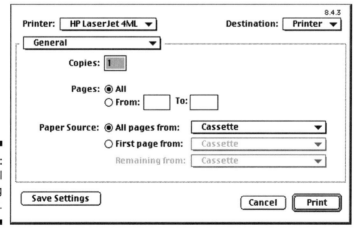

Figure 7-13: The General Print dialog box.

The Print dialog box has a pop-up menu that offers seven options (see Figure 7-14). Let's look at these options and their suboptions one at a time.

Figure 7-14:
The Print dialog box's pop-up options menu.

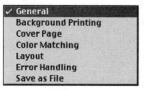

```
✓ General
  Background Printing
  Cover Page
  Color Matching
  Layout
  Error Handling
  Save as File
```

The Print⇨General dialog box

The choices you make in the Print⇨General dialog box are

- How many copies to print
- Which page numbers to print
- Automatic or manual feed paper
- Which printer to use for this print job
- Destination: printer or PostScript file
- And whether to save these settings permanently

TIP

Try pressing the Tab key and watching what happens. The active field will jump to each of the text fields in the dialog box in rotation. Shift-Tab makes the active field jump backward. Try it; you'll like it.

Copies

How many copies do you want to print? The Print dialog box defaults to one copy in most applications, so you'll probably see a 1 in this field when the dialog box appears. Assuming that's the case, don't do anything if you only want to print one copy. If you want to print more than one copy of your document, select the 1 that appears in the Copies field and type in a new number (see Figure 7-15).

Figure 7-15:
To print 13 copies, replace the 1 with 13.

Copies: ▐1▐

Copies: |13|

Pages

Which pages do you want to print? All of them? Or just some? This option is easy. If you want to print your entire document, click the All radio button. If you only want to print a specific page or range of pages, type their numbers in the From and To text entry boxes.

For example, say you have a ten-page document. You print the whole thing and then notice a typo on page 2. You fix the typo and then print only page 2 by typing a 2 in both the From and To fields, as shown in Figure 7-16.

Figure 7-16:
Here's how to print only the second page of a document.

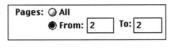

You can type any valid range of pages into the From and To fields.

Paper source

Your choices are Paper Cassette or Manual Feed for your first page or all your pages.

If you plan to use the paper in your printer's paper tray, choose Cassette. If you plan to feed a single sheet, choose Manual Feed.

If you want the first page to come from one place and the remaining pages to come from another, click the appropriate radio button and make the appropriate choices from the pop-up menus.

It's that simple.

Destination: printer or PostScript file

The pop-up menu in the dialog box's upper right corner lets you choose to print to your printer or create a PostScript file on disk instead. When you choose File, the Print button becomes a Save button. When you click the Save button, a standard Save dialog box appears.

Save Settings

This button saves the current settings and makes them the default for future print jobs. If everything is just as you like it, click this button and all future print jobs will use these settings.

The Print⇨Background Printing dialog box

Choosing Background Printing from the Print dialog box's pop-up menu lets you turn background printing on or off, and set a print time if you so desire (see Figure 7-17).

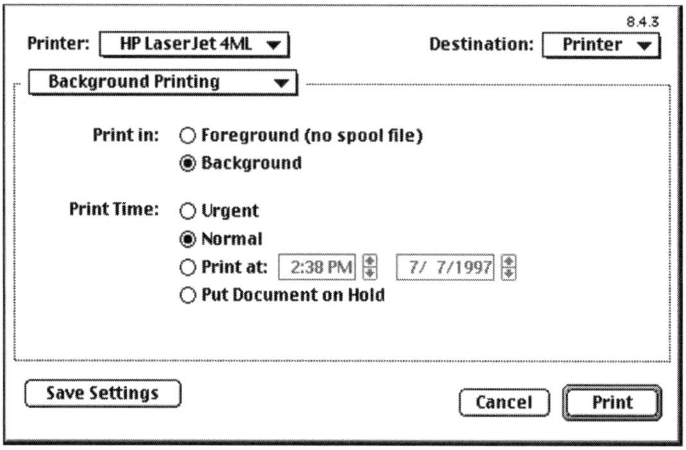

Figure 7-17:
The Print dialog box's Background Printing options.

```
                                                          8.4.3
  Printer:  [ HP LaserJet 4ML  ▼ ]      Destination:  [ Printer ▼ ]
  [ Background Printing          ▼ ]
  ┌──────────────────────────────────────────────────────────────┐
  │                                                                │
  │      Print in:   ○ Foreground (no spool file)                  │
  │                  ◉ Background                                   │
  │                                                                │
  │   Print Time:    ○ Urgent                                      │
  │                  ◉ Normal                                      │
  │                  ○ Print at:  [ 2:38 PM ⬍ ]  [ 7/ 7/1997 ⬍ ]   │
  │                  ○ Put Document on Hold                        │
  │                                                                │
  └──────────────────────────────────────────────────────────────┘
  [ Save Settings ]                        [ Cancel ]  [ Print ]
```

Print in foreground or background

Background printing has been around for a while. It's the thing that allows you to continue using your Macintosh while it's printing. Wonderful stuff.

It didn't used to be that way. In the bad old days, in the pre–System 6 era when there was no background printing, you sat and waited until the printing was done before you could use your Mac again.

Under Mac OS 8, background printing is turned on unless you specifically turn it off. You may notice your Mac feeling a little twitchy or jerky when a document is printing in the background. That's normal. Ignore it. After a while, you hardly notice it at all. And it's much better than the alternative — being unable to work until your print job is done.

Print time

To set a printing time for your document (see Figure 7-17).

Click the radio button next to your desired print time priority. Here's what the priorities mean:

- ✔ The Normal option prints the document now. If other documents are in the print queue, it takes its place behind documents printed before it.

- ✔ The Urgent option prints the document now but places it ahead of any documents in the print queue.

- ✔ The Print at option lets you choose a specific time. When you click its radio button, you can adjust the time and date.

- ✔ The Put Document on Hold option lets you prepare a document for printing but not print it at this time.

The Print⇨Cover Page dialog box

Clicking the Before Document or After Document radio button (see Figure 7-18) adds a page at the beginning or end of your print job. The cover page contains your name, the program and document names, date and time, and printer name. In other words, a page that looks like pretty much like this:

User: Bob LeVitus
Application: ClarisWorks
Document: Brief Bio (WP)
Date: Tuesday, August 14, 1994
Time: 3:54:02 AM
Printer: HP LaserJet 4ML 1

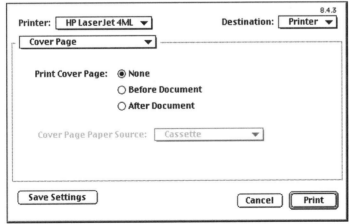

Figure 7-18:
The Print dialog box's Cover Page options.

I may have used this feature once in the past ten years. I suppose if you're on a network sharing a printer, there might be a reason to waste trees by printing useless pages with hardly anything on them. But unless you must have a cover page, leave the None button selected and save a tree.

The Print⇨Color Matching dialog box

Here's where you choose from Black and White, Color/Grayscale, or ColorSync Color Matching for your output (see Figure 7-19). Use your best guess.

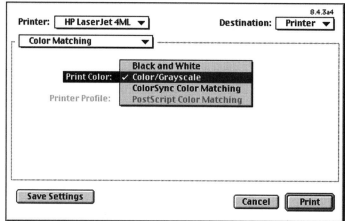

Figure 7-19:
The Print
dialog box's
Color
Matching
options.

The Print⇨Layout dialog box

Choose the number of pages per printed sheet, and whether or not you prefer a border (see Figure 7-20).

The Print⇨Error Handling dialog box

This dialog box provides options in case a PostScript error occurs; leave it alone unless you have a reason to change it.

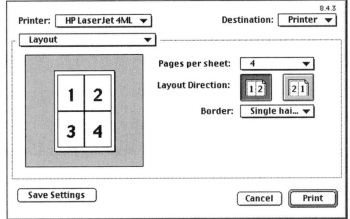

Figure 7-20:
The Print dialog box's Layout options.

The Print⇨Save As File dialog box

These options let you save your file as a PostScript file on disk. One pop-up menu lets you choose between raw PostScript and several flavors of Encapsulated PostScript. Another pop-up menu lets you include no fonts, all fonts, or only nonstandard fonts. (Nonstandard fonts are fonts other than the ones the Install Mac OS program installs.) Choose whichever setting is appropriate for the recipient of your document.

The safest bet is to include all fonts, just in case. The downside to this solution is that the PostScript file will be much larger than the original. For example, a SimpleText file used only 5K of disk space in its original form (that is, saved as a SimpleText document). When saved as a PostScript file with all fonts included, it grew more than tenfold, requiring a whopping 80K of disk space.

Several things can inflate the size of the PostScript file. Including all fonts adds a lot of K. High-resolution images add a lot of K. And long documents use a lot of K. It's common for color artwork or page layout documents printed to disk as PostScript files to be larger than a high-density floppy disk. So if you plan to save a PostScript file to your hard disk and then copy it to a floppy disk, you may have to use a backup or compression utility to segment the file so that it will fit on several floppy disks.

I can't tell you much about the PostScript Level and Data Format choices; ask the people to whom you're sending the file if they have a preference.

One last thing . . .

StyleWriter and StyleWriter II users, as well as users of other inkjet printers and/or non-PostScript printers, may see slightly different versions of the Print and Page Setup dialog boxes. The differences should be minor enough not to matter.

The Hip New Thing: Desktop Printers

Desktop printers are unique and a huge improvement over earlier printing schemes; the new architecture for printing makes the entire experience easier.

What is a desktop printer, anyway?

A desktop printer is an icon on your desktop that represents a printer that is connected to your computer. It's created automatically when you select a printer in the Chooser DA. To print a document, drag its icon onto a desktop printer (see Figure 7-22).

In Figure 7-21, when I release the mouse, Great American Novel will print.

Figure 7-21:
Drag and
drop
printing
with
desktop
printer
icons.

Technically, SimpleText, the application that created the Great American Novel document, will launch, and its Print dialog box will open automatically. Click the Print button, or press Return or Enter, and the document will print and then SimpleText will quit automatically.

What if SimpleText isn't available? If you have a translator that can open SimpleText documents, you'll see a dialog box where you can choose another application. If you don't have a compatible application or translator, you'll see an error message telling you that the document cannot be opened.

You create new desktop printers with the Chooser desk accessory.

Using desktop printers

Before I talk about using desktop printers, I need to tell you why you should use desktop printers. Three words: It saves steps. Rather than open a document, choose File⇨Print, and diddle around in the Print dialog box, you can drag that document onto a desktop printer, click Print (or press Return or Enter), then go out for a Jolt cola or whatever. In a word, it's easy. No muss, no fuss. Just drag and drop and click (or press), and in a few moments, paper starts popping out of your printer.

So basically, you use desktop printers by dragging documents onto them. As long as the application that created the documents is available, they'll be printed after you click Print (or press Return or Enter) with no further ado.

Another handy use for desktop printers is to create desktop printers for special kinds of print jobs. For example, create one for envelopes that uses the landscape, manual feed, and black and white settings. Create another for grayscale portrait mode printing. And so on. Just drag your file onto the appropriate desktop printer (be sure and give it a descriptive name) and you'll avoid all those messy adjustments in the Page Setup and Print dialog boxes.

But there's more to using desktop printers than just drag and drop. When you select a desktop printer (by single-clicking it), a new Printing menu appears in the menu bar, as shown in Figure 7-22. To view the print queue, open the desktop printer icon. (In case you forgot, you open an item by double-clicking its icon or by selecting its icon and choosing File⇨Open [Command-O].)

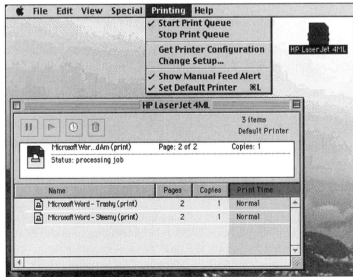

Figure 7-22:
The Desktop Printer window and menu.

You'll notice a set of tape recorder-like icons in the Desktop Printer window. From left to right these are stop the print queue, start the print queue, set the print time for the selected item or items, and delete the selected item from the queue. Also note that you can click any of the column heads — Document Name, Pages, Copies, or Print Time — to change the sorting order of the items in the list.

In Figure 7-22, there are three Microsoft Word documents in the queue. Bad American Novel is currently printing. Clicking the stop button would suspend the printing of Bad American Novel until I chose to resume. Clicking the delete button would permanently remove Bad American Novel from the printing queue, and it would never print.

So what do the menu commands do?

- **Start Print Cue and Stop Print Queue** are like the Play and Pause buttons on your VCR. To pause the printing process and be able to resume where you left off later, choose Stop Print Queue. To resume, choose Start Print Queue.

- **Get Printer Configuration** brings up a dialog box that provides information about your printer and its fonts.

- **Change Setup** lets you choose another PPD (PostScript Printer Description) file for this printer.

- **Show Manual Feed Alert** lets you decide whether or not your Mac pauses to ask you to insert a sheet of manual feed paper before a manual feed print job. A check mark beside this item means it's turned on.

- **Set Default Printer** lets you decide, if you have more than one printer attached, which one will be the default printer (that is, the one that's selected when you choose Print) in the Print dialog box.

One last thing about these here desktop printers: You can choose your desktop printers from the pop-up menu in the Print dialog box! That's right, the Print To pop-up menu in the Print dialog box gives you a choice of any printer that appears on your desktop. No more trips to the Chooser! Hooray!

What is QuickDraw GX? (And Should I Use It?)

Here's Apple's pitch about QuickDraw GX from when System 7.5 was the rage several years ago: "QuickDraw GX is setting the stage for the next generation in graphics. QuickDraw GX greatly extends and expands the graphics capabilities of the Macintosh, creating a new standard for desktop graphics computing and reaffirming the place of Macintosh as the premier publishing platform in the personal computer industry. It offers significant improvements to all customers, from generalist users to publishing professionals."

Here's Apple's pitch today: "Prompted by our new dual OS strategy — Mac OS and Rhapsody — Apple has reevaluated the graphics and printing architectures of Mac OS. Beginning with Mac OS 8 and QuickDraw GX 1.1.6, Apple provides a unified operating system printing architecture, standardizing on classic (non-GX) QuickDraw printing and printer drivers. With the unified printing architecture, QuickDraw GX printer drivers and QuickDraw GX printing extensions will not be supported in Mac OS 8 and future Mac OS releases."

Basically this means that QuickDraw GX is dead and the only people who need it are those who have QuickDraw GX-specific programs. You know who you are. Otherwise (that is, most of you), don't even bother installing it.

Font Mania

To a computer user, *font* means typeface. Although professional typographers will scream, we'll go with that definition for now.

Each font looks different. There are tens of thousands of different fonts available for the Macintosh. You can buy single fonts and font collections anywhere you can buy software. There are also plenty of shareware and public domain fonts available from online services and user groups. Some people have thousands of them.

How to install fonts

This is a very short section. To install any font except a Type 1 font, drag it onto your System Folder icon. When you drag a font onto your System Folder icon, your Mac asks if you want to place it in the Fonts folder. Click OK.

When you click OK, the deed is done and the font is installed. To remove a font, drag it out of the Fonts folder (which is in the System Folder). After a font is installed, it appears in the Font menu of all your applications.

You can store fonts anywhere on your hard disk, but a font will only be available in an application if it's in the Fonts folder when you launch that application.

Type formats

There are four different kinds of fonts that you need to know about:

- ✔ *Bitmap* fonts, unlike other font formats, come in different sizes. You need a separate bitmap file for each size of the font that you want to display or print.

- ✔ *TrueType* fonts come with Mac OS 8. They are the Apple standard issue and are in wide use on Macs as well as on Windows machines. These fonts are scalable, which means that there is only a single outline for the font, and your Mac makes it bigger or smaller when you choose a bigger or smaller font size in a program.

- ✔ *Type 1* fonts, sometimes referred to as PostScript Type 1 fonts, are the standard for desktop publishing on the Mac. There are tens of thousands of Type 1 fonts available (and not nearly as many TrueType fonts exist).

  Type 1 fonts come in two pieces, a bitmap font suitcase and a second piece, called a printer font. Some Type 1 fonts come with two, three, or four printer fonts. They usually have related names.

- ✔ *TrueType GX* is the latest font format. Very few of these were ever produced, and with GX dead, probably few more will ever be.

Font advice in brief

You don't need to know a thing about font types. Really. When you get a font, just drag it (or all of its parts) onto your System Folder icon.

If you have a lot of fonts and need help managing them, try Adobe's ATM Deluxe.

Chapter 8

File Sharing for the Rest of Us

• •

• •

Computer networking has a well-deserved reputation for being complicated and nerve-wracking. The truth is, there's nothing scary or complicated about sharing files, folders, and disks (and printers, for that matter) among computers. As long, of course, as the computers are Macintoshes.

If you have more than one computer, file sharing is a must. It's fun, it's easy, and it's way better than SneakerNet[*].

Your Macintosh includes everything you need to share files and printers. Everything, that is, except the printers and the cables. So here's the deal: You supply the printers and cables, and I'll supply the rest.

This chapter is kind of unusual. I don't show you how to actually share a file until the next-to-the-last section. The first four sections provide an overview and tell you everything you need to know to share files successfully. Trust me, there's a method to my madness. If you try to share files without doing all of the required prep work, the whole mess becomes confusing and complicated — kind of like networking a pair of PC clones.

So just follow along and don't worry about why you're not sharing yet. You'll share soon.

[*]SneakerNet: Moving files from computer to computer on a floppy disk; i.e., walking from one computer to the other with floppy disk in hand.

What It Is

Macintosh file sharing lets you use files, folders, and disks from other Macs on the network as easily as if they were on your own local hard disk.

Devices connected directly to your computers, such as hard disks or CD-ROM drives, are *local*. Devices you access (share) over the network are *remote*.

File sharing also lets any computer on the network access (if you desire) your files, folders, and disks as easily as if they were on someone else's local hard disk.

Finally, file sharing lets you *link* programs on your computer to programs on other computers. Why would you want to do that? You'll find out.

For our purposes, a network is two or more Macs connected by LocalTalk-compatible cables.

This chapter assumes you're working on a small network, the kind typically found in a home or small business. There are also huge corporate networks, spaghetti-like mazes with thousands of computers and printers connected by cable, phone, infrared link, and ISDN, complete with confusing-sounding hardware such as routers and hubs and hublets and transceivers and netmodems. That kind of network *is* complicated, even if the computers are Macs. And, of course, this chapter isn't about that subject.

If you're part of a mega-monstrous corporate network and you have questions about your particular network, talk to the P.I.C. (person in charge, a.k.a. your network administrator).

If you're trying to *build* one of these mega-networks, I regret to inform you that you'll need a book a lot thicker than this one.

Portrait of a LocalTalk Network

This chapter describes my office network. It consists of two Macintoshes and a network laser printer. (By the end of the chapter, that's not all we'll be sharing, if you know what I mean.)

This two-person network is merely an example. In real life, a network can and often does have dozens or hundreds of users. Regardless of whether your network has two nodes or two thousand, the principles and techniques in this chapter are the same.

My little network looks like what's shown in Figure 8-1.

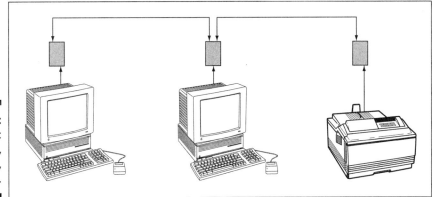

Figure 8-1:
Left to right:
My Mac,
Lisa's Mac,
the printer.

The black lines between the devices are cables; the gray box near each device is a connector. You need one connector for each device and enough cable to run between them. We happen to use the Apple LocalTalk Locking Connector Kits (part number M2068) and Apple Locking Cable Kits (M2066). LocalTalk connectors look something like Figure 8-2.

Figure 8-2:
The plug
coming out
the far side
goes into
the modem
or printer
port of your
Mac. The
two holes
(ports) on
the near
side are
where you
connect
your Apple
Locking
Cables.
(Don't laugh
— I drew
this picture
myself!)

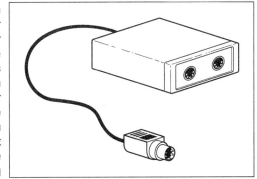

We could have used PhoneNet connectors from Farallon instead of the Apple connectors. The big difference is that PhoneNet connectors use regular telephone cord from Radio Shack (or Target or anywhere) instead of expensive Apple Locking Cables. PhoneNet connectors are also less expensive than Apple LocalTalk connectors. Finally, PhoneNet connectors perform as well as (if not better than) Apple's LocalTalk connector. So why did I use the Apple cables? Because they were here. They came with my loaner computer. If I were paying my own money, I'd have gone with PhoneNet instead.

When discussions of networks take place, you're likely to hear the words AppleTalk, EtherTalk (or Ethernet), TokenTalk, and/or LocalTalk bandied about with great regularity. The first three are *protocols,* a kind of language networks speak. The last, LocalTalk, is a collection of wires and connectors. I'll talk more about this aberration in a moment.

Support for the AppleTalk protocol, and for LocalTalk, is built into every Mac. Your Mac includes all the software and ports that you need to set up an AppleTalk network; all you have to provide are LocalTalk-compatible cables and connectors (such as the Apple or Farallon products mentioned earlier).

LocalTalk is an aberration. It's not a protocol even though it sounds like one. In the old days, Apple referred to both the wires and the protocol as AppleTalk. Then one day a few years ago, Apple decreed that AppleTalk was a protocol and LocalTalk was the wires and connectors.

I suppose disassociating the protocol and the wires makes sense. Still, LocalTalk sounds like a protocol (AppleTalk, EtherTalk, TokenTalk), even though it's not. Anyway, LocalTalk refers to the physical connections that an AppleTalk network uses.

Got it? AppleTalk, EtherTalk, and TokenTalk are protocols, the languages that the network speaks. LocalTalk is a collection of physical parts — connectors (LocalTalk connectors), ports (like the modem or printer port), and cables (LocalTalk-compatible cables) — that hook the machines together.

Getting Turned On

The first thing to do is turn AppleTalk on. No network activity can take place until it's on.

1. Open the Chooser (Apple menu⇨Chooser).

2. Click the Active radio button to turn on AppleTalk (see Figure 8-3).

Figure 8-3:
Click the
AppleTalk
Active radio
button in
the Chooser
desk
accessory.

3. Close the Chooser by clicking its close box in the upper-left corner or by choosing File⇨Close (Command-W).

4. Open the AppleTalk control panel (Apple menu⇨Control Panels⇨ AppleTalk) and choose the appropriate connection from the pop-up menu (see Figure 8-4).

Figure 8-4:
Choose the
appropriate
connection
from the
AppleTalk
control
panel's
pop-up
menu.

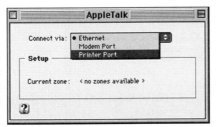

If you're using a small network, that's all there is to getting started.

If your network has multiple zones, you'll also have to choose a zone in the AppleTalk control panel at this time.

Zones are mini-networks connected together. Once a network gets to about 50 users, zones help network managers keep network traffic under control. If you have zones, there's probably somebody around to ask if you need to know more.

5. Close the AppleTalk control panel by clicking its close box in the upper-left corner or by choosing File⇨Close (Command-W).

Setting Up File Sharing

Okay. AppleTalk is on, and you're ready for a quick game of Name That Mac before you turn file sharing on.

Get a network identity

1. Choose Apple menu➪Control Panels➪File Sharing.

   The File Sharing control panel opens (see Figure 8-5).

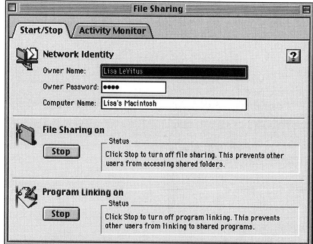

Figure 8-5:
The File Sharing control panel for Lisa's Mac.

2. Type in all three pieces of information in the Network Identity section at the top: your name, a password, and a name for your Mac.

   - **Owner Name:** This one should be self-explanatory — type your name.

   - **Owner Password:** Your password can be any combination of up to eight letters and numbers. When you click anywhere outside the Password field, the letters or numbers in your password turn into bullets, as shown in Figure 8-5.

   - **Computer Name:** Select a computer name that's unique and memorable. Lisa's Macintosh is a better choice than Mac.

You can press the Tab key to move from field to field in the File Sharing control panel.

Turn file sharing and program linking on

File sharing and program linking each have a Stop/Start button. It's a toggle: If it's turned on, the button reads "Stop." If it's not turned on, the button reads "Start." Turn file sharing and program linking on, if they're not on already, by clicking each section's Start button.

The status of file sharing and program linking appears to the right of their buttons, as shown in Figure 8-5. Both are presently on. How do I know? The buttons read Stop, and the status boxes to the right of the buttons say that they're on.

You want your File Sharing control panel to look like Figure 8-5, so if file sharing and program linking aren't on, click their Start buttons (click each one once). In other words, if *your* buttons say Start, click them. If they say Stop, don't click them.

Program linking lets certain Macintosh programs exchange information with other programs. Programs implement linking in various ways, and not all programs can link. See the documentation that came with your program to see if linking is supported and how to use it.

There is no penalty for turning program linking on, so I keep it running — even though I can't recall ever using it — in case I need it someday. You allow or disallow program linking for specific users in the Users & Groups control panel (more on that subject in a second).

If program linking is not on (in the File Sharing control panel), other users on your network cannot program link even if the Allow user to link to programs on this computer check box is checked in the appropriate user window of the Users & Groups control panel.

Users and Groups and Guests (Oh My!)

Macintosh file sharing is based on the concept of users and groups. Shared items — disks or folders — can be shared with no users, one user, or many users. Access to items on your local hard disk is entirely at your discretion. You may configure your Mac so that nobody but you can share its folders and disks, so that only one other person can share its folders and disks, or so that many people can share its folders and disks. People who share folders and disks are called *users*.

Users

Before you can go any further, you need to create user identities for the people on your network. You perform this little task with the Users & Groups control panel. I'm going to demonstrate on Lisa's Mac:

1. Open the Users & Groups control panel (Apple menu⇨Control Panels⇨Users & Groups).

   A Users & Groups window appears, as shown in Figure 8-6. If you haven't previously created users or groups, two users appear in the window:

   Owner: Lets you configure sharing for the owner of your Mac, the person whose name appears in the Owner Name field of the File Sharing control panel. This icon should have your name on it.

   Guest: Lets you configure a guest account for your Mac.

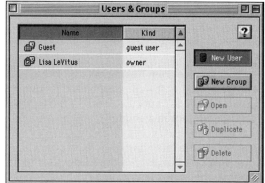

Figure 8-6:
The Users
& Groups
window.

2. Click the New User button to create a new user.

3. Rename the new user something meaningful.

4. When you create a new user, you have the option of assigning a password. If network security is unimportant to you (if only people you trust use the network), it's okay to leave the password field blank. You can also use the Allow user to change password check box to give your new user more control over his or her password. If you leave this box unchecked, the owner of the Mac has control over this user's password.

5. Click the Users & Groups window and then open the item with your name on it (the name that you typed in the Owner Name field of the File Sharing control panel).

6. Pull down the pop-up menu at the top of the window and choose Sharing.

7. Open the new user's item and choose Sharing from the pop-up menu.

If you arrange things so that you can see both users' windows, you should see something similar to Figure 8-7. Use the following descriptions to determine how to configure the check boxes.

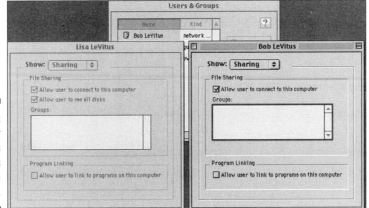

Figure 8-7:
The user privileges windows for Lisa and me.

The check boxes set the privileges of each user. Because Lisa and I are partners and want full access to each others' computers, we check both choices:

- ✓ **Allow user to connect to this computer:** Lets the user connect to this Mac from a remote Mac (as long as he or she knows the proper password).

- ✓ **Allow user to see all disks:** This choice is only available for the owner of the Mac. It means you can see every file on your hard disk if you connect from a remote machine.

After you close the user window, that user is said to be *registered*. In a forthcoming section, I discuss the three categories of users on the network; registered users are one of the three.

Groups

Groups are a convenient way to deal with a bunch of users at once. In the preceding example, I set privileges for a single user, Lisa. Say I want to create a group so that I can assign the same privileges to everyone in our family: Lisa; our daughter, Allison, and our son, Jacob, who occasionally use our computers; and myself. First, I open the Users & Groups control panel

(Apple menu⇨Control Panels⇨Users & Groups). Next, I create new user items for Allison and Jacob. Then I create a new group (by clicking New Group) and name it LeVitus Family. Finally, I drag the icons for Lisa, Bob, Jacob, and Allison onto the group icon. The group icon inverts as shown in Figure 8-8.

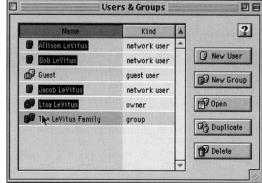

Figure 8-8:
Creating a
group for
the LeVitus
family.

If you open a group window and look inside, you see items representing the individual users. (see Figure 8-9). Opening one of the user items is the same as opening it in the Users & Groups window. In other words, the Jacob LeVitus item in the LeVitus Family group window is like an alias of the Jacob LeVitus item in the Users & Groups window.

Giving privileges to a group is the same as giving those same privileges to each individual member of the group.

Be our guest

Notice the icon in your Users & Groups window called Guest. The Guest icon represents any users who haven't been assigned individual access privileges. Use this icon to allow or disallow guests to connect to your shared folders or disks. Even when guest access is turned on, no one but you has access to any of your folders or disks until you specifically share them. I'll talk about assigning access privileges to disks and folders in the next section.

Removing users or groups

To remove a user or group item from the Users & Groups window, drag it to the Trash. It's that simple.

Figure 8-9:
Opening
either
Jacob
LeVitus
item — the
one from
the Users &
Groups
window or
the one in
the LeVitus
Family
group
window —
brings up
the user
privileges
window for
Jacob
(lower
right).

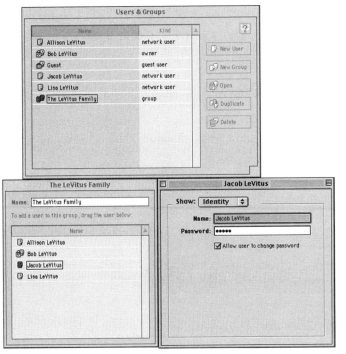

Access and Privileges (Who Can Do What)

Now that file sharing is on and you've created users and/or groups for your networks, you're ready to begin deciding who can use what.

Sharing a folder or disk

To share a folder or disk with another user, take the following initial steps.

1. Select the folder or disk icon and choose File⇨Sharing.

   The access privileges window for the selected item opens (see Figure 8-10).

2. Click the Share this item and its contents check box.

   If you want to be the owner of the folder, leave the Owner pop-up menu alone (more about ownership in a sec).

3. Choose a user or group from the User/Group pop-up menu (the LeVitus Family group in Figure 8-10).

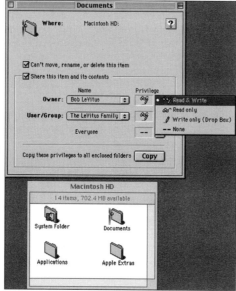

Figure 8-10:
The access
privileges
window
for the
Documents
folder on
Hardy Boy.

4. For the owner and each user or group, choose access privileges from the pop-up menus. Each of the access categories is explained in the following sections.

You may not see exactly what's in Figures 8-9 and 8-10 on your screen. Well, of course you won't. I'd be surprised if your network's users were named LeVitus. But there are other differences you might see as well:

✔ If you've selected a folder inside another shared folder, the check box at the top says "Use enclosing folder's privileges" instead of "Share this item and its contents."

✔ If you've selected a folder on another computer, the Owner and User/Group areas are text entry boxes, not pop-up menus.

✔ If you've selected a folder that someone else owns, all the pop-up menus are dimmed.

Setting access privileges

The pop-up menus to the right of the Owner and User/Group pop-up menus control the access. In other words, they control who can use what and how much they can use it.

There are three categories of users on the network:

✔ **The owner:** The owner of a folder or disk can change the access privileges to that folder at any time. The name in the Owner Name field of the File Sharing control panel is the default owner of shared folders and disks on that machine. Ownership may be given away (more on that in a moment).

✔ **A registered user or a group:** A registered user has access to shared disks and folders over the network as long as the user or group has been granted access by the folder or disk's owner. A registered user is any user who has an entry in the Users & Groups control panel. A group is nothing more than a bunch of registered users.

✔ **Everyone:** This category is an easy way to set access privileges for everyone at once — the owner, registered users and groups, and guests.

The access privileges pop-up menus (the ones with icons, to the right of the Owner, Registered User, and Everyone items) let you control how much access each type of user has to the shared folder or disk. If you click one, you'll see the privilege description that corresponds to the icon.

You can choose from four kinds of access for each user or group:

✔ **Read & Write:** A user with read and write access can see, add, delete, move, and edit files, just as if they were stored on his or her own computer.

✔ **Read only**: A read-only user can see and use files that are stored in a shared folder, but can't add, delete, move, or edit them.

✔ **Write only (Drop Box):** It's like the label says; a user with write-only access can drop files into your shared folder or disk.

✔ **None:** With no privileges, a user can neither see nor use your shared folders or disks.

Useful settings for access privileges

Here are some ways you can combine access privileges for a folder or disk:

Allow everyone access

Figure 8-11 shows the settings that allow access for everyone on a network.

Allow nobody but yourself access

Figure 8-12 shows the appropriate settings that allow only the owner access.

Allow one person or one group access

Figure 8-13 shows the settings that allow only one person or group (in addition to the owner) access.

Figure 8-11:
Let everyone on the network open, read, and change the contents of this shared disk or folder.

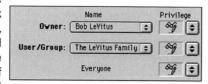

Figure 8-12:
Let nobody except the owner see or use the contents of this shared disk or folder.

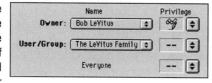

Figure 8-13:
Let the owner and a single user or single group see, use, or change the contents of this shared disk or folder.

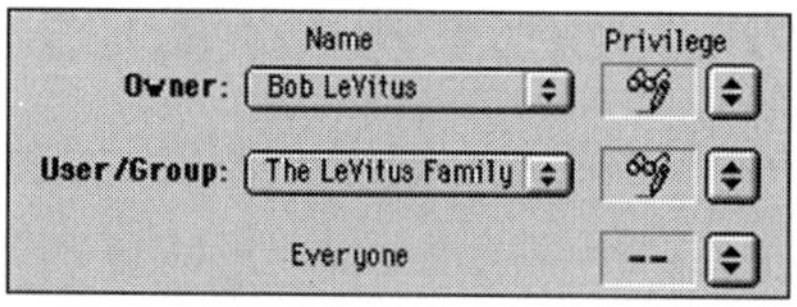

Allow others to deposit files and folders without giving them access (a drop box)

Figure 8-14 shows the settings that allow users to drop files or folders without being able to see or use the contents of the disk or folder.

After a file or folder is deposited in a drop folder, the dropper cannot retrieve it, as he or she doesn't have access privileges to see the items in the drop folder.

Figure 8-14:
No users can see or use the contents of this shared folder or disk, but they can deposit files or folders of their own in it.

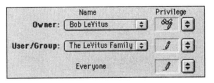

Read-only bulletin boards

Figure 8-15 shows the settings that let everyone access the contents of the disk or folder without giving them the ability to make changes.

Figure 8-15:
Everyone can open and read the files and folders in this shared folder or disk, but only the owner can make changes.

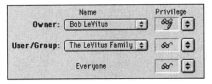

The two other privileges

There are two more items in the access privileges window. At the top, the Can't move, rename, or delete this item check box protects the folder from being moved, renamed, or deleted by users whose privileges would otherwise allow them to move, delete, or rename that folder. (This check box doesn't appear in the access privileges window for disks.)

The Copy these privileges to all enclosed folders option, at the bottom of the access privileges window, does exactly what its name implies. This feature is a fast way to assign the same privileges to many subfolders at once.

The Actual Act of Sharing

Okay, this is the moment you've all been waiting for. You've done everything leading up to the big moment: sharing is set up, users and groups are registered, and access privileges are assigned.

If you've been following along, you know how to do all of the prep work and more. So make sure that you've shared at least one folder on your hard disk and that you have full access privileges to it. Now go to another computer on the network, and I'll show you how to access that folder remotely.

Interestingly, file sharing doesn't have to be activated on the other machine. A Mac can access shared files over the network even with file sharing turned off. If file sharing is turned off, you can't create users and groups or assign access privileges, but you can access a remote shared disk or folder if you have been granted enough access privileges by its owner, even with file sharing turned off on your Mac.

If file sharing is turned off on your Mac, though, others won't be able to access your disk or folders, even if you've shared them previously.

Connecting to a shared disk or folder

Continuing my little network example, I'm going to access the Documents folder on Lisa's Mac, which Lisa owns but has granted me full access to (see Figure 8-16).

On my computer, I choose Apple menu⇨Chooser and then click the AppleShare icon.

AppleTalk, of course, is active on my machine. If it's not, I won't be able to use the network. While file sharing doesn't have to be turned on for me to access a remote disk or folder, AppleTalk does.

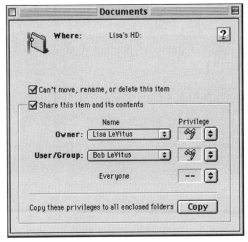

Figure 8-16:
The Documents folder on Lisa's HD. I have full privileges, so I'm able to access this folder from my (remote) computer.

I select Lisa's Macintosh in the Chooser's file server list and then click OK (see Figure 8-17).

After I click OK, the Connect dialog box appears. Because I'm the owner of this Mac, my name appears in the Name field. I type in my password and then click OK (see Figure 8-18).

I now encounter another dialog box where I can select one or more items to use. Because that single folder, Documents, is the only folder on Lisa's Mac that has been shared with me, it's the only one that appears in Figure 8-19.

I click OK, and the Documents icon appears on my desktop, as shown in Figure 8-20.

The unique icon for the Documents folder clearly indicates that this is a shared folder accessed over the network. Those are, of course, wires coming out the bottom of the icon. This icon is what you see whenever a remote disk or folder is mounted on your desktop.

If there are multiple items in the item selection dialog box (refer to Figure 8-19) and you want to select more than one, click the first item, hold down the Shift key, and click once on each item that you want to add to the selection. After you've selected all the items that you want to use, click the OK button, and they are all mounted on your desktop.

Connecting automatically at startup

If I wanted the Documents folder, which is on Lisa's Macintosh, to appear automatically on *my* Mac's desktop every time I turn it on, I would click the check box to the right of Documents in Figure 8-19.

I only expect to use this folder occasionally, so I won't.

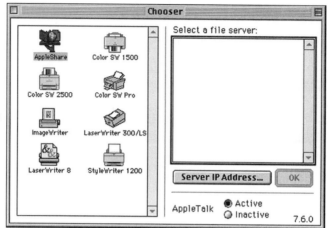

Figure 8-17:
The Chooser on my Mac as I connect to Lisa's Mac.

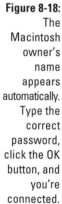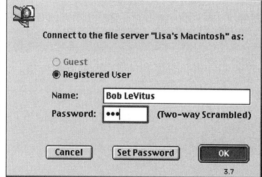

Figure 8-18:
The Macintosh owner's name appears automatically. Type the correct password, click the OK button, and you're connected.

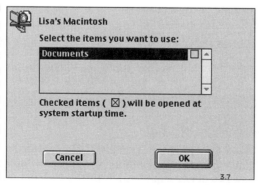

Figure 8-19:
The last dialog box before the Documents folder on Lisa's hard disk appears on my desktop.

Figure 8-20:
The
Documents
icon, which
represents
a shared
folder from
Lisa's hard
disk,
appears on
my desktop.

Reopening the remote Documents folder quickly and easily

Now that I've mounted Lisa's Documents folder on my desktop for the first time, I can make it easier to use in the future by creating an alias for it. Next time I want to use the Documents folder, I open the alias, and the Connect dialog box appears. I type in my password and the folder appears (is mounted) on the desktop. No Chooser; no other dialog boxes; no muss and no fuss.

If you use remote folders often, mount each one on your desktop, create an alias for each one, and put the aliases in a folder called Remote Folders. Move the Remote Folders folder to your Apple Menu Items folder, and you'll be able to mount these remote folders on your desktop almost instantly.

Getting on your own computer from a remote computer

Because Lisa is the owner of her computer, if she walks over to my computer, she can mount her entire hard disk on my desktop. She has checked the Allow user to see entire disk check box in the sharing pane of her user item in the Users & Groups control panel. In other words, after she opened the icon representing herself in her Users & Groups control panel, she gave herself the privilege of seeing her entire disk remotely by choosing the appropriate options.

Anyway, if Lisa were at my Mac and wanted to use her hard disk, she'd do almost the same things that I did to mount the Documents folder on my desktop, with one small difference.

Here's how she'd do it: First, she'd walk over to my Mac. Then she'd select Apple menu⇨Chooser. In the Chooser, she'd select her Macintosh from the list of servers. Now, here's where the procedure is a little different: When the password dialog box appears, it has the owner's name in it, as shown back in Figure 8-18. She would delete the "Bob" part and replace it with "Lisa." Then she would click OK. After typing her password, instead of seeing a list of folders, she'd see her hard disk in the next dialog box. (If Lisa had logged on as a guest or used my name and password, she'd have seen the Documents folder instead of her hard disk in the dialog box.)

Here's a great tip for Lisa. If she plans to use her hard disk while working at my Mac, there's an even easier way. Before she leaves her computer, she should make an alias of her hard disk and copy it to a floppy disk. When she gets to my computer, all she has to do is insert that floppy and open the alias of her hard disk. The Connect dialog box will appear, and as long as she types the correct password, her hard disk will mount on my desktop. Neat.

This technique is often called office-on-a-disk. If you work in a largish office and find yourself trying to connect to your hard disk from someone else's computer, carry one of these office-on-a-disk floppies with you at all times.

Disconnecting from a shared folder or disk

When you finish using the shared disk or folder, close any open files or programs on the shared disk or folder and then disconnect using one of these three methods:

- ✔ Select the shared disk or folder icon and choose File⇨Put Away (Command-Y).
- ✔ Drag the shared disk or folder icon to the Trash.
- ✔ If you're done working for the day, choose Special⇨Shut Down. Shutting down automatically disconnects you from shared disks or folders.

A Few Other Things You Ought to Know

That's the gist of it. But there are still a few aspects of file sharing you might want to know about. For example, how do I know who is using the network? How do I change my password? How can I unshare a folder or disk? And how do I connect to my shared computer remotely via modem?

The answers to these and other fascinating questions await you. Read on.

Monitoring file sharing

When file sharing is on, you can see what's going on out on the network with the Activity Monitor within the File Sharing control panel (see Figure 8-21).

A list of connected users appears at the top, and a list of shared folders and disks appears at the bottom. To disconnect a user at any time, select his or her name in the list and then click the Disconnect button. A dialog box appears asking you how many minutes until the selected user is disconnected (see Figure 8-22).

Type in a number and click OK. When that amount of time has passed, the user will be disconnected. The shared disk or folder icon will become grayed out on the user's desktop, indicating that the item is no longer available. The disconnected user will see a dialog box saying that he or she has been disconnected (see Figure 8-23).

In the dialog box shown in Figure 8-22, if you set the number to zero and click OK, the user is disconnected immediately.

The Activity Monitor at the bottom of the screen tells you how much activity there is on the network. If yours is always up in the busy range, you may need to rethink your network strategy.

AppleShare file servers can ease network traffic, and so can hardware add-ons like hubs and routers. If your network appears busy in the Activity Monitor most of the time, you should beef up your network with one or more of the aforementioned items.

Figure 8-21:
The Activity
Monitor
portion of
the File
Sharing
control
panel tells
you what's
happening
on the net.

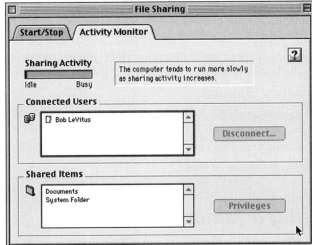

Figure 8-22:
Type in a number and click OK; the user will be disconnected after that many minutes have passed.

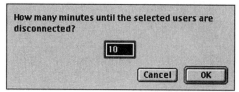

How many minutes until the selected users are disconnected?

10

Cancel   OK

Figure 8-23:
If you see this dialog box, you've been disconnected.

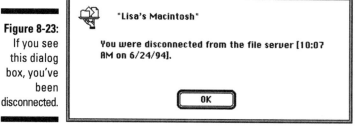

"Lisa's Macintosh"

You were disconnected from the file server [10:07 AM on 6/24/94].

OK

Changing your password

You can change your password at any time.

1. Open the File Sharing control panel (Apple menu⇨Control Panels⇨ File Sharing) from your own computer.

2. If the Activity Monitor tab still shows, click the Start/Stop tab to get back to the main file sharing window.

3. Delete your old password.

4. Type in a new password.

5. Close the File Sharing control panel.

Your new password is now in effect.

Unsharing a folder or disk

To unshare a folder or disk you own, merely select it, choose File⍓Sharing, and uncheck the Share this item and its contents check box. The folder or disk becomes inaccessible over the network as soon as you close the Sharing window.

Logging on remotely via modem

Mac OS 8 offers Apple Remote Access at no extra charge. It used to be an "additional-cost add-on." This change is a very good thing.

What remote access means is that if you're at another location with a Mac and modem, and your Mac has a modem that's been configured for remote access (I'll show you how in a moment), you can access your home hard disk from the remote Mac!

Before you can use remote access, you have to install it (see Appendix A). Remote access is not automatically installed because many users never need its functionality.

Preparing your Mac for remote access

Preparing your Mac so that you can log onto it remotely is simple. Because remote access uses the same Users & Groups and File Sharing control panels as network file sharing, if you've followed along so far this chapter, you're almost ready for remote access. There's just one last thing to do:

1. Open the Remote Access Setup control panel (shown in Figure 8-24).

2. Choose your modem from the pop-up list.

3. Turn your modem speaker on or off by clicking the appropriate radio button.

4. Select your dialing method by clicking the appropriate radio button.

5. Leave the Ignore dial tone and Use MNP 10 check boxes unchecked (if you can't make things work, try checking one or both later).

6. Close the Remote Access Setup control panel.

That's it! Your Mac is now ready for registered users to access it remotely.

Figure 8-24: The Remote Access Setup control panel.

Getting files from your Mac while you're on the road

When you installed Apple Remote Access, a Remote Access Client folder was created on your hard disk. Inside it are two items: Read Me and Remote Access Client. I strongly recommend you read the one called Read Me. Go on, do it now. There may be something important in there that isn't in here.

Okay, now take the one called Remote Access Client with you when you travel. It only weighs about 300K so it easily fits on a floppy disk.

Upon arriving in your remote location, copy Remote Access Client to the hard disk of the Mac you're using to connect to your home Mac. Launch Remote Access Client. Fill in the fields for your name, password, and the phone number of the modem connected to your home Mac (see Figure 8-25).

Save this connection, if you expect to use it again, by choosing File⇨Save (Command-S).

If you click the Save my password option, you don't have to type your password when you connect. On the other hand, people who gets their hands on this document can connect to your home computer and wreak havoc with your files. So don't check it unless you're certain that you won't misplace the disk with the Remote Access Client document on it.

That's it. Almost. There are two other things you need to know about before you're a PhD in remote access: the Options dialog box and the DialAssist control panel.

Figure 8-25:
Fill in the blanks and then press Connect to mount your home computer's hard disk on this remote computer's desktop.

	Untitled	
Connect As:		
● Registered User ○ Guest		
Name: Bob LeVitus		
Password: •••••••		
☐ Save my password		
Connect To:		
Number: 15125556666		
☐ Use DialAssist Setup...		
Options...	Connect	

The Options dialog box, shown in Figure 8-26, lets you specify whether and when to redial, choose an alternate phone number, and specify whether and when you want to be reminded of your connection if you forget.

DialAssist is a control panel that helps you remember and dial complicated phone number sequences. If you click the check box Use DialAssist and then click the Setup button, the DialAssist control panel opens (see Figure 8-27).

If dialing home involves anything more complicated than dialing a 9 before your phone number — a country code, long-distance access number, credit card number, or whatever — check out DialAssist.

Figure 8-26:
Remote
Access
Client's
Options
dialog box.

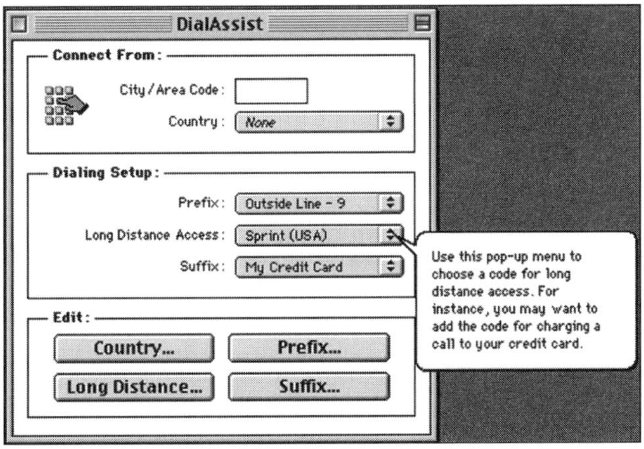

Figure 8-27:
The
DialAssist
control
panel
helps you
remember
and dial
stuff like
your credit
card or
long-
distance
access
number.

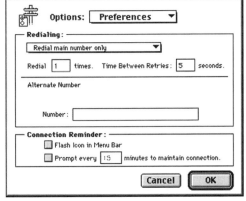

Notice that DialAssist has Balloon Help, so if you need to know more about how a feature works, turn it on. A nice touch.

After you've used DialAssist's pop-up menus to create your custom dialing string, you can preview the results in the Remote Access Client window.

There. That's it! You know how to share files with the best of them, no matter where you are.

Chapter 9

Memory and Other Seemingly Complicated Arcana

• •

In This Chapter

▶ Running out of RAM

▶ The Memory control panel

▶ The disk cache

▶ Virtual memory

▶ The RAM disk

▶ Memory-related troubleshooting

• •

*T*he Mac lets the user — that's you — get along fine without knowing much about memory. Many users go through their entire lives with a Macintosh without knowing anything more than "it has 32 megs in it."

On the other hand, a working knowledge of the way your Mac's memory works can be invaluable in getting the most out of your Mac.

In other words, you don't have to know this stuff, but it's likely to come in handy someday. It's not particularly complicated or particularly technical, so it wouldn't hurt to just jump right in.

Baby, Baby, Where Did Our RAM Go?

RAM is the TLA (three-letter acronym) for Random Access Memory. RAM is the special kind of memory in which your System software and applications live while your Mac uses them. System software (including most extensions and control panels) loads into RAM on startup; applications load into RAM when you open them.

Your Mac probably came with 8, 16, or 32 megabytes of RAM. Depending on what you want to do, that amount may or may not be enough.

If you never plan to do anything more than use a single program that doesn't require a massive amount of RAM (that is, not Photoshop or PageMaker, both of which require at least 6MB and 10MB of RAM respectively) and never plan to use two or more programs at once, a 16-meg Mac may let you squeak by.

If you have 32MB or less of RAM, read this chapter and Chapter 14 very, very carefully. The less RAM you have, the more important it is to manage it wisely.

If you want to keep a word processor, a calendar, a phone book, and a graphics program all open at the same time, a 16MB Mac may not have enough RAM for you. I actually consider 32MB the functional minimum for using Mac OS 8 effectively.

The simple rule is that the more stuff you want to run at once, the more RAM you're gonna need. If you have programs that require a lot of RAM, you'll need enough RAM to run them and your System software simultaneously. You'll also need even more RAM if you want to keep several programs open at the same time.

Go ahead: Add more RAM

You can add more RAM to most Mac models easily and relatively inexpensively (between $5 and $10 per megabyte today, but prices change quickly, so check around before you buy).

If you are so inclined, you can install RAM yourself with a minimum of technical skills. Memory comes mounted on cute little printed circuit boards called SIMMs (fancy acronym for single in-line memory module) or DIMMs (fancy acronym for dual in-line memory module) that snap into little printed circuit board–holders inside your Mac. Installing RAM yourself will, of course, void your warranty. (On the other hand, if your Mac is more than 366 days old, it doesn't have a warranty.)

If you are technologically challenged and never want to lift the lid off your Mac (I don't

blame you), you can have RAM installed for you at any Apple dealer. But this service costs significantly more than doing it yourself.

I'm a klutz. I don't repair things around the house. But I've managed to install RAM upgrades in several Macs without incident. It's not terribly difficult, and it doesn't require soldering or other specialized skills. If you can turn a screwdriver, you can probably handle the task.

If you do decide to go the do-it-yourself route, I recommend TechWorks (800-234-5670 or 512-794-8533). Their prices are fair, their support and manuals are superlative, and they offer a lifetime guarantee on every RAM chip they sell.

Essentially, you should remember that three things use RAM:

- The System and Finder
- Extensions and control panels
- Applications

The first, the System and Finder, you have no control over. That dynamic duo is going to chew up almost 8 megabytes of RAM no matter what you do.

You do, however, have control over extensions, control panels, and applications, and you can use this control to make the most of the memory you have.

Okay. RAM is used *primarily* for three things. There's other stuff — PRAM (parameter RAM), debuggers, rdev and scri files — that could be rattling around in there, using up small amounts of your RAM. But their impact on the amount of RAM that you have to work with is negligible, so they're not important to this discussion. Besides, most people will never need to know what a scri file is.

Sigh. Okay, just this once. A *scri file* is a special kind of extension that automatically loads before all other extensions. The old System Update 3.0 that you should have been using with System 7.1 (but don't need with Mac OS 8) is a scri file. So is Apple's WorldScript Power Adapter.

System software memory theory: where some of the RAM goes . . .

To observe how RAM is being used on your Mac, look at the About This Computer window (Apple menu⇨About This Computer).

Figure 9-1 shows a Mac running Mac OS 8. No extensions or control panels are loaded. The System software uses 7.7MB of RAM.

How do you get Mac OS 8 alone to load, without loading any extensions or control panels? Easy. Hold down the Shift key during startup until you see the "Extensions Off" message on the Welcome to Mac OS 8 screen. Memorize this tip; it's a good thing to know. If you run into memory problems (that is, if you see error messages with the word *memory* in them), starting up with your extensions turned off will enable you to run your Mac so that you can pinpoint problems related to any of your control panels or extensions.

Figure 9-1:
Mac OS 8
alone,
with no
extensions
or control
panels
loaded,
uses 7.7MB
of RAM on
this Mac.

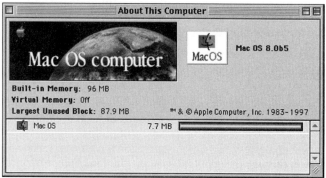

On this 96MB Mac, after the System software eats up its share of RAM, 87.9MB of RAM is available for extensions, control panels, and applications.

Your mileage will vary and you'll probably see a slightly different number on your Mac. Don't worry about it. The System software for each Mac model requires slightly different amounts of RAM.

When I restart my Mac the old-fashioned way, without holding the Shift key down, the extensions and control panels load as usual, and the System software expands to take up a whopping 12.4MB (see Figure 9-2). See what I mean about 16MB being the functional minimum? If you only have 16MB of RAM, you have less than 4 megabytes available for running applications. That's not enough. You'll need more RAM or virtual memory (covered soon).

Figure 9-2:
Mac OS 8,
with its full
comple-
ment of
extensions
and control
panels
loaded at
startup,
uses
12.4MB of
RAM.

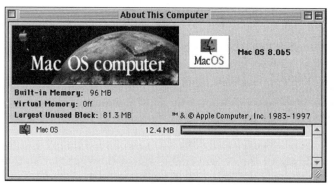

This situation often causes confusion. When you look at the bar for System software in the About This Computer window, it displays not only the RAM used by your System and Finder but also the RAM used by your extensions and control panels that load at startup.

There's no way to tell how much of that bar is the System and Finder and how much is the extensions and control panels. The important thing is that the System software bar tells you how much combined RAM the System, Finder, extensions, and control panels use.

If you're good at math, you can figure out that loading the full complement of Mac OS 8 extensions and control panels costs 4.7MB of RAM.

12.4MB – 7.7MB = 4.7MB.

On my 96-meg Mac, I'm left with almost 83 megabytes available for applications.

You can free up a bit more RAM for applications by turning off extensions and control panels in the Extensions Manager control panel. Read Chapter 14 for details on exactly how much RAM each extension and control panel uses and what happens if you turn them off.

Application memory theory: where the rest of the RAM goes

If you haven't read the first part of Chapter 4, which explains the About This Computer item in the Apple menu and provides you with your first glimpse of memory management, you should do so now. There's a very important technique there — how to adjust Application memory — and I'm not going to waste space repeating it.

Sigh. I guess I have to repeat at least part of it. This *is,* after all, a chapter about memory management.

When you launch an application, the application grabs a chunk of memory (RAM). You can see how big a chunk of RAM it grabs by going back to the Finder after you launch it and choosing Apple menu⇨About This Computer (see Figure 9-3).

The beginning of Chapter 4 has a lengthy discourse on changing the amount of RAM a program grabs when you launch it and why you may want to do so. If you weren't paying attention, you diddle a program's RAM usage by selecting its icon and either choosing File⇨Get Info or using the keyboard shortcut, Command-I (see Figure 9-4).

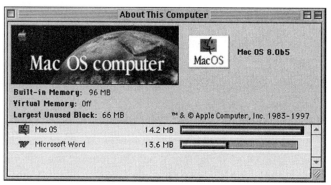

Figure 9-3:
Microsoft
Word, being
somewhat
of a RAM
hog, grabs
13.6MB of
RAM when
I launch it.

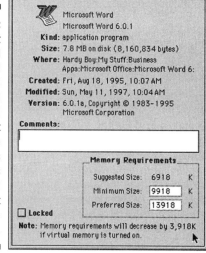

Figure 9-4:
Microsoft
Word
grabbed
13.6MB
of RAM
when I
launched it
because
that's
what its
Preferred
Size was set
at (more
or less).

Here's a brief review of what these memory sizes mean:

✔ The Suggested Size is the size the manufacturer of the program recommends. In most cases, the Preferred Size should be set to at least this amount. You can't change the Suggested Size.

✔ The Minimum Size is the smallest amount of memory the program needs to run. It is usually (but not always) slightly smaller than the Suggested Size.

✔ The Preferred Size is the amount of memory the application requests (and will get as long as there is that much memory available when the application is launched). Your Mac doesn't let you set the Preferred Size lower than the Minimum Size.

When you try to open an application, if the available RAM (Largest Unused Block in the About This Computer window) is less than the Preferred Size but more than the Minimum Size, the program launches. But its performance may be degraded, or you may encounter memory-related errors.

In summation

Make sure that you're clear on this theory stuff before you move on to execution. RAM is used by three things: System software (and Finder), extensions and control panels, and applications.

You can make more RAM available for your programs by holding down the Shift key at startup, which disables all extensions and control panels.

You can fiddle with the amount of RAM that a program uses in its Get Info box.

Everything else you need to know about memory involves the Memory control panel, which you're about to meet.

The Shift-key-at-startup technique is wonderful, but it's absolutely absolute. Either your control panels and extensions are on, or they're off. The Shift key provides no way to turn some off and leave others on. When they're all off, you lose the ability to share files, to use desktop printers and the CD-ROM drive, and much more.

That's why Apple provides the Extensions Manager control panel, which has received a total face-lift in Mac OS 8. You use it to selectively disable and enable control panels and extensions. As I keep saying, this dandy tool is discussed in Chapter 14, a chapter designed to help you figure out which extensions and control panels you truly need. You'll find out how much precious RAM and disk space each control panel and extension uses, and you'll also discover how to get rid of the ones that you don't want (both temporarily and permanently).

In other words, Chapter 14 may be the most useful chapter in this book.

Memories Are Made of This: The Memory Control Panel

You configure memory-related functions for your Mac in the Memory control panel, which is in the Control Panels folder. You open the Memory control panel by choosing Apple menu⇨Control Panels⇨Memory.

Here's a look at the Memory control panel's components, which are for the most part unrelated.

Cashing in with the disk cache

The *disk cache* (pronounced "cash") is a portion of RAM set aside to hold frequently used instructions. In theory, if you set a reasonable-size cache, say 5 percent of your total RAM, your Mac should feel like it's running faster. In reality, many people can't tell the difference.

The first important thing to know is that the size of the disk cache is added onto the RAM used by the System software. Therefore, memory assigned to the disk cache is not available for programs to use. In Figure 9-2, the System software is using 12.4MB of RAM. The disk cache is set to 1,024K.

If I increase the size of the disk cache to 2,048K (see Figure 9-5) and restart the Mac, the System software balloons to 13.5MB (see Figure 9-6).

Figure 9-5: The disk cache is increased to 2,048K; see the results in the next figure.

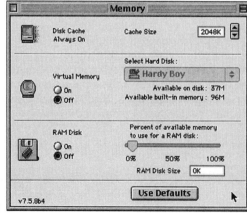

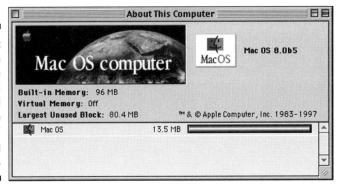

Figure 9-6:
The System
software
uses 1.1MB
more RAM
than before
("before"
being
Figure 9-2).

Those of you who caught the math thing a few pages ago have certainly noticed that the numbers here don't add up correctly. 13.5MB – 12.4MB = 1.1MB, which does not equal 1MB or 1,024K as it should.

The vagaries of RAM usage are well known. The amount of RAM that System software uses changes from hour to hour, seemingly at random. I opened About This Computer three times today and got three different numbers, ranging from a low of 12.4MB to a high of 15.2MB.

In other words, RAM usage is not a precise science. Take all numbers in this chapter with at least one grain of salt.

How to set your disk cache

If RAM usage is an imprecise science, telling you how to set your disk cache is imprecise science *fiction*. Bearing that in mind, here's some excellent advice on figuring out the best setting for you.

As I said, some people don't notice the speed improvement provided by a larger disk cache. So first you must determine whether you can tell the difference in speed by cranking the disk cache size way up. Here's how to crank up the disk cache size:

1. Choose Apple menu⇨Control Panels⇨Memory to open the Memory control panel.

2. Click the upward-pointing arrow on the button labeled Cache Size repeatedly until it won't increase any further (see Figure 9-7).

Figure 9-7:
Click the
up-arrow
repeatedly
until it won't
go any
higher; then
click the
down-arrow
two times.

3. Click the down-arrow two or three times (so you leave enough RAM available to open an application).

4. Restart your Mac.

You now have a huge disk cache, larger than you would actually use in real life. But I want you to exaggerate its effects for this experiment.

When your Mac gets back to the Finder, proceed to Step 5.

5. Open the System Folder, noticing how long it takes for the window to appear completely.

6. Close and then reopen the System Folder window, again noticing how long it takes to appear on-screen.

The difference in speed (the System Folder should have opened noticeably faster the second time) is a result of the increased size of the disk cache.

You should also notice a speed improvement when you scroll through documents. Launch your favorite application and scroll around a document for a while.

If you don't notice any speed improvement in the Finder or in your favorite application, return to the Memory control panel, set Cache Size to its lowest setting (96K or 32K), and be done with it.

If you notice (and like) the speed improvement, you still have a little more work to do. As you may remember, memory assigned to the disk cache is not available for applications. So you want to set the disk cache to the lowest possible number that still feels fast to you.

To lower the disk cache, repeat the preceding steps, lowering the disk cache one click each time. Restart after each change. Then close and reopen the System Folder two times and note the difference in speed the second time.

When you begin to notice sluggishness when closing and opening or when scrolling through documents, then you've discovered your threshold. Return to the Memory control panel, increase Cache Size one click, and be done with it.

The old rule of thumb about the disk cache is to allow 32K per megabyte of RAM. I've always thought that this suggestion was bunk, as many people can't tell the difference between a 32K disk cache and a 1,024K disk cache. And why should they waste a megabyte of perfectly good RAM? So I've always encouraged people to try the experiment I've just described and see for themselves.

That said, I have to admit that the disk cache in Mac OS 8 feels a bit zippier than earlier disk caches. I notice a definite speedup with the disk cache set to 2,048K. Under System 7.1 and earlier versions, the speedup didn't feel as great.

For what it's worth, I'm leaving mine set to 2 megs (2,048K) for now and may even bump it up to 3 or 4 megs. Because I've got oodles of RAM (96MB!), that still leaves me plenty of RAM for applications, so I'm willing to trade a meg or two of RAM for the speedup. Once again, your mileage may vary.

It's not real, it's virtual (memory)

Virtual memory works better in Mac OS 8 than ever before.

The truth is that you should have enough real RAM to use your favorite application or applications (if you like to keep more than one program running) comfortably. You should have enough real RAM to open all the documents and programs you need.

If you can't afford that much RAM, consider Connectix RAM Doubler 2, which does what virtual memory does but does it better and faster without using any space on your hard disk, for about $50 (see the "RAM Doubler 2" sidebar). If you can't manage to find $50, virtual memory isn't that bad.

You access virtual memory via the Memory control panel, as shown in Figure 9-8. Just click the On radio button and use the arrows to the adjust the total amount of memory you will have after you restart your Mac. (Yes, you have to restart if you want to turn virtual memory on, turn virtual memory off, or change virtual memory settings. Sorry.) In Figure 9-9, after making the appropriate adjustments in the Memory control panel and restarting, my 96MB Mac thinks that it has 128MB.

Virtual memory works by setting aside space on your hard disk that acts as RAM. It actually creates a very big, invisible file on your hard disk equal to the amount of virtual memory in use plus all the installed RAM! So if you

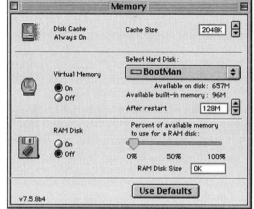

Figure 9-8:
Making a
96-meg
Mac think
that it has
128MB.

Figure 9-9:
After
restarting,
this Mac
acts as if it
has 128MB
of RAM.

have a 32MB Mac and want to make it think it has 64MB using virtual memory, you'll have an invisible 64MB file on your hard disk taking up space. For me the cost is even higher — I start out with a 97MB invisible file as soon as I turn virtual memory on.

Figure 9-10 shows how much hard disk space virtual memory is using on my Mac. Of course, I had to know that the file was named VM Storage in order to use Find File to show it, but that's neither here nor there.

So now you know that virtual memory eats up some hard disk space, but it does have some benefits. First, virtual memory lets your Mac think that it has more RAM than it actually does. This additional, almost magical RAM, is most effective in allowing you to run several small programs than one large program. Second, turning virtual memory on, even if you only set it to add 1 megabyte of virtual memory, allows many applications to run using less RAM on Macs with PowerPC processors.

Figure 9-10:
One downside of virtual memory: an invisible file on your hard disk taking up 128 megs of space.

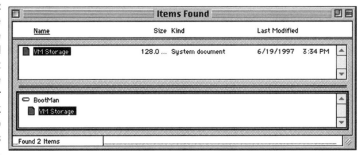

Go back and take another look at Figure 9-4. See that little note at the bottom that says "Memory requirements will decrease by 3,918K if virtual memory is turned on in the Memory control panel"? It'll disappear (and Microsoft Word will require about 4MB less RAM to run) with virtual memory turned on. This tip alone makes it worth turning on VM even if you only set it to 1MB.

For what it's worth, programs also require less RAM under RAM Doubler 2.

RAM Doubler 2

If you need to have more RAM but can't afford the chips, then consider RAM Doubler 2, an alternative virtual memory program from Connectix Corporation. It installs with a single click and magically transforms your 8MB Mac into a 16MB Mac (or your 32MB Mac into a 64MB Mac, or whatever). Its speed is much better than that of Apple's virtual memory. It doesn't require a permanent, invisible file on your hard disk, and it works with almost everything virtual memory works with. It's kind of like virtual memory without any of the side effects.

I'd be remiss if I didn't mention that if any single program has its Preferred Size set higher than the amount of free RAM installed in your Mac, performance will more than likely be degraded. Even so, in the same situation, the degradation from Apple's virtual memory will likely be worse. While RAM Doubler 2 is pretty miraculous, even miracles have limitations.

If you like virtual memory, you'll like RAM Doubler 2 even better. Even if you hate virtual memory, you may like RAM Doubler 2. If you need more RAM but can't afford it right now, give RAM Doubler 2 a try. It's the next best thing to real RAM.

Better still, buy 32MB of real RAM. You'll feel better after you do.

Faster than a speeding bullet: It's a RAM disk

A RAM disk enables you to use part of your installed RAM as a temporary storage device, a virtual disk made of silicon. Using a RAM disk is much, much faster than any other kind of disk and, if you're using a battery-powered Mac, it's much more energy efficient.

Many Macintoshes include a RAM disk feature. To find out if yours is one of them, open your Memory control panel. If you see RAM disk controls like those shown in Figure 9-11, your Mac has the RAM disk feature.

Figure 9-11:
If your Mac supports the RAM disk feature, you'll see these controls in your Memory control panel.

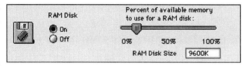

Memory assigned to a RAM disk is not available for opening programs or loading extensions and control panels. So unless you have 32 or more megabytes of RAM, a RAM disk is probably not practical. Even with 32MB, it probably won't be that useful.

RAM disks are wickedly fast while you use them, but they are temporary. When you shut down your Mac (or if the power is interrupted to a non-PowerBook Mac), the contents of a RAM disk are wiped out. In addition, certain kinds of System crashes can erase a RAM disk's contents. The contents of a RAM disk do, however, survive a restart.

Even so, you should never store your only copy of a file on a RAM disk. If you save files on a RAM disk, make sure to copy them to your hard disk every so often — just in case.

Creating a RAM disk

To create a RAM disk, click the On button in the RAM Disk portion of the Memory control panel (refer to Figure 9-11) and drag the slider to choose the percentage of the available memory that you want to use for your RAM disk. Close the control panel and restart your Mac. The new RAM disk appears on your desktop (see Figure 9-12).

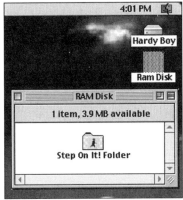

Figure 9-12: A RAM disk acts like any other disk, only faster. Much faster.

Erasing a RAM disk

There are three ways to erase the contents of a RAM disk. One, of course, is to shut down your Mac. You'll see a warning that the contents of the RAM disk will be lost; when you click OK, it's gone.

You can also erase a RAM disk by doing one of the following:

- ✔ Selecting the RAM disk's icon and choosing Special⇨Erase Disk
- ✔ Dragging everything on the RAM disk to the Trash and then choosing Special⇨Empty Trash

Resizing or removing a RAM disk

To resize a RAM disk, use the slider in the Memory control panel to choose a new size; then restart your Mac.

The contents of a RAM disk are lost when you resize it, so copy anything important to your hard disk before you resize.

To remove a RAM disk, click the Off button in the Memory control panel and then restart your Mac. The RAM disk must be empty or the Off button is disabled.

Good things to try with a RAM disk

Some applications run a lot faster when they're on a RAM disk. Copy your favorite game to a RAM disk and give it a try.

Your Mac runs screamingly fast if your System Folder is on a RAM disk. You need at least 16 megs of RAM to create a RAM disk big enough for your System Folder.

It is possible to use a RAM disk containing just a System and a Finder as your startup disk. It's not very useful, but it is possible. Here's how you do it:

1. Create a RAM disk large enough to hold your System and Finder (about 10MB).

2. Create a new folder on the RAM disk. Name it System Folder.

3. Copy the System file and the Finder file from the System Folder on your hard disk to the newly created System Folder on the RAM disk.

4. Open the Startup Disk control panel and click your RAM disk's icon to designate it as the startup disk.

5. Restart your Mac.

Your Mac boots up from the RAM disk instead of your hard disk.

While this particular execution won't do much for you, if you have enough RAM to create a 15MB or 20MB RAM disk, you can add a few extensions and control panels to the System Folder on the RAM disk and have a relatively useful, blindingly fast startup disk.

Another thing to try is moving your favorite application to the RAM disk and running it from there. Many applications — including Web browsers — run significantly faster from a RAM disk. And storing your Web browser's cache of recently viewed pages on a RAM disk makes pages appear blazingly fast the second time you visit them.

And there you have it. More than you really need to know about RAM and your Macintosh!

Part III
U 2 Can B A Guru

The 5th Wave   **By Rich Tennant**

IF BOB DYLAN HAD PURSUED A CAREER IN COMPUTERS

"PUT HIM IN FRONT OF A TERMINAL AND HE'S A GENIUS, BUT OTHER-
WISE THE GUY IS SUCH A BROODING, GLOOMY GUS HE'LL NEVER
BREAK INTO MANAGEMENT."

In this part . . .

1 discuss thousands of tips, tricks, and techniques that make using your Mac easier and more fulfilling. More succinctly, this part is about how things work and how you can make them work better.

After two chapters full of tips and tricks, I'll crawl through the Control Panels folder and discuss each and every control panel and its recommended settings.

Moving right along, I'll next delve into automating your Mac using AppleScript, complete with some easy-to-follow info that's guaranteed to get you scripting with the best of them.

Next, in what may be the most useful chapter in the book, I look at every single file installed with Mac OS 8. I'll tell you who needs it, how much RAM it uses, how much disk space it uses, and most important of all, how to get rid of it safely if you don't need it.

And finally, I introduce you to the World of the Wide Web, with an introduction to your Internet tools, including that new pup on the block, CyberDog.

Chapter 10

Sure-Fire, Easy-to-Use, No (Or Low)-Cost Timesaving Tips

● ●

In This Chapter

▶ Flying fingers

▶ In living color — or not

▶ Contextual menus: They're great in context

▶ Getting your Views under control

● ●

Some of what you're about to read has been mentioned somewhere in the first nine chapters already. But this chapter isn't a blatant attempt at upping my page count. No siree. This chapter is here because, by now, you lust for speed.

Now that you understand the basics, if you're normal, you wish your Mac worked faster. (You're not alone — all users wish that their Macs worked faster at some time, even those with Power Mac 9600 MPs or Motorola Starmax 5000/300s.) So in this chapter, I'll cover things that can make your Mac at least seem faster, most of which won't cost you a red cent.

Let Your Fingers Do the Flying

One way to make your Mac faster is to make your fingers faster. Here are a couple of ways:

Use those keyboard shortcuts

I know I've told you this tip already, but the less often you remove your hand from the keyboard to fiddle with the mouse, the less time you'll waste. Learn to use those keyboard shortcuts. Memorize them. Make your fingers memorize them. The more keyboard shortcuts you use, the faster you'll get done with what you are doing. Trust me.

Learn to type better

Learning to type faster may be the very best way I know to make your Mac faster. As a Macintosh consultant and trainer, I get to spend a lot of time with beginners. And almost all of them are lousy typists. When they complain that their computer is too slow, I ask them to perform a task for me. Then I perform that same task for them. I can type about 50 words per minute, and I type without looking at the keyboard. I always accomplish the task in less time; if the task involves a lot of typing, I accomplish it in much less time.

Because you're there and I'm here, I can't provide you with as dramatic an illustration. But trust me, typing fast saves you time at your Mac — a lot. And this speed gain isn't just in word processors and spreadsheets. Once you're a decent touch-typist, you'll fly when you use those nifty keyboard shortcuts that I mention so frequently.

There are several fine typing programs out there, and any one of them will do just fine. Most cost under $30 by mail order and are worth every penny. I happen to like a program called Mavis Beacon Teaches Typing (from The Software Toolworks) for a number of reasons. First, it allows you to choose whether there should be one space or two after a period. The correct answer, of course, is one — at least if you're typing on a Mac.

What? You learned to put two spaces after a period in your high school typing class? Well, you learned wrong, at least if you're going to use a computer. The double-space after punctuation is a throwback to the days when typewriters were king and we had no personal computers or printers. Because typewritten text is monospaced (that is, all letters are the exact same width), a double-space after a punctuation mark looked better than a single space.

With the advent of the computer and laser printer, most fonts are no longer monospaced (Courier and Monaco *are* monospaced). Today, on most personal computers, most fonts are spaced *proportionally*. In other words, some characters are wider than others. The width of a space in a proportionally spaced font is just the right size to use a single space after punctuation. If you use a double-space, it looks unattractive.

Mavis Beacon Teaches Typing (or any of the typing programs) will teach you to type significantly faster in just two weeks. If you give it about 30 minutes per day of your undivided attention, you will learn to type quickly without looking down. Mavis Beacon includes timed speed and accuracy drills (see Figure 10-1), as well as a typing game (see Figure 10-2) where you try to type fast enough to keep your computerized opponent's car in the rearview mirror and not ahead of you. The program keeps track of your drills and lets you see graphs and charts of your progress at any time.

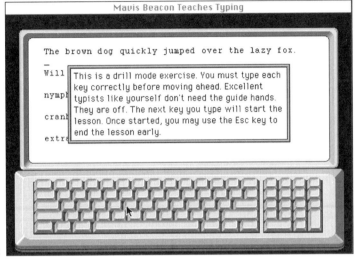

Figure 10-1:
A typing drill in the Mavis Beacon Teaches Typing program.

Figure 10-2:
A game in the Mavis Beacon Teaches Typing program.

The important thing isn't how the typing program works or which program you buy. You simply need to commit the time. Just remember: The easiest way to speed up your Mac is to speed up your fingers. Honest. Trust me, it's not as stupid as it sounds.

End of sermon.

The Mac is not a typewriter

The Macintosh is more of a typesetting machine than a typewriter. So when you use a Macintosh, you should follow the rules of good typography, not the rules of good typewriting. If you want your documents to look truly professional, in addition to putting single spaces after punctuation, you need to understand the difference between inch and foot marks (" and ') and typographer's quotation marks (' and ' or " and "). You also need to know when and how to use a hyphen (-), an en dash (–), and an em dash (—).

In other words, the Mac is not a typewriter. If you want to make your documents look more elegant and professional, get ahold of Robin Williams's excellent book *The Mac Is Not a Typewriter* (Peachpit Press). It's wonderful, easy to understand, and covers all the stuff I just mentioned (and much more) in great detail.

Why Living Color May Not Be So Great

Chances are good that your Macintosh has a color monitor (most do). And chances are also good that you keep that monitor set to the maximum number of colors it supports. That may be a mistake.

Monitor settings

Your screen consists of thousands of square dots (more than 300,000 for the average Mac monitor) known as *pixels* (an acronym of sorts for picture element). Most 13- or 14-inch monitors display a picture that is 640 pixels wide by 480 pixels high — more than 300,000 pixels on the screen for your Mac to deal with. Larger monitors have more pixels; smaller monitors have fewer.

The number of colors that you choose to display on your monitor has a significant impact on how quickly your screen *updates*. The more choices your Mac has to make about the color of each pixel, the longer it takes for the screen to update completely so that you can continue your work.

When I say *update,* I'm talking about the amount of time it takes for your screen to paint all the pixels their proper color or colors after opening or closing an icon or document. For example, when you open a color picture in a graphics application or open a window in the Finder, the screen updates until every element is drawn on-screen in its proper place and in its proper color.

Some people call screen updating screen *redrawing*. It means the same thing: the time you spend waiting for Finder windows to draw themselves completely, or the time it takes for documents to appear completely in their windows on-screen. When your screen is updating, you have no choice but to wait for it.

(You might sometimes hear this scourge referred to as *refreshing,* but that term is incorrect in this context. *Screen refresh rate* is a technical term, measured in hertz [Hz], that has to do with the video hardware. Even so, people use the three words — update, redraw, and refresh — more or less interchangeably.)

How quickly your screen updates depends on a few things, mostly CPU speed, hard disk speed, and video circuitry (built-in or on a video card).

You shouldn't find it surprising that much of what's in the rest of this chapter is about making your screen update faster no matter what CPU, hard disk, or video gear you have.

I admit that the faster your Mac, the less difference the techniques in this chapter will make to your overall performance. If you've got a Mac with a PowerPC 603/603e/604/604e chip, try my suggestions out for a while and see if you think they're worth it. Because your Mac has relatively high performance, screen updating is relatively speedy, even with some of the options mentioned in this chapter turned on.

You be the judge.

Depending on your video card or internal video, you will be able to choose from black and white, 4 colors, 16 colors, 256 colors, thousands of colors, or millions of colors.

You choose the number of colors that you want your screen to display in the Monitors & Sound control panel, which is shown in Figure 10-3.

The Power Macintosh 9500 (whose Monitors & Sound control panel is displayed in Figure 10-3) has a video card that can display millions, thousands, or 256 colors at once on my 20" monitor.

Most Macs today can display a maximum of millions of colors on a 14" monitor using built-in video circuitry. And many of these Macintosh models can be upgraded to display thousands or millions of colors on larger monitors by adding an inexpensive VRAM (video RAM) chip.

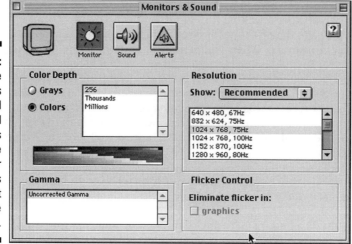

Figure 10-3:
The
Monitors
& Sound
control
panel lets
you choose
the number
of colors
you want
to see
on-screen.

If you want more colors than your Mac model supports (even with additional VRAM), or you want to use a larger monitor, you may need to purchase a video card that supports that combination of colors and size. Video cards range from a low of a couple of hundred dollars to several thousand dollars. For the big bucks, you can get a superfast, accelerated video card capable of powering a 21" monitor set to display millions of colors, with bells and whistles such as virtual desktops, hardware zoom and pan, and resolution switching.

If you choose the Black & White option, each pixel on the screen has only two options: to be black or white. If you choose 256 colors, each pixel on-screen can be any of 256 possible colors. If you choose millions of colors, each pixel on-screen can be any one of millions of possible colors. Unfortunately, not all Macs (mine included) offer Black & White as an option these days.

As you might expect, the more choices each pixel has, the more processing time your Mac requires to update the screen. So the more colors you choose in the Monitors control panel, the more sluggish your Mac will feel. Scrolling in many programs is much faster if you choose the Black & White option. And in some programs, 256 colors is faster than thousands or millions of colors.

So here's my advice: Unless your application requires color, set your monitor to Black & White (if Black & White is even offered) for maximum performance. When you're using your word processor or spreadsheet, you probably don't need color anyway. Why make your Mac slower if you don't have to?

Use 1-bit color for speed and 8-bit color for games. Use millions of colors only if you need them (for Photoshop, PageMaker, and so on).

In computerese, the number of colors that your monitor displays is often referred to as *bit depth* (or sometimes, *pixel depth*). In a nutshell, bit is short for binary digit, the smallest unit of information that the computer can understand. The bit depth describes how many bits of information can be sent to each pixel.

Here are the English translations for the most common bit depths:

- ✔ 1-bit means black and white.
- ✔ 8-bit means 256 colors.
- ✔ 16-bit means thousands of colors.
- ✔ 24-bit means millions of colors.

Window color considerations

If you choose to display colors on your monitor, the window color, as chosen in the Appearance control panel (shown in Figure 10-4), has a slight impact on your Mac's apparent speed.

Figure 10-4: The Appearance control panel. Set both Accent Color and Highlight Color to Black & White for slightly improved perfor- mance.

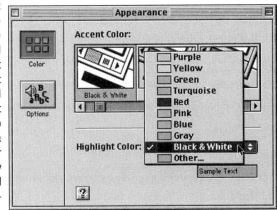

The Accent Color setting manages the color of your window borders, scroll boxes, and scroll arrows. For all the same reasons mentioned previously, the Black & White option is faster than any of the colors.

I have to admit that this adjustment won't make much difference in your Mac's speed, but it makes a little. The older and slower your Mac, the more it'll help.

Contextual menus: They're great in context

While we're on the topic of speed and shortcuts, don't forget about those delightful new contextual menus. Just hold down the Control key and click any item in the Finder.

My personal fave is the Move To Trash shortcut. That's good. But why isn't there a keyboard shortcut for it? That's bad.

A Mac with a view — and preferences, too

The View Options and Preferences windows (shown in Figure 10-5 and accessed via View⇨View Options and Edit⇨Preferences) are other places where your choices affect how quickly your screen updates in the Finder.

The View Options window is, like our old friend the contextual menu, well, contextual. Depending upon what is active when you choose it from the View menu, you'll see one of three similar versions (shown left to right in Figure 10-5): folders in icon or button views, the desktop, and folders in list view.

Geneva: It's not just a city in Switzerland anymore

Let's start with the one speed improvement you can make in the Preferences window (Edit⇨Preferences). Using the Geneva 9 font in the Finder will be slightly faster than using most other fonts, as Geneva 9 is one of the fonts that your Macintosh stores in its ROM (read-only memory).

One thing's for sure: If you select a third-party PostScript font in an uninstalled size, it will definitely be slower than Geneva 9. And it will look uglier.

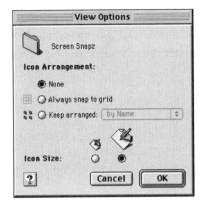
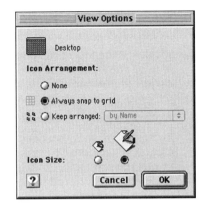

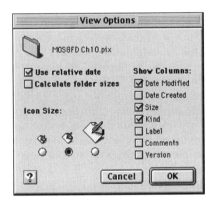

Figure 10-5:
Your
choices in
the View
Option and
Preferences
windows
can make
your Mac
feel faster.

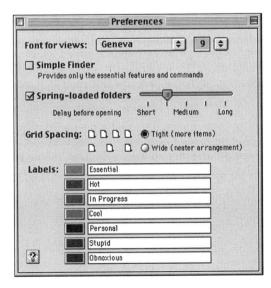

When bigger isn't better

The smaller the icon, the faster the screen updates. In the View Options windows, the little tiny icon on the left is the fastest; the big, horsey-looking icon on the right is the slowest. (In list view, the one in the middle is, of course, in the middle.)

It doesn't pay to calculate folder sizes

I recommend that you deactivate Calculate folder sizes (that is, uncheck or clear its check box) to make the screen redraw faster in the Finder. At least, to me, the screen feels like it redraws faster with this feature turned off. This feature is only offered for windows that sport one of the list views, for obvious reasons.

Actually, the Finder is kind of smart about the Calculate folder sizes option. If you try to do anything in the Finder — make a menu selection, open an icon, move a window, and so on — while folder sizes are calculating, the Finder interrupts the calculation and lets you complete your task before it resumes calculating. So, in theory, you should never notice a delay when Calculate folder sizes is on.

Try the Calculate folder sizes option both on and off. I don't know about you, but I find any noticeable delay unacceptable, and I notice a delay when it's turned on, even on very fast Macs. Maybe this feature is just annoying and not actually slowing things down, but I can't stand having it on. If I want to know how big a folder is, I select it and select the Get Info command from the File menu (Command-I).

Getting ahead-er and other stuff

The Show Columns check boxes in the View Options window for list views — Date Modified, Date Created, Size, Kind, Label, Comments, and Version — have a slight impact on screen update speed when you open a Finder window in list view. The fewer items you have checked, the fewer items there are for the Finder to draw. As a result, the Finder updates windows faster.

The impact of these seven items on screen updating is pretty small, so your choice should be made based on what information you want to see in Finder windows, not on whether choosing them will slow your Mac down. Play around with these options if you like, but unless your Mac is very slow, you probably won't notice much difference between on and off.

If you don't need it, turn it off or toss it out

A whole forthcoming chapter is devoted to showing you how to turn off or eliminate Mac OS 8 features that you don't need or want. Read it carefully. Features like AppleTalk, File Sharing, and QuickDraw GX and 3D use prodigious amounts of memory and can also slow down your Mac's CPU. If you don't need 'em, don't let 'em clog up your Mac. Read Chapter 14 carefully and then fine-tune your Mac for the best performance.

What Else Can I Do?

If you've tried every trick in the book (or at least in this chapter) and still think that your Mac is too slow, what can you do? Here are four suggestions:

- ✔ Get a new, faster model or upgrade yours. Apple and other companies keep putting out faster and faster Macs and Mac compatibles at lower and lower prices. From time to time, Apple offers reasonably priced upgrades that can transform your older, slower Mac into a speedy new one.

- ✔ Get an accelerator. I only offer this suggestion because one of you out there is considering it. I beg you, *don't do it.* I've rarely known an accelerator owner who hasn't discovered an incompatibility somewhere along the line.

- ✔ Get an accelerated graphics card. Rather than attempting to accelerate your CPU, an accelerated graphics card is designed specifically to speed up one thing: the screen update rate. These things work, blasting pixels onto your screen at amazing speeds. They're extremely popular with graphic arts professionals who would otherwise suffer agonizingly slow screen redraws when working with 24-bit graphics.

- ✔ Get a new hard disk. Depending on the speed of your Mac, a faster disk may provide a substantial speedup.

Chapter 11

Advanced Techniques for Beginners

In This Chapter

▶ Modifying your Apple menu

▶ Using startup items

▶ Tweaking the Control Strip

*I*n the last chapter, I showed you how to make your Mac faster. In this one, I show you ways to make it better. Indeed, if you haven't guessed already, this chapter is about ways to make your Mac easier to use.

Souping Up Your Apple Menu

A customized Apple menu is an absolute must in my book. It's the fastest, easiest, most happening way to manage your Mac. If you don't put your Apple menu to work for you, you're missing out on one of the best things in the Mac OS.

The items in your Apple menu are sorted alphabetically by your Mac, so they appear in alphabetical order in the Apple menu. If you understand how the Macintosh sorts items in a list, you can use this knowledge to your advantage.

Remember, everything in your Apple Menu Items folder appears in your Apple menu.

If you want an item to appear at the top of the Apple menu, precede its name with a number (or a space).

In Figure 11-1, I forced the first four items on the menu to be Hardy Boy (an alias of my hard disk), Documents (an alias of my Documents folder), Desk Accessories (which I created back in Chapter 5) and Control Panels, by preceding each one's name with a number. Because the Macintosh sorting algorithm sorts numbers before letters, these items now appear before the first alphabetical entry (Automated Tasks) in numerical order.

Notice that I chop the word "alias" off the end of my aliases. This is strictly a personal preference; I feel that having that extra five letters tacked onto a file's name is unsightly.

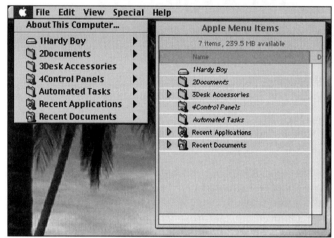

Figure 11-1:
Controlling the order of items in the Apple menu with numbers.

Space cowboy

A second, slightly prettier way to accomplish the same sort is to precede the item names with one or more spaces instead of numbers, as demonstrated in Figure 11-2.

In Figure 11-2, Hardy Boy has four spaces before its name; Documents has three spaces before its name; Desk Accessories has two spaces before its name; and Control Panels has a single space before its name.

Divide and conquer

You can create dividers in your Apple menu using the same principle. Say I want a dividing line after Control Panels. I just use the principles of Macintosh sorting to create a divider line of dashes using an empty folder (see Figure 11-3).

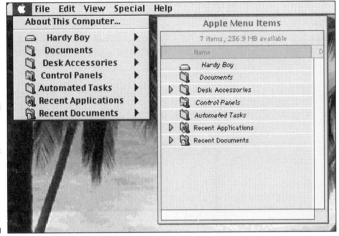

Figure 11-2: Controlling the order of items in the Apple menu with spaces.

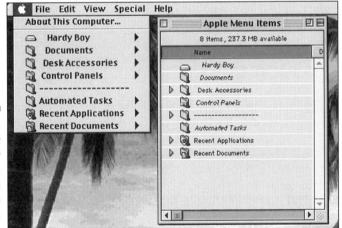

Figure 11-3: An empty folder becomes a divider in the Apple menu.

The divider appears between Control Panels and Automated Tasks because the hyphens (the empty folder's name) sort after spaces but before letters (or numbers).

Instead of using an empty folder, make an alias of the Clipboard in your System Folder and use it for a divider instead. Using Clipboard aliases makes dividers at least somewhat useful because you can choose one instead of using the Finder's Show Clipboard command. Just create an alias of the Clipboard, rename it ------, and toss it in your Apple Menu Items folder.

There are plenty of interesting characters on your Mac keyboard that you can use instead of spaces to force a specific sorting order. The bullet (•, which you create by typing Option-8) sorts after the Z, so items with names preceded by a bullet will sort at the bottom of the list after items starting with a Z (see Figure 11-4).

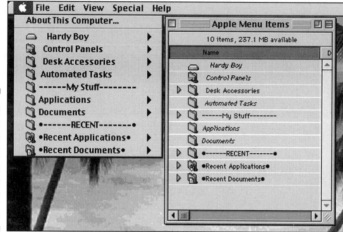

Figure 11-4:
You can even use unusual characters to reorder your Apple menu.

Notice in Figure 11-4 that all the folder aliases in the Apple menu have hierarchical submenus. This feature is what makes all of my organizational tips so great. You can organize your Apple menu so that you can quickly get to any file on your hard disk.

Look, ma, no dividers!

If you want your dividers to look even spiffier, you can make them appear without an icon at all, just like what's shown in Figure 11-5. This trick is strictly cosmetic, but I think it looks cool.

Here's how to make icon-less dividers:

1. Open any graphics program and use its selection tool to select a patch of white about 1 inch square. Choose Edit⇨Copy to copy the white square to the Clipboard.

2. Jump back to the Apple Menu Items folder and select the divider's icon.

3. Choose File⇨Get Info (Command-I).

   The Get Info window for that icon appears.

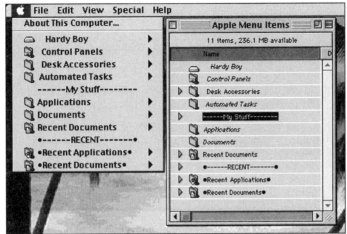

4. Click the icon in the Get Info window.

   A border appears around it.

5. Choose Edit⇨Paste (Command-V).

   The patch of white, which is invisible on the desktop and in the Apple menu, becomes the icon for the divider.

Neat, huh?

All these sorting and organizing tricks are easy once you get the hang of the way the Mac sorts items in folders. And the principles you learn here work in any window.

I use my sorting tricks in most of my folders. In Figure 11-6, I force the most frequently used item (Outgoing Comms '97) to the top of the list by preceding its name with a space, and I force less important items (Books Done.sit, Other Done.sit, and Proposals Done.sit) to the bottom by preceding their names with a grave accent (`).

When you press the tilde key (usually found in the upper-left corner of the keyboard), your Mac types a grave accent (`) if the Shift key isn't down; it types a tilde (~) if the Shift key is held down. The tilde sorts after the Z in the Macintosh sorting scheme. (To be perfectly precise, the tilde sorts after the grave accent, which sorts after the Z.) Figure 11-7 shows other characters that sort after the tilde; these include ™ (Option-2) and • (Option-8). But the accent/tilde is handy, being right there in the corner of my keyboard.

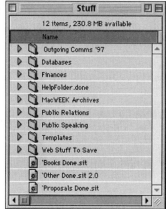

Figure 11-6:
Use a space or a grave accent before a file's name to force it to the top or bottom of the list, respectively.

Figure 11-7:
Option characters like ° (Option-Shift-8), • (Option-8), ™ (Option-2), and ∞ (Option-5) sort after both Z and the grave accent.

Rather than have me tell you about file sorting, why don't you give it a try for yourself? So go to your Mac right now (unless you've been there all along) and try all the tips you just learned.

If the stuff you've read so far in this chapter is not making sense or not working for you:

1. Choose View⇨As List.

2. Choose View⇨Sort List⇨By Name.

These sorting tips only work in windows viewed as lists and sorted by name.

If you're in the list view but it's not sorted by name, merely click the word Name under the window's title bar.

Start Up Your Mornings Right

This section presents a pair of techniques for making your Mac start up better. The Startup Items folder tip is the most useful, but the other one, which closes all open windows automatically at startup, can be convenient as well. Both are techniques worth knowing.

On becoming a (startup) item

Don't overlook the convenience of the Startup Items folder in your System Folder. Everything in this special folder will launch automatically at startup.

Think about that for a second. What's the first thing you do after you turn on your Mac and the desktop appears? If your answer begins with the word "Open" or "Launch," you can save yourself some effort by putting an alias of the launched or opened item in the Startup Items folder. It will then launch automatically at startup.

If you work with a single database or spreadsheet file every day, why not put an alias of it in the Startup Items folder? Then when you turn on your Mac, that document automatically appears on the screen. Or if the first thing you do each morning is check your e-mail, put an alias of your e-mail program in the Startup Items folder.

You can even put a sound in the Startup Items folder. Thereafter, that sound will play as the Finder appears.

For this trick to work, the sound must be stored in the System 7 sound format. You can tell if a sound is in this common format by opening the sound file. If the sound is a System 7 sound, you will hear it play when you open it. Other sound file formats (such as AIFF, WAV, and so on) will do nothing or display an "application can't be found" error message when you open them.

Most sounds floating around Mac circles these days are in the System 7 format.

The new Stickies feature is neat to have around all the time. If you put an alias of Stickies in the Startup Items folder, your sticky memos will always be available (see Figure 11-8).

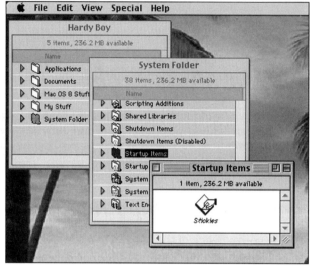

Figure 11-8:
When I start up my Mac, Stickies launches automatically.

Stickies knows that you're likely to want to use it all the time, so it's got a preference setting that not only puts an alias of it in the Startup Items folder, but it also makes sure that it launches into the background, making the Finder the active application at startup.

To use this feature, launch Stickies, choose Edit⇨Preferences, and check both the Launch at system startup and ...in the background check boxes (see Figure 11-9).

Not all programs are as considerate as Stickies; the items in the Startup Items folder launch alphabetically, using that same Macintosh sorting order that I talk about in the previous section. And under ordinary circumstances, the last item to launch would be the active application at the end of the startup sequence.

Stickies can launch itself and then make the Finder the active application.

Figure 11-9:
Click both Launch at system startup and ...in the background.

So if you want the Finder to be the active application at startup and you've got several items in your Startup Items folder, just make sure that Stickies loads last and that you've checked the ...in the background check box in Stickies' preferences.

In other words, precede Stickies' name with a few Zs (or a tilde or bullet) to make it the last item in the list when you view the Startup Items window by name (see Figure 11-10).

Figure 11-10:
By making
Stickies
launch last,
we can take
advantage
of its ability
to make the
Finder
active at
startup.

Control Strip Poker

One relatively new feature that can save you time and effort is the Control Strip, which (if it's turned on in the Control Strip control panel) appears somewhere on your screen.

With the Control Strip, you can adjust your Mac's speaker volume, change monitor bit-depth and resolution, select a printer, and turn file sharing and AppleTalk on and off, all without visiting a control panel or the Chooser.

On becoming a (Control Strip) item. Or not.

You'll find out more about the Control Strip in Chapter 12, but for now, here are a couple of things you should know:

Control Strip modules live in a folder in your System Folder named (what else?) Control Strip Modules. If a module is in this folder at startup, it appears in your Control Strip on-screen.

Apple provides seven Control Strip items (see Figures 11-11 and 11-12). If you don't want or need some of them, you can delete them (that is, trash 'em) and make your Control Strip even shorter and more efficient. But they're handy if you need to do the things they do.

Figure 11-11:
The full complement of Apple-supplied Control Strip modules as seen in the Control Strip itself.

 One last thing: There are many freeware and shareware Control Strip modules available. For example, my bookmark program, URL Manager Pro, includes a module that lets me perform a number of actions right from my Control Strip.

Figure 11-12:
The full complement of Apple-supplied Control Strip modules as seen in the Control Strip Modules folder.

Chapter 12

Control Tweaks

● ●

In This Chapter

▶ Instructions on tweaking every single control panel

▶ Lots of pictures

● ●

*T*he Control Panels folder contains (what else?) your control panels. What exactly are control panels? They're usually little mini-programs that control a single aspect of your Mac's operation.

I've talked about some of the control panels (Memory, Sharing Setup) earlier in this book, but because Mac OS 8 includes about 40 control panels for most Macs, in this chapter, I'll go through them one at a time, in alphabetical order, describing and suggesting settings for each and every one.

After a brief AppleScript interlude in Chapter 13, I continue this discussion in Chapter 14, "What Can Stay and What Can Go," with a full disclosure of how much memory and disk space each control panel uses and how to remove or temporarily disable ones that you don't need. I even explain why you might want to do this stuff.

I've included *no-brainer* settings at the end of many sections for those of you who just want to know how to set the thing and don't care what it does or why. These no-brainer settings are not the gospel, but they're a good place to start. (You can always come back and change them later after you figure out what they are and what they do.)

Appearance

Mac OS 8's new Appearance control panel replaces the old Color and Windowshade control panels and adds a couple of twists, including a first-ever (at least in Apple System software history) opportunity to have your menus appear in a font other than Chicago (Charcoal).

Click the Color button on the left side of the screen (see Figure 12-1), and you can select your windows' accent color and the highlight color of selected text.

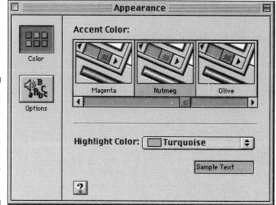

Figure 12-1:
The
Appearance
control
panel's
Color
settings.

Click the Options button on the left side of the window shown in Figure 12-2, and you can (for the first time ever) choose from a whopping two System fonts to be used in menus and other Mac communications with you (prompts, dialog boxes, and so on) and set two preferences dealing with collapsing windows. Finally, you can choose whether or not to use the "System-wide platinum appearance."

With the exception of System-wide platinum appearance, these are all very personal choices. Do you prefer Aquamarine to Sapphire? Whooshing sounds when you "roll up" windows? Or not?

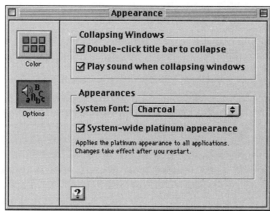

Figure 12-2:
The
Appearance
control
panel's
Options
settings.

System-wide platinum appearance (see Figure 12-3) is not merely cosmetic, it also offers a great time-saving advantage. Turning it on allows you to drag windows in *all* applications by their edges (with it turned off, you can only move a window by dragging its title bar). This, if you ask me, is a very good thing.

Figure 12-3: System-wide platinum appearance turned off (left) and on (right). You can't drag the window on the left around by its edges. And note that you only get the collapse box when System-wide platinum appearance is turned on.

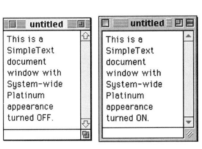

Appearance no-brainer setting: Accent color: Your choice. Highlight color: Your choice. Double-click title bar to collapse: On. Play sound when collapsing windows: On. System Font: Anything other than Chicago (in other words, Charcoal). System-wide platinum appearance: Definitely on.

Don't forget, the no-brainer settings are merely suggestions. For example, if you hate the whoosh of collapsing windows, by all means turn it off.

Apple Menu Options

The Apple Menu Options control panel has two functions:

✔ It turns the hierarchical submenus on or off.

✔ It lets you specify how many recent documents, applications, and servers your Mac should track.

The first function controls whether or not folders (and aliases of folders as well as disks) in the Apple menu display their contents when you highlight them. Put another way, the Submenus on/off switch (actually, a pair of radio buttons) turns the little triangles on and off. It works while the control panel is open, so try each choice and then pull down the Apple menu to see the results.

The second function requires that you check the Remember recently used items check box. When you do so, your Mac will remember the specified number of documents, applications, and servers for you. You'll find the remembered items in the similarly named folders in the Apple menu (see Figure 12-4).

Figure 12-4: The Apple Menu Options control panel and it's two offspring: heirarchical submenus in the Apple menu and the Recent Items folders at the bottom of the Apple menu.

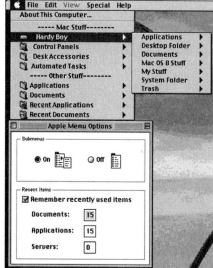

The Mac remembers these items by creating aliases and putting them in the appropriate Recent Items folder. All three Recent Items folders are in the Apple Menu Items folder.

The Mac uses FIFO (first in, first out) to limit the number of items in each folder according to your choices in the Apple Menu Options control panel. Say you set the number of documents to 20. When you open document 21, document 1 is forgotten. More long-windedly, when you open document 21, your Mac creates an alias for document 21. It then deletes the alias for document 1 so that there are again only 20 items in the folder, as you requested.

All of this stuff is done invisibly, without your knowledge or intervention.

Apple Menu Options no-brainer setting: Submenus: On. Documents: 15. Applications: 15. Servers: 0 (unless, of course, you're connected to a server, in which case it's your call).

AppleTalk

The AppleTalk control panel (see Figure 12-5) lets you choose how and where to network your Mac or Mac compatible. Its main function is to let you select ports — Printer, Modem, Ethernet (if you have it; I do), or Remote Only for dial-in connections, as I discussed way back in Chapter 8.

Figure 12-5:
The AppleTalk control panel lets you choose where your network connection connects.

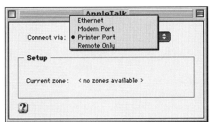

But wait, there's more! You can choose Edit⇨User Mode, promote yourself to Administration level, and then password-protect your network settings and much more. If you do that, you'll have access to an Options button that lets you turn AppleTalk on and off. (Big deal. As you surely remember, you can also turn AppleTalk on and off in the Chooser desk accessory.)

Or choose File⇨Get Info (Command-I) to learn more than you need to know about your Mac and its addresses and software version numbers, which may someday come in handy.

Finally, choosing File⇨Configurations (Command-K) lets you create, rename, import, or export your specific configurations.

The AppleTalk control panel is particularly useful for PowerBook users who may have more than one network setup they'd like their Mac to remember. But the rest of us will probably use this control panel once and then forget about it forever.

At least now you can say you know what it is and what it does. Don't forget that Mac OS Help is only a keystroke (that would be Command-?) away.

AutoRemounter (PowerBooks Only)

This control panel deals with what happens to shared disks that you have mounted on your PowerBook desktop when you shut down or put your Mac to sleep. It's shown in Figure 12-6. Sleeping, restarting, and shutting down all have the same effect on shared disks: The network connection is broken. With AutoRemounter, you have some control over what happens when you wake up or start up. Without it, you'd have to manually reestablish the network connection to each shared disk.

Figure 12-6:
Auto-
Remounter
can (duh)
remount
volumes
automatically
after
shutdown
or sleep.

Note that this control panel only matters if you mount disks or volumes over a network; stand-alone Macs need never even open it.

The Remount Shared Disks choices are mutually exclusive (you can select only one of the these choices at a time):

✔ **After Sleep:** This option automatically remounts any shared disks on your desktop after you put your Mac to sleep.

✔ **Off:** This option disables the AutoRemounter control panel completely.

The Connect to Disks By choices are:

✔ **Automatically Remounting:** This option automatically remounts any shared disks on your desktop after you shut down, restart, or sleep (based on your selection in the Remount Shared Disks section) but does *not* require a password for the disk to be remounted.

✔ **Always Requiring Passwords:** This option automatically remounts any shared disks on your desktop after you shut down, restart, or sleep (based on your selection in the Remount Shared Disks section) but *does* require a password before the disk is remounted.

Don't choose the Automatically Remounting option if the contents of shared disks are confidential. Someone else could awaken or restart your computer; selecting this option gives that person access to files on the remote disks. Choose the Always Entering Passwords option instead so that other users will only gain access to remote disks if they know the password.

Just a reminder that choices are, by their nature, mutually exclusive when you see a set of radio buttons. Radio buttons always signify that only one choice may be active at any time.

AutoRemounter no-brainer setting: If you don't use File Sharing, click the Off button and forget it. If you use File Sharing, click Always and Automatically Remounting. (Choose Always Entering Passwords if your office is secure and you don't want to have to type your password each time a disk is remounted.)

Brightness

This control panel lets you adjust the brightness of some monitors, mostly PowerBook and Duo models. The Install Mac OS program is smart and usually doesn't install this control panel unless your monitor supports it (most don't).

If the Brightness control panel was installed inadvertently on a Mac that doesn't support it, and you try to open it, an error message like the one in Figure 12-7 tells you that your Mac can't use this control panel. No big deal. Just trash it and forget it.

For those of you who can use the Brightness control panel, all I can say is that very few people have ever cast their gaze upon it and lived to tell the tale. Suffice it to say that this control panel has a slider bar to control screen brightness, and it gives you the option of setting up a keyboard shortcut to do the same thing. So few Macintosh users need to worry about this control panel that I won't expose them to the curse by presenting a screen shot.

Figure 12-7:
You get this
message if
your Mac
can't use
the
Brightness
control
panel.

> The control panel "Brightness" cannot be used with this Macintosh.
>
> OK

ColorSync System Profile

ColorSync is a color-matching technology that ensures color consistency between screen representation and color output. It is of no importance unless you are also using the ColorSync color-matching system on your printing devices and scanners.

I thought not.

So this control panel's settings are totally irrelevant. Nothing whatsoever will happen if you change them.

ColorSync System Profile no-brainer settings: Don't touch it.

Control Strip

Show or hide the Control Strip by choosing the appropriate radio button in this control panel.

Use the Control Strip's built-in hide and show feature (demonstrated in Figure 12-8) to collapse and expand the strip on-screen. Click the little nub to expand it again.

Control Strip no-brainer settings: Click the Show Control Strip radio button.

Figure 12-8:

Figure 12-8:
Click at
either end
of the
Control
Strip
(circled,
top) to
collapse it
to a little
nub on-
screen
(bottom).

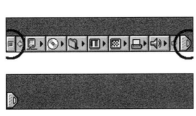

Date & Time

The Date & Time control panel lets you configure your Mac's internal clock, which many programs use, and configure the menu bar clock (see Figure 12-9).

Figure 12-9:
Set your
Mac's
internal
clock (and
the menu
bar clock) in
the Date &
Time
control
panel.

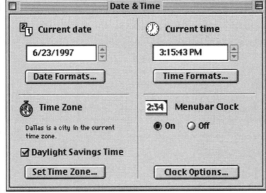

To set the date or time

Click the number that you want to change in the Current date or Current time field. The number is highlighted when you click it, and a pair of arrows appears. Increase the selected number by clicking the up arrow; decrease it by clicking the down arrow. You can also use the arrow keys on the keyboard to increase or decrease the number. Or you can type a new number right over the selected number.

Use the Tab key to move from number to number. Month, day, year, hour, minute, second, and AM/PM are selected in sequence when you press the Tab key. If you want to move backward through the sequence, press Shift-Tab. As long as you hold the Shift key down, you'll cycle through the numbers in reverse order as you press Tab.

Time and date formats

Your choices in the Date or Time Formats dialog boxes will be seen anyplace your Mac displays the date and time: in the menu bar, in programs that date or time stamp documents, in the Finder (creation and modification dates), and so on.

To change formats, click the appropriate button. The Date Formats dialog box (shown in Figure 12-10) lets you change the punctuation marks in the long date and the dividers in the short date.

Figure 12-10: The Date Formats dialog box. Apple thinks of everything, doesn't it?

> **Date Formats:** U.S.
>
> **Long Date**
> Prefix: [   ]
> [Weekday ▼] [,]
> [Month   ▼] [   ]
> [Day   ▼] [,]
> [Year   ▼] [   ]
> ☐ Leading zero for day
>
> **Short Date**
> [Month/Day/Year ▼]
> Separator: [/]
> ☐ Leading zero for day
> ☐ Leading zero for month
> ☑ Show century
>
> **Samples**
> Thursday , January 2 , 1992
> Thu , Jan 2 , 1992
> 1/2/1992
>
> [Cancel]
> [OK]

You can change the display order of both long and short dates. Use the Weekday, Month, Day, or Year pop-up menu to change the order of the long date; click the Month/Day/Year pop-up menu to choose a different order for the short date.

The Time Format dialog box lets you choose a 12-hour or 24-hour clock and a bunch of other stuff, as Figure 12-11 shows.

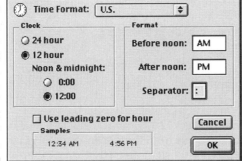

Figure 12-11:
The Time
Format
dialog box,
which
probably
doesn't
need any
changing.

The rest of it

The Daylight Savings Time check box sets the clock forward one hour (checked) or backward one hour (unchecked).

The Set Time Zone button lets you choose your time zone from a scrolling list.

Type the first letter of a big city near you to scroll to that city's name in the list.

Is this thrilling or what?

Finally, the Clock Options button lets you do all kinds of fun stuff with your menu bar clock (shown in Figure 12-12). You can set the clock to chime on the hour or quarter-hour, and you can select custom fonts and colors.

Figure 12-12:
If you're a
tweak freak,
you'll have a
field day
with all the
menu bar
clock's
options.

Apple's menu bar clock is based on Steve Christensen's popular freeware menu bar clock, SuperClock, which many Mac users loved and revered long before Apple began including it back in System 7.5.

Desktop Pictures

This control panel, shown in Figure 12-13, lets you select a decorative pattern for your desktop. To choose from the 48 (down from 74 in Mac OS 7.6) available patterns, click the left and right arrow buttons on the window (or use the left-arrow and right-arrow keys on the keyboard). When a pleasing pattern appears, click the Set Desktop button.

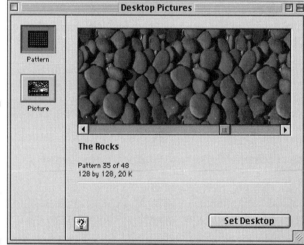

Figure 12-13: Desktop Pictures gives you a choice of 48 fancy desktop patterns.

 I lied: Desktop Patterns is an application, not a control panel. If you don't believe me, view the Control Panels folder's window by kind. Why did Apple choose to place it in the Control Panels folder? I don't know, but it seems like as good a place for it as any. Actually, in Mac OS 8, there are at least a dozen items that are actually applications, even though they live in the Control Panels folder.

The technical difference is that a control panel may load some of its code at startup (when you see the little icons march across the bottom of the screen). An application doesn't load anything until you open it.

But wait, there's more! If you click the Pictures button on the right, you can choose from four included pictures or any PICT file of your own. Just click the Select Picture button (if it says Remove Picture, click it once. It'll change to Select Picture and provides an Open dialog box). You then find four starter pictures in the Sample Desktop Pictures folder within the Apple Extras folder. Or use any PICT file of your own. Play around with the different positioning options available from the pop-up menu (it says "Position Automatically" in Figure 12-14).

Desktop Pictures is a vast improvement over earlier versions of the System, which offered only a handful of ugly patterns with a maximum of eight colors. The Desktop Pictures control panel, er, application, works in grayscale and looks great in thousands or millions of colors as well.

This functionality was previously available in third-party commercial and shareware programs like Wallpaper, Screenscapes, DeskPICT, and others, so it's nice that Apple is finally giving us this functionality for free.

Dial Assist

No cop-out, but this little doohickey was covered in clear and loving detail back in Chapter 8. Let's not waste trees, okay?

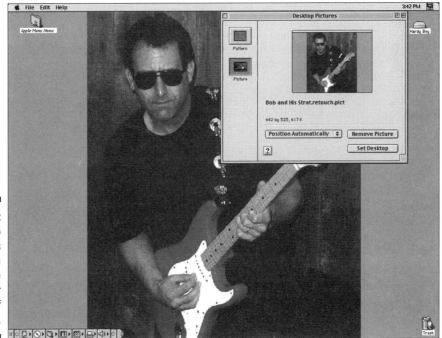

Figure 12-14:
Desktop Pictures lets you have a big picture as your desktop if you prefer.

Editor Setup (OpenDoc Only)

If you installed OpenDoc, you have an Editor Setup control panel. As with the man behind the curtain in *The Wizard of Oz,* pay no attention to it now. (It's covered extensively in Chapters 15 and 16, if you can't stand the suspense.)

Energy Saver

Almost all recent Mac models (and clones) are said to be *Energy Star compliant* — they can turn themselves off at a specific time or after a specified idle period. If your Mac supports this feature, the Energy Saver control panel is installed when you install Mac OS 8. (If your Mac doesn't support this control panel but it was somehow installed and you try to open it, you'll see an error message haughtily informing you that your Mac can't use it. No problemo. Trash the dastardly Energy Saver control panel and be done with it.)

In the top part of the dialog box, you can choose to have your computer go to sleep (a low-power mode) or shut down automatically after so many minutes of idle time (kind of like a killer screen saver).

The first time you restart your Mac after installing Mac OS 8, a helpful dialog box tells you that you now have Energy Saver and asks if you'd like to configure it now. Nice, eh?

To turn this feature on, move the slider until the appropriate time displays beneath it. To turn it off, slide the slider to Never. Figure 12-15 shows this little gadget.

Click the Show Details button and you'll see two additional sliders to control your display and hard disk sleep patterns separately.

And if you click the Scheduled Startup and Shutdown button at the top of the Energy Saver window, you can choose to have your Mac start up or shut down once at a specific time, or you can set up a recurring shutdown (for example, shut down every day at 11:29 p.m., just in time for Dave).

If you're not around when one of these shutdowns occurs and you have unsaved work in any application, you'll see a dialog box asking if you want to save your changes. The Mac won't shut down until you click a button in this dialog box. In fact, if you click the Cancel button in this dialog box, the shutdown is canceled along with the Save dialog box.

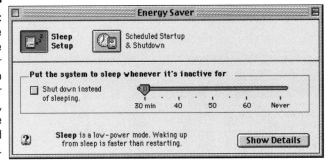

Energy Saver no-brainer settings: Drag the slider to 30 or 45 minutes for sleep (not shutdown); then remember to turn your Mac off manually when you're not going to need it for a while.

Extensions Manager

Extensions Manager is another program that's been around for years as freeware but made its first appearance as an Apple product in System 7.5 and was overhauled extensively for Mac OS 7.6. Extensions Manager lets you turn extensions, control panels, startup items, and shutdown items on and off easily.

There's a longer, more technical discussion of why you need Extensions Manager, along with some tips, in Chapter 14. For now, here's how you use it.

Extensions and control panels load into memory if they're in the Extensions or Control Panels folders at startup. Without Extensions Manager (or one of its third-party counterparts such as Now Software's Startup Manager, Inline Software's INITPicker, or Casady & Greene's Conflict Catcher), you would have to move an extension or control panel out of its special folder manually and then restart your Mac to disable it — which, as you might guess, isn't much fun.

You still have to restart your Mac, but you can use Extensions Manager to turn individual control panels and extensions on and off without moving them manually.

You can work with Extensions Manager in the Finder by opening its icon or choosing Apple menu⇨Control Panels⇨Extensions Manager. Or you can work with it at startup, before any control panels or extensions load.

To open Extensions Manager at startup, hold down the spacebar on your keyboard until the Extensions Manager window appears (see Figure 12-16).

Figure 12-16:
The
Extensions
Manager
window lets
you turn
control
panels,
extensions,
startup
items, and
shutdown
items off and
on at will (at
startup).

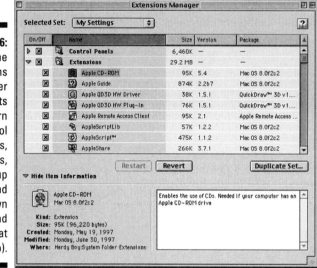

Regardless of which way you open it, you choose which items you want to turn on or off by clicking the box before their name (an X means the item is turned on). Your choices remain in effect until you change them in the Extensions Manager window.

You can create *Sets* with Extensions Manager, groups of extensions and control panels that you want to use simultaneously. To create a set, click items in the list until the ones that you want turned on have Xs and the ones that you want turned off don't. When everything is just the way you like it, choose File⇨New Set. You'll be asked to name the set. After you do, the set will appear in the Sets menu as a custom set along with the preinstalled sets — Mac OS All and Mac OS Base. Sets can be quite convenient, as I explain in Chapter 14.

When you finish making your selections or creating sets, close the Extensions Manager window. If you used the spacebar to open Extensions Manager at start up, your Mac will start up with only the X-ed items loaded; if you're in the Finder, click Extensions Manager's Restart button for your selections to take effect.

The Mac OS Base set turns on only the most essential control panels and extensions, turning off memory hogs like QuickDraw 3D and QuickDraw GX (see Chapter 14 for details). Using it may regain some of your precious RAM for other purposes.

You can also turn on or off the entire Extensions, Control Panels, Startup Items, or Shutdown Items folders by clicking the On/Off box next to their names. In other words, turning off the Control Panels folder in Extensions Manager turns off all of your control panels at once. You'll find Duplicate Set, Delete Set, and Rename Set commands in the File menu. They do what they sound like they do.

Finally, if you click an item in the Extensions Manager window (Apple CD-ROM is selected in Figure 12-16), some information about it will appear in a box in the lower-right corner of the window. Though Chapter 14 does a more thorough job of explaining this stuff, the little box in the corner will do in a pinch if your copy of *Mac OS 8 For Dummies* isn't handy.

File Sharing

The File Sharing control panel, new to Mac OS 8, combines the features of two older control panels, File Sharing Monitor, and Sharing Setup. This is where you turn File Sharing on and off, and find out which items on your local disk are currently being shared, how much network activity there is, and who is currently connected to your hard disk. It's shown in Figure 12-17.

I won't waste any more of your time with this one; it was covered in great detail in Chapter 8, in case you've forgotten.

General Controls

This is the big fellow, the granddaddy of all control panels. Figure 12-18 doesn't do it justice.

A whopping six different options are managed by General Controls.

Desktop options

The Show Desktop when in background check box determines whether the Finder shows through in the background when you've got another application open. Unchecking this option makes Finder windows and icons disappear

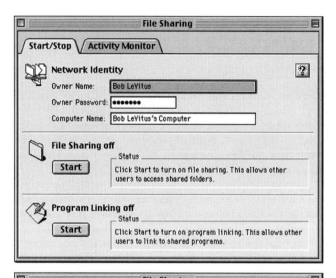

Figure 12-17:
The File
Sharing
control panel
turns sharing
on and off
(Start/Stop
tab) and tells
you what's
being shared
and who is
connected
(Activity
Monitor tab).

when other programs are active, which means that the only way to switch to the Finder is to choose it from the Application menu. In other words, if you click outside of a word processor window, you don't pop into the Finder.

Checking the Show Desktop when in background option makes it more convenient to return to the Finder from other programs by clicking the desktop or a Finder window, but this feature may be more confusing for beginners.

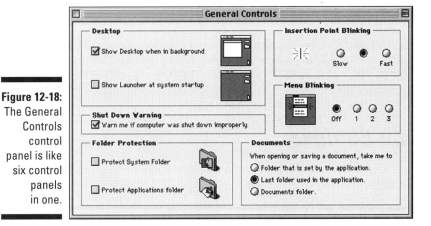

Figure 12-18:
The General
Controls
control
panel is like
six control
panels
in one.

The Show Launcher at system startup check box governs whether the Launcher is active. I ranted about Launcher in Chapter 6, so I won't bore you with my vitriol. Suffice it to say that I don't find it very useful, but beginners might.

Shut Down Warning

If this check box is checked, you'll see a warning like the one in Figure 12-19 when you restart your computer after a crash, freeze, power interruption, or improper shutdown.

Figure 12-19:
Your Mac
will scold
you if you
shut down
improperly
(or crash —
like it's your
fault!).

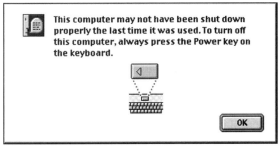

This computer may not have been shut down properly the last time it was used. To turn off this computer, always press the Power key on the keyboard.

OK

Folder Protection

If the Folder Protection check boxes are checked, items in those folders (System or Applications or both) can't be renamed or deleted.

Insertion Point Blinking

This option sets the speed at which the text insertion point, a flashing vertical line, blinks in documents. Your choices are Slow, Medium, or Fast. I like Medium or Fast because I find it easiest to see the cursor that way. Your mileage may vary.

Menu Blinking

This option controls whether or not menu items flash when you select them, and if they flash, how many times.

Off is the fastest setting.

Documents

This set of radio buttons determines what folder will be active in Open and Save dialog boxes:

- ✔ **Folder that is set by the application:** This option brings up the Open or Save dialog box ready to save or open files in the folder that contains the program you're using or whatever folder that program ordinarily defaults to, often the last folder you opened or saved a file from/to. So if you're using ClarisWorks and you choose File⇨Save or File⇨Open, the list of files you see in the Open or Save dialog box will be the contents of the ClarisWorks folder or perhaps the last folder you saved a file into.

- ✔ **Last folder used in the application:** This option brings up the Open or Save dialog box ready to save or open a file in the last folder you saved to or opened a document from. In other words, your Mac remembers for you. Many programs do this automatically (see "Folder that is set by the application" above). Clicking this setting makes sure every application does it.

- ✔ **Documents folder:** This option will bring up the Open or Save dialog box ready to save or open a document in the Documents folder.

General Controls no-brainer settings:

For beginners: Show Desktop when in background: Off. Show Launcher at system startup: On. Shut Down Warning: On. Folder Protection: On for both. Insertion Point Blinking: Fast. Menu Blinking: 3 times. Documents: Documents folder.

For more advanced users: Show Desktop when in background: On. Show Launcher at System Startup: Off. Shut Down Warning: Your call. Folder Protection: Off for both. Insertion Point Blinking: Fast. Menu Blinking: Off. Documents: Last folder used.

Keyboard

The Keyboard control panel modifies how your keyboard responds to your keystrokes. It's shown in Figure 12-20.

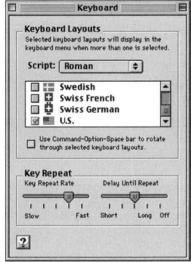

Figure 12-20: The Keyboard control panel governs how your keyboard responds.

The Keyboard Layouts section allows you to choose a different keyboard layout for languages other than United States English.

The Key Repeat Rate sets how fast a key will repeat when you hold it down. This feature comes into play when you hold down the dash key to make a line or the * key to make a divider.

The Delay Until Repeat option sets how long you have to hold down a key before it starts repeating.

Because changes to the Keyboard control panel take place immediately, you can open it and a word processor and experiment with its settings until you are comfortable.

Keyboard no-brainer settings: Look at Figure 12-20. Duplicate its settings. If you live somewhere other than the United States and see a familiar-sounding keyboard layout in the lower part of the window, select it.

Do not under any circumstances click the check box in the middle unless you have good reason to use foreign keyboard layouts on occasion. The Command-Option-spacebar keyboard shortcut, when turned on, can cause unpredictable behavior if you later forget you've turned it on. Use this thingie with caution, especially if you use Photoshop (which uses Command-Option-spacebar as the shortcut for Zoom Out).

Launcher

Launcher (see Figure 12-21) is Apple's cheesy little file launcher. It lets you open items in its window with a single click, which saves you the trouble of rummaging through folders. The Launcher window's buttons reflect the contents of the Launcher Items folder in your System Folder.

To add an item to Launcher, drag it onto the Launcher window, which automatically creates an alias for that item in the Launcher Items folder. To delete an item from Launcher, hold down Option and drag the item from the Launcher window to the Trash.

Figure 12-21:
The Launcher window contains single-click launch buttons for each item in the Launcher Items folder.

Whatever is in the Launcher Items folder appears as a button in the Launcher window. Single-clicking the button opens the item, which can be a file, a folder, a document, or a control panel, or (better idea) an alias of a file, a folder, a document, or a control panel.

If you want Launcher to start up automatically, there's an option for that very thing in the General Controls control panel.

If you like Launcher, read up on how to make it better in Chapter 6.

Launcher is even less necessary now that the Finder has single-click buttons in any window. Why they don't retire this old hag is a mystery to me.

Mac OS Easy Open

Mac OS Easy Open (MEO) is the enabling technology that lets you choose another application to open a document when you don't have the actual application that created it. Figure 12-22 provides a demonstration. To get this picture, I deleted every copy of SimpleText on my hard disk and then tried to open a SimpleText document called Read Me.

Figure 12-22:
This
translation
dialog box is
part of
Mac OS
Easy Open.

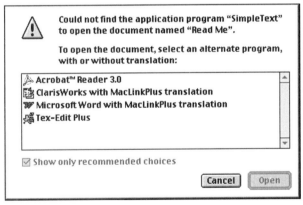

> ⚠️ Could not find the application program "SimpleText" to open the document named "Read Me".
>
> To open the document, select an alternate program, with or without translation:
>
> - 🅰 Acrobat™ Reader 3.0
> - 📄 ClarisWorks with MacLinkPlus translation
> - 📝 Microsoft Word with MacLinkPlus translation
> - 📄 Tex-Edit Plus
>
> ☑ Show only recommended choices
>
> [Cancel] [Open]

If MEO isn't turned on or isn't installed, instead of this dialog box, you see an error message telling you that an application couldn't be found for this document.

The four check boxes in this control panel manage how the translation dialog box works (see Figure 12-23).

Figure 12-23:
The Mac OS
Easy Open
control
panel.

If you check Always show dialog box, you must confirm your translation preference every time you open a document. In other words, if this item is checked, you see the dialog box shown back in Figure 12-22 every time you open a SimpleText file. If you uncheck this option, the second time (and every time thereafter) that you open a SimpleText file, it will automatically launch into the selected alternate program.

If you check the Include applications on servers option, MEO will look on all network volumes currently mounted for an application that can open the document.

If you don't have a high-speed network (such as Ethernet or Token Ring), launching a remote program can take a long, long time. You might want to consider leaving this option off unless you really, really need it.

The Auto pick if only 1 choice option picks the appropriate program to open the file automatically (without the dialog box) if you only have one program capable of opening that file.

The Translate 'TEXT' documents option, when turned on, evaluates all plain text files to see if they should be translated before opening. This increases your ability to read documents from other computers (DOS/WinDoze, mainly), but may slow down the opening of Mac-created plain text documents. If you don't associate with people who use DOS or WinDoze, leave it unchecked for sure.

The Delete Preferences button deletes any links that you've created between documents and applications. Why would you need to delete preferences? If the Always show dialog box option isn't checked and a document always launches the wrong application, click Delete Preferences. The next time you try to open that document, you'll get a dialog box allowing you to choose a different application. In other words, the Delete Preferences button makes MEO forget any connections between documents and applications previously created in a translation dialog box.

Macintosh Easy Open Setup no-brainer settings: Automatic document translation: On. Always show dialog boxes: Off. Include applications on servers: Off. Auto pick if only 1 choice: On. Translate 'TEXT' documents: Off.

MacLinkPlus Setup

If you chose to install the optional MacLinkPlus translators when you installed Mac OS 8, you'll have a MacLinkPlus Setup control panel in your Control Panels folder. My advice is, don't change a thing and don't mess with it unless someone or some software manual instructs you to. Okay?

Map

A lame little control panel that's virtually useless. I'm not gonna waste your time with it. Figure 12-24 shows a picture, just for kicks.

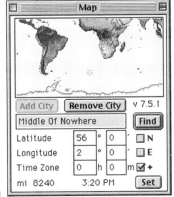

Figure 12-24: The mostly useless Map control panel.

Memory

See Chapter 9, which covers nothing else.

Memory no-brainer settings: Cache Size: 128K. Virtual Memory: On and set to at least one megabyte more than your installed RAM. Ram Disk: Off.

Modem

The Modem control panel (shown in Figure 12-25) lets you choose which port your modem is connected to, as well as sound and dialing options (only available for internal modems, alas).

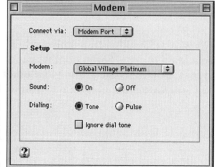

Figure 12-25:
The Modem
control
panel.

Monitors & Sound

Here's where you control your Mac's monitor and audio options.

Monitor

Click the Monitor button at the top of the window. You can now select the number of colors in the Color Depth scrolling list and Grays or Colors by clicking the appropriate radio button. If your monitor and video card support what is known as MultiSync, you can also change resolutions, as shown in Figure 12-26. Finally, some monitors let you adjust their gamma settings, which makes white look slightly different.

Sound

Click the Sound button at the top of the window. You can adjust all of your Mac's sound levels by dragging the appropriate slider. (Some options shown in Figure 12-27 may not be available on all computer models.)

Alerts (beep sounds)

Click the Alerts button at the top of the window. Now you can choose your Mac's System Alert sound, also known as its beep sound (see Figure 12-28). The slider on the right controls System Alert (that is, beep) volume.

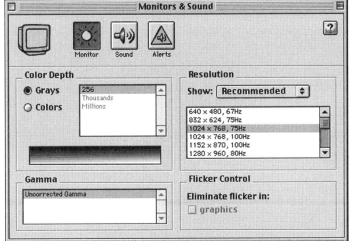

Figure 12-26:
The
Monitors &
Sound
control
panels with
the Monitor
button at the
top selected.

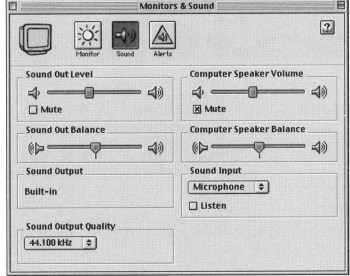

Figure 12-27:
The
Monitors &
Sound
control
panels with
the Sound
button
selected.

If you have a microphone that works with your Mac, or have sounds you've downloaded or traded with others, you can add additional beep sounds using the SimpleSound desk accessory (for microphone recording) or by dragging any sound file onto the System Folder icon (for stored sounds).

Figure 12-28:
The
Monitors &
Sound
control
panel with
the Alerts
button
selected.

Don't believe me? Here's how to record your own sound (microphone required, of course).

First choose Apple menu⇨SimpleSound.

1. Click the Add button.

   A recording dialog box appears (see Figure 12-29).

Figure 12-29:
SimpleSound's
record-your-
own-beep-
sound
dialog box.

2. Click the Record button.

3. Make your noise or sound.

4. Click the Stop button.

5. Name the sound.

Bingo. That's it. Your new sound appears in the list of sounds. Select it now as your beep sound if you like. See. Told you it was a piece of cake (as long as you have the microphone).

Mouse

This control panel, shown in Figure 12-30, sets the mouse-tracking and double-click speeds.

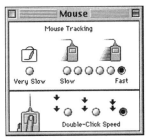

Figure 12-30: The Mouse control panel, where speed is king.

The Mouse Tracking setting governs the relationship between hand movement on the mouse and cursor movement on the screen. Fast mouse-tracking settings send the cursor squirting across the screen with a mere flick of the wrist; slow mouse-tracking settings make the cursor crawl across in seemingly slow motion, even when your hand is flying. Set it as fast as you can stand it. I like the fastest speed, as shown in Figure 12-30. Try it. You may like it.

The Double-Click Speed setting determines how close together two clicks must be for the Mac to interpret them as a double-click and not two separate clicks. The leftmost button is the slow setting. It lets you double-click at an almost leisurely pace. The rightmost is the fast setting (which I prefer). The middle button, of course, represents a double-click speed somewhere in the middle.

Changes in the Mouse control panel take place immediately, so you should definitely play around a little and see what settings feel best for you.

Mouse no-brainer settings: Mouse Tracking: Moderately fast to fast. Double-click speed: Middle setting.

Numbers

Use this control panel to change the decimal and thousands separators (the period and comma in $1,000,000.00) as well as the symbol used to denote currency ($ in the U.S., £ in England, and so on). Figure 12-31 shows the Numbers control panel.

Figure 12-31: Because you'll probably never see your own, here's a peek at my Numbers control panel.

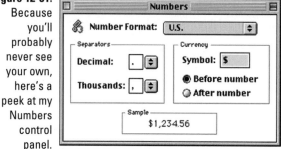

You could go through your entire life without ever needing to open the Numbers control panel.

OpenDoc Setup

OpenDoc Setup controls how OpenDoc works on your Mac OS machine. The top part determines how much memory each OpenDoc document consumes when created, the bottom part controls when OpenDoc is turned on and off.

See the "What's open, Doc?" sidebar in Chapter 15 for info on OpenDoc.

OpenDoc Setup no-brainer settings: See Figure 12-32. Make yours look like that.

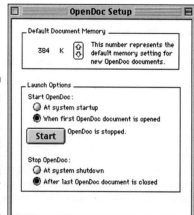

Figure 12-32: OpenDoc Setup control panel. Make yours look like this for best results.

PC Exchange

PC Exchange manages which Macintosh program launches when you open documents created on that other kind of computer, running that other operating system, MS-DOS (see Figure 12-33).

Figure 12-33:
If I open
a DOS
document
that has the
.TXT suffix,
PC Exchange
tells
SimpleText
to launch
and open the
document.

Apple throws in this application assignment — .TXT documents open in SimpleText — for free. If you'd prefer to read DOS files in a program other than SimpleText, click the application assignment to select it and then click the Change button (see Figure 12-34).

In the Change dialog box, you can change the three-letter suffix, the application program that you want to use to open that type of document, and the type of document.

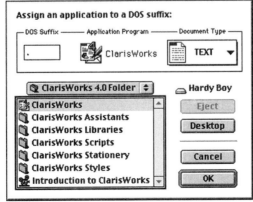

Figure 12-34:
ClarisWorks
will now
launch when
I open a DOS
document
that has the
.TXT suffix.

If you click the Document Type pop-up and nothing happens, the type is set already for that document and you can't change it.

To remove an application assignment, select it by clicking and then click the Remove button.

Double-clicking an application assignment opens the dialog box, just as selecting it and then clicking the Change button does.

The Add button in the PC Exchange control panel brings up the same dialog box shown in Figure 12-34. To create a new application assignment, make your choices in the dialog box and then click OK. Use the Options button to tell PC Exchange to work on other SCSI devices such as external hard drives or Zip, Jaz, or SyQuest drives.

ppp

PPP is point-to-point protocol. It's how most Mac users communicate with the Internet. And Mac OS 8 is the first version to include it.

I hate to disappoint you, but that's all you're going to get for now. We'll talk about this little puppy ad nauseam in the upcoming CyberDog chapter (that being Chapter 15). Stay tuned.

QuickTime Settings

This one's a no-brainer. It's probably already configured properly, in which case, leave it alone. Just check to make sure it's set as follows:

First choose AutoPlay from the pop-up menu if it's not already selected; then click both check boxes — Enable Audio CD AutoPlay and Enable CD-ROM AutoPlay. This enables your Mac to automatically start playing all audio CDs and some CD-ROM titles.

Now choose Music from the pop-up menu and make sure that QuickTime Music Synthesizer is checked.

That'll do it. Close it and forget it.

Remote Access Setup

This control panel is present only if Remote Access is installed. See Chapter 8 for the gory details.

Sharing Setup

Ditto! Chapter 8 again!

Speech

(This control panel is available only if you install PlainTalk.)

Choose Voice from the Options pop-up menu (see Figure 12-35) to select the voice your Mac will use for speech-to-text applications. Now choose a voice from the 22 wild and wacky selections in the Voice pop-up. To check out your handiwork, click the speaker icon. Each voice says something different. My favorite is Fred, who says, "I sure like being inside this fancy computer." If you think that's fun, try this: Launch SimpleText, type a few words and then select them, then choose Sound⇨Speak Selection (Command-H). Cute, eh?

Figure 12-35:
The Speech control panel — choose from 22 wild and wacky voices and make them talk slower or faster.

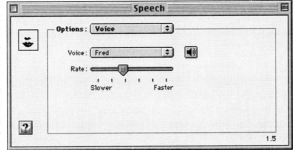

For a really good time, choose Talking Alerts from the Options pop-up menu and click both check boxes (as shown in Figure 12-36). Choose the Random from the list option from the Speak the phrase pop-up menu and then close the Speech control panel. The next time a program puts an alert box up on the screen ("Save changes to the document 'untitled' before closing?"), your favorite voice will speak it for you.

Figure 12-36:
This one will
really make
you puke;
set yours
like mine
and your
Mac will
speak alerts
to you.

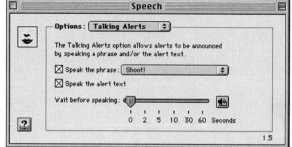

Even cuter. Here's my guess: You'll leave it turned on for maybe a week.
Or less.

Startup Disk

With this control panel, you choose which hard disk or hard disk volume (if
you've partitioned your hard disk) should act as the startup disk when more
than one drive with a System Folder is connected to the Mac (see Figure 12-37).

Figure 12-37:
This Mac
has three
hard disks
attached.
Hardy Boy is
selected, so
it's the
startup disk.

TCP/IP

Sorry to disappoint again, but you'll have to read Chapter 15 if you want to
know about this alphabet soup (and PPP too).

Text

Another control panel you'll never need. Unless, of course, you have a version of Mac OS 8 other than the United States version. If you use more than one language on your Macintosh, you can choose between them in this control panel, which is shown in Figure 12-38.

Figure 12-38:
You'll probably never need to touch the Text control panel, so here's what it looks like.

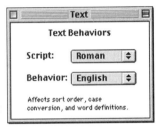

Users & Groups

I'm sorry if I sound like a broken record, but I covered this one in great detail back in Chapter 8. If you need to know, that's where to go.

Web Sharing

I hate to sound like a broken record again, but you'll learn more than you can stand about this control panel in Chapter 15. Leave it turned off for now.

Chapter 13

How to Write an AppleScript in 21 Minutes

(The chapter title is, of course, a takeoff on Viki King's wonderful book about that other kind of script writing, *How to Write a Movie in 21 Days*.)

AppleScript is like a tape recorder for your Mac. It can record and play back things that you do, such as opening an icon or clicking a button.

Describing AppleScript to a Mac beginner is a bit like three blind men describing an elephant. One man might describe it as the Macintosh's built-in automation tool. Another might describe it as an interesting, but often overlooked, piece of enabling technology. The third might liken it to a cassette recorder, recording and playing back your actions at the keyboard. A fourth (if there were a fourth in the story) would assure you it looked like computer code written in a high-level language.

They would all be correct. AppleScript is the Mac's built-in automation tool (at least in System 7.5 and later, it's built in). It is a little-known (at least up to now) enabling technology. It is like a cassette recorder (for programs that support AppleScript recording). And scripts do look like computer programs (which could be because they are computer programs).

I call AppleScript a *time and effort enhancer*. AppleScript, if you just spend the time and effort it takes to learn it, will save you oodles of time and effort.

Therein lies the rub. This stuff isn't simple. There's no way in heaven I'm going to teach you how to use AppleScript in the next nine pages. Entire books have been written on the topic, for gosh sake!

And don't kid yourself. AppleScript is complicated and will take some effort to master. So rather than try to teach you how to use it, I'll try to show you what AppleScript can do for you, and I'll get you to the point where you can write a simple script of your own, all in about 21 minutes.

What the Heck Is an AppleScript, Anyway?

In the broadest sense, AppleScript is an enabling technology that lets you record and play back complex sequences of Macintosh events occurring in the Finder, in programs, or in any combination of the Finder and programs. In a narrower sense, AppleScript now makes it possible to automate multi-step sequences, such as changing the bit depth of your monitor. What used to take at least three steps . . .

1. Open the Monitors control panel

2. Click a number of colors

3. Close the Monitors & Sound control panel

. . . can now be performed instantly and effortlessly with one script. This feature may not sound like much, but it can sure save you time and effort. The more often you perform a task each day, the more you should consider automating it (if, of course, it can be automated — not all tasks can be automated, as you'll soon see).

The AppleScript components are installed automatically when you install Mac OS 8. (I'll discuss the components one by one after a brief rant.)

 AppleScript has been around for a few years, but before System 7.5 it wasn't included in Apple System software releases. Instead, it came in separate Scripter and Developer packages at additional cost. So it never really caught on with the masses.

In the meantime, many forward-thinking developers have incorporated AppleScript support into their programs. Better still, that number is growing faster now that AppleScript is part of the System software.

Power users have been clamoring for this stuff for years. It's finally here, and it's only going to get better and more powerful as time goes on and more people get copies for free.

I encourage you, if you really want to master your Macintosh, to learn at least a bit of basic scripting. This chapter is a start, but your investment of time spent learning AppleScript will be repaid tenfold in time you save performing your daily tasks. And at the very least, some of the canned scripts that Apple provides — such as the one that turns file sharing on and off or adds an items alias to your Apple menu — can save you time and effort every day.

The Script Editor requires at least 700K of free memory (Largest Unused Block in the About this Computer dialog box). If you don't have enough memory to use it, quit all open applications and try again. If that doesn't do it, open the Extensions Manager control panel, select the Mac OS 8 minimum option from the pop-up menu, and then restart your Mac. (Don't forget to turn this stuff back on later.)

What the Mac OS Installer Installs and Where It Installs It

Mac OS 8 includes a bevy of AppleScript-related items in various places on your hard disk. Some are essential to AppleScript's operation; the rest are merely convenient. Before you learn how to use them, here are your tools.

The AppleScriptLib and AppleScript extensions

(In the Extensions folder, which is in the System Folder)

These extensions are installed in the Extensions folder (in the System Folder). They are the engine that make AppleScript work. If they're not in the Extensions folder at startup, AppleScript won't work. They require no care or maintenance.

The Scripting Additions folder

(In the System Folder)

This folder contains add-on parts of the AppleScript system. AppleScript is modular, so you can add new commands to AppleScript by merely dropping a new item into the Scripting Additions folder. Leave it be.

AppleScript Guide

(In the AppleScript folder, which is in the Apple Extras folder)

This item consists of a pair of SimpleText documents, Using AppleScript part 1, and Using AppleScript part 2.

Why is Using AppleScript in two parts? Because there's a limit to the size of SimpleText documents, and there's more stuff you need to know than can fit in a single document file. That's why. I think.

It doesn't matter why there are two of them. If you want to learn AppleScript, I strongly recommend that you read them. Both. They're dry, but not as boring as they look, once you get started.

Script Editor

(In the AppleScript folder, which is in the Apple Extras folder)

Script Editor is the program with which you edit scripts. Duh. We'll play with it in a minute.

The Automated Tasks folder

(In the AppleScript folder, which is in the Apple Extras folder)

The Automated Tasks folder contains several useful scripts. Open and read the About Automated Tasks SimpleText document at your earliest convenience; it explains each of the tasks, so I won't waste the space.

There's an alias of the Automated Tasks folder in your Apple Menu Items folder (Mac OS 8 put it there for you — isn't that thoughtful?), so you can select any of these useful scripts right from the Apple menu.

Keeping the more-is-more theme, you'll also find a folder called More Automated Tasks. They're more "advanced" than the plain old automated tasks; useful, but complicated to explain.

Please note that Apple may have changed the names of some of the scripts before this book went to press. Also note that Apple will probably add and remove some scripts that the Installer installs as time goes by. So if you can't seem to find on your hard drive some of the scripts that I mention on the next few pages, there's nothing wrong with your System. Apple just changed the software.

But wait, there's more

If you want to use AppleScript with programs other Mac OS 8 (much but not all of which is scriptable), they have to be AppleScript *enabled,* which means that they have to be adapted by their developers to work with AppleScript.

There are three levels of AppleScript support found in applications: scriptability, recordability, and attachability. Programs can support one, two, or all three levels.

Unfortunately, there is no easy way of telling whether a program is AppleScript enabled at all, much less if it's recordable or attachable. For what it's worth, the Finder supports all three levels.

Here are brief descriptions of the three levels of AppleScript support that you may find in third-party programs:

Scriptable programs

Scriptable means that the program can follow instructions sent by AppleScript scripts. Scriptable apps are the most common kind. If a program proclaims that it supports AppleScript, it's at this level at least.

Unfortunately, it's up to the developer to decide how much of the program is actually scriptable, so some programs are more scriptable than others. Microsoft Excel, FileMaker Pro, PageMaker (limited support), and Now Up-to-Date/Now Contact are a few scriptable programs I know of.

Recordable programs

Recordable programs go scriptable programs one better. Recordable means that you can record your actions in the program and automatically create an AppleScript script for future playback based on what you did within the program. Few programs are recordable yet.

Attachable programs

Attachable programs are even rarer than recordable ones. Attachable means that the program will let you attach a script to an item or element in a document, such as a cell in a spreadsheet, a button in a database, or a rectangle in a drawing. The Finder is attachable because you can attach a script to an icon.

What it all means

At this point, you should know at least this much:

- ✔ AppleScript is a kind of recording and playback mechanism for repetitive tasks on your Mac.
- ✔ Some programs, most notably Mac OS 8's Finder, can be scripted to do some things under script control.
- ✔ A few programs can record and attach scripts.

Notice I didn't say *understand* up there, I said *know*. To develop true understanding would require far more pages than I have. But I had to mention this stuff so that when you try to use a script with a nonscriptable (or nonrecordable or nonattachable) program, you have at least a vague idea of why it's not working.

Writing a Simple Script

I agonized for a long time over this section. I wanted to teach you something useful, but it had to be easy enough to show in just a few pages.

I've realized that it can't be done. If a script is useful, it's going to require more explaining than I have space for. (And most of the easy, useful scripts are already done for you and thoughtfully placed in the Automated Tasks or More Automated Tasks folder.) So instead, I'm going to show how to write a script that's totally dumb but fun to watch.

If you want to see smart scripts, open any of the ones in the Automated Tasks or More Automated Tasks folder (in the AppleScript folder in the Apple Extras folder) and examine it closely.

1. Launch the Script Editor application.

   A new, untitled script appears on the screen.

2. Type **My first stupid script** in the description field at the top of the document window.

3. Click the Record button.

   After a brief pause, your screen should look more or less like Figure 13-1. Notice the tiny image of a cassette tape where the Apple menu's Apple logo used to be. It flashes to let you know that you're recording.

Figure 13-1:
Ready to
record a
script.

4. Make the Finder active by clicking the desktop or any open windows or choosing Finder in the Application menu.

5. Close all open windows (Option-click any window's close box, press the Option key and choose File⇨Close All, or use the keyboard shortcut Command-Option-W). If there are no open windows on your screen, ignore this step.

6. Create a new folder on the desktop (File⇨New Folder or Command-N).

7. Open the new, untitled folder and then click its title bar and drag it to a new location. The farther you drag it, the better.

8. Click the zoom box (the first of the two boxes on the far right side of the title bar) of the untitled folder window. Click it again.

9. Drag the folder to another new location.

10. Return to the Script Editor application and click the Stop button.

That's it! You've written your first script. It should look something like Figure 13-2. Don't save it yet. (As you'll see in a moment, there are choices yet to make about *how* to save your script.)

To see how your script works, click the Run button. Watch closely, as it happens fast. If you blinked and missed it, run the script again. It switches to the Finder, closes all open windows, creates a new folder, moves it, grows it, grows it again, and then moves it again.

I'm fudging a little when I say that you wrote a script. Actually, you recorded a script. If you had *written* it, you would have typed all the stuff between "tell application Finder" and "end tell" from memory, without actually performing the actions.

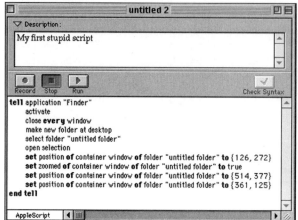

Figure 13-2:
Your first
script.

In fact, the most effective way to use AppleScript is a combination of record-ing and writing. First record your actions, then analyze the script, and then try to figure out ways to perform each action more efficiently by typing in different commands and trying them. To reach this level of scripting mas-tery, you'll need to know a lot more about the AppleScript language than this chapter can teach you.

Okay. You can return to the Finder and trash those untitled folders (one was created each time you ran the script).

So that's how to record a script.

There is one more thing you should know: Unfortunately, many control panels are not scriptable.

If a Script Is Any Good, It Should Be Saved

There are a three different ways to save a script. If you choose Save or Save As from the File menu in the Script Editor, a pop-up menu in the Save dialog box gives you your choices (see Figure 13-3).

- ✔ The Text option creates a text file of your script. This script can be opened in any text editor for editing, or reopened by Script Editor.

- ✔ The Compiled Script option creates a Script Editor file. You can open, run, or modify the file with the Script Editor program.

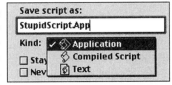

Figure 13-3:
So many
ways to
save a
script.

✔ The Application option creates a self-running script that executes when you open its icon.

The files in the Automated Tasks folder are scripts saved as applications.

If the Never Show Startup Screen check box is unchecked in the Save dialog box, your script will display a startup screen with a Run button before it executes, as shown in Figure 13-5.

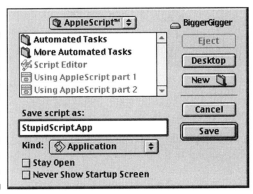

Figure 13-4:
If you save
your script
as an
Application,
you have
even more
choices to
make.

If you check the Stay Open check box, the script application remains open until you quit it. Scripts saved with this option usually look for something to happen and then perform an action.

The Alert When Folder Changes script in the More Automated Tasks folder is one of these stay-open-and-watch applications.

Run Only means the saved file can't be edited. You would use the Save As Run Only command (in the File menu) if you had a spiffy script that you didn't want others to see or modify. Anyway, a Run Only script can never be modified. If you choose Save As Run Only instead of Save or Save As, the resulting file will be a Run Only application or compiled script (you can't save a Run Only text file). This script can never be modified or changed.

Figure 13-5:
You can
eliminate
this startup
screen by
checking
the Never
Show
Startup
Screen
option in the
Save dialog
box, as
shown in
Figure 13-4.

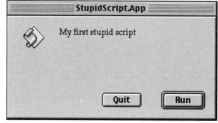

Chapter 14

What Can Stay and What Can Go

*T*his chapter is by far the most useful chapter in the book. In this chapter, I go through the entire System Folder one item at a time. I show you how much RAM each item uses, how much disk space it occupies, and what (if any) side effects will occur if you delete or disable it.

There are no substitutes for RAM or hard disk space. But no matter how much you have, there will come a day when you need more of one or the other or both.

Yes, there are Band-Aids like Virtual Memory or RAM Doubler (for making your Mac think it has more RAM than it does) or StuffIt SpaceSaver or other compression software (for making your hard disk think it's bigger than it is). And yes, I think you can use programs like that safely most of the time.

Most of the time. RAM Doubler doesn't pose much threat, as it doesn't really deal with files or the file system. Compression software, on the other hand, adds another layer of complexity to your Mac. It's always expanding and compressing files in the background, reading and writing from the hard disk. So there's more chance for errors to occur. And all compression software extracts a noticeable performance penalty, slowing down your Mac anywhere from a little to a lot, depending on the compression software, your Mac model, and the speed of your hard disk.

My advice: Resort to those devices if you must, but *real* RAM and hard disk space are much better.

Reclamation Theory

RAM and hard disks are expensive. Therefore, I created this chapter, a first, I believe, in System software book history, a chapter dedicated to telling you how to get rid of the deadweight among the 65 or so megabytes of files (assuming a full install of Mac OS 8 and all its optional bells and whistles) in your System Folder by deleting or disabling.

Let's face it: Mac OS 8 puts a lot of files on your hard disk even if you don't choose one of the optional installations. If you do install all of the options, it installs a whopping 545 files and folders, give or take a few. Not everybody needs every single one of these files; many of them can be deleted to free up (reclaim) hard disk space.

And another thing: Many control panels and extensions load into RAM at startup. So not only do they take up disk space, extensions and control panels can use up your valuable RAM too.

I'll go through the System Folder and see what each item costs you in terms of RAM and disk space, and what, if any, repercussions will be felt if you trash or disable the item.

This chapter lists every item that Install Mac OS can install, including all the Custom installation options like QuickTime 3D, OpenDoc, Cyberdog, Remote Access, and so on. So unless you've installed every one of the custom options (see Appendix B), you may not see every file or folder mentioned in this chapter. You're forewarned.

Life After Death: The Truth about Restoring Deleted Files

Before I can show you how to save RAM and disk space, I need to briefly cover a couple of important topics: backing up and reinstalling.

Other benefits of a lean, mean System Folder

There are a bunch of other benefits to keeping your System Folder lean and mean:

✔ The Apple menu submenu for the Control Panels folder will be shorter.

✔ The Control Panels folder will contain fewer items and thus be easier to manage.

✔ The Chooser will be less cluttered when you get rid of printer drivers you'll never need.

✔ Your Mac may start up and run faster if you don't load unneeded extensions and control panels.

Back up first

If you don't have a backup and you don't have a set of Mac OS 8 install disks or the CD-ROM, DO NOT DELETE ANY FILES! I repeat: If you don't have a backup and a set of Mac OS 8 install disks or CD, DON'T TRASH ANYTHING.

That said, if you're faithful about making backups (you should be, as you've heard me harp about it enough times by now; read Appendix B again if you're still unclear), you can delete files with relative impunity. If you decide you miss them, restore them from your backup.

Beware if you only have one backup set of disks or cartridges. Your backup software may keep a *mirror image* of your hard disk on the backup media. In other words, when you delete a file from your hard disk, the backup software may delete it from the backup disk(s). Read your backup software manual carefully.

Install Mac OS: Restorer of lost items

Any System software file you delete can be restored if you have a set of Mac OS 8 install disks or the CD-ROM. The degree of difficulty you'll encounter (and the amount of time it will take you) depends on what you need to restore.

To reinstall any extensions or control panels you delete, just run Install Mac OS (see Appendix A) and reinstall anything and everything in one fell swoop.

Certain other Mac OS functions, such as Apple Remote Access, OpenDoc, Cyberdog, and others, can be installed individually. Click the Customize button in Install Mac OS and you'll see what's what.

I still want to know why I can't install just the Find File extension (or any other single extension or control panel) using the Custom Install option. Apple?

Anyway, that's all you need to know at this time. It's okay to trash any piece of Mac OS 8 as long as you have a set of Install disks (or the CD-ROM) so that you can reinstall it if you discover you need or want it.

Another thing to consider if you have a Zip, Jaz, SyQuest, or optical disk drive — perform a full install on a cartridge and set it aside for a rainy day. That way if you delete something and later want it back, you can just drag it over rather than performing a complete reinstallation.

Just a thought . . . Now let's move on and discover. . . .

What, Exactly, are Extensions and Control Panels?

Control Panels and Extensions appear first and second in the chapter because they make the most difference in reclaiming disk space and RAM. (I'll cover the rest of the System Folder later in the chapter.)

Extensions and control panels are a type of System software file with a special property: If they are not in the Control Panels or Extensions folder at startup, they do not load and/or will not function. (Or at least most won't. A few control panels can be used even if they aren't in the Control Panels folder at startup.)

Apple isn't the only one to make extensions and control panels. Many popular third-party programs, including famous names like After Dark, QuicKeys, and Now Utilities, are extensions or control panels.

Most extensions and control panels grab a certain amount of RAM when they load at startup. If you choose Apple menu➪About This Computer right now, you'll see how much RAM they're using by looking at the bar for your System software, which includes the RAM used by all loaded extensions and control panels.

Some control panels can be run from a floppy disk. In other words, if you're really tight on hard disk space, you can copy certain control panels, such as Color or Date & Time, to a floppy disk and open the copy on the floppy if you need to change color, date, or time. Alas, this feature is only available with a handful of control panels. The rest must be in the System Folder at startup or they won't work. When in doubt, try it out.

Disabling 'em all with the Shift key

You can disable all control panels and extensions by holding down the Shift key during startup until you see the "Extensions Disabled" message appear beneath the "Welcome to Mac OS" greeting. That's what I've done in Figure 14-1. So my naked System software uses 7MB of RAM, leaving me 88.5MB available for running applications (the Largest Unused Block in Figure 14-1).

Figure 14-1:
No extension or control panels loaded = 7MB used by my System Software.

Sharp-eyed readers will notice that there's half a megabyte of RAM missing in Figure 14-1 (96 – 7 = 89, not 88.5). That's the result of something called *memory fragmentation*. In simple terms, some programs don't release all the RAM they used when you quit them. There are two solutions: Restart your Mac, or buy so much RAM the little bits you lose to memory fragmentation won't bother you.

Having lots of RAM is way cool. I never get "not enough memory to open the program" messages any more — even with seven programs open at the same time.

Discriminating disabling with Extensions Manager

When I use the Extensions Manager control panel to turn on all the Mac OS 8 extensions and control panels (by choosing Mac OS 8.0 All from the Selected Set pop-up menu), the System software uses 10.8MB of RAM, leaving me less RAM for programs (the Largest Unused Block in Figure 14-2). Note that RAM used by System Software includes RAM grabbed at startup by optional stuff like QuickDraw 3D, OpenDoc, and so on.

Figure 14-2:
With all the
extensions
and control
panels
turned on,
the System
software
eats up
more RAM.

In the bad old days, disabling extensions and control panels was a messy affair that entailed moving them out of the Extensions or Control Panels folder manually and rebooting. It wasn't long before a wide variety of third-party extension/control panel managers appeared on the market. Prior to System 7.5, almost everyone I know used one.

Here's an example of why you might want to: You can reclaim a whopping 3 megs of RAM just by disabling the GXGraphics extension (which you probably don't need). That's what this chapter is about and why I feel it may be the most important part of this book.

In the rest of the chapter, when I say how much RAM you'll save by disabling an extension or control panel, I mean that's how much RAM you'll save by turning it off (that is, unchecking it) in the Extensions Manager control panel. (Of course, you'll also save that amount of RAM if you delete the file totally.)

The disk space measurement for each file is the size shown in list view in the Finder. The Power Macintosh 9500 I used had a 2-gigabyte hard disk. If you have a larger disk, the files may occupy slightly more space on your disk than the numbers shown in this chapter, due to something called file allocation blocks, which is complicated and not important.

In other words, your mileage may vary — and my disk-size figures are just estimates provided for your convenience. Or, in other, other words, many of the files that weigh 32K on my 2-gig drive will weigh 16K or less on hard disks smaller than mine because of that file allocation block thing you don't need to know about.

The same goes for my RAM measurements. Your mileage may vary slightly. I measured RAM usage with a wonderful shareware extension/control panel manager called Symbionts, of which I'm proud to be a registered owner. If you use other software to measure RAM usage, your numbers may be slightly higher or lower.

One final thing: I performed all the testing for this chapter using a freshly installed copy of Mac OS 8 and all its optional parts. If you have other files in your System Folder, they're not part of the Mac OS.

In your System Folder, you'll see several folders with "(disabled)" after their names, such as Control Panels (disabled) and Extensions (disabled). Leave them alone. They are used by the Extensions Manager to disable control panels and extensions by moving them into these folders. *Remember, if the control panel or extension isn't in the Control Panels or Extensions folder at startup, it doesn't load.*

Control Panels

These control panels were covered in depth in Chapter 12. If you don't understand the cryptic comments or side effects, try rereading that control panel's entry in Chapter 12.

Appearance

Disk Space: 228K
RAM Used: 0
Side effects if disabled or deleted: Loss of control of window color, system font and collapsing windows.
Comments: I'd keep it, especially until you've played with it enough to know how you'd like your Mac to look.

Apple Menu Options

Disk Space: 65K
RAM Used: 42K
Side effects if disabled or deleted: Loss of Apple menu submenus and recent item tracking.
Comments: I'd keep it. I love submenus and recent item tracking. Unless I were terribly RAM-constrained (using an 8MB or even a 16MB Mac), I would never even consider disabling it, much less deleting it.

AppleTalk

Disk Space: 260K
RAM Used: 0
Side effects if disabled or deleted: Possible loss of printing and network services (shared disks, e-mail, and so forth).
Comments: If you're on a network, you definitely need it. If you have a printer connected, you definitely need it. Because it uses no RAM, I'd say leave it alone unless you're horribly short of disk space, in which case you may trash it. (But trust me, you'll probably want it back soon for one reason or another.)

Auto Remounter (PowerBook)

Disk Space: 33K
RAM Used: 11K
Side effects if disabled or deleted: Loss of capability to automatically remount disks after sleep or shutdown.
Comments: You only need it if you have a PowerBook you connect to a network. Otherwise, turn it off in Extensions Manager or trash it.

ColorSync System Profile

Disk Space: 33K
RAM Used: 0
Side effects if disabled or deleted: Loss of capability to use ColorSync.
Comments: Get rid of it unless you use ColorSync on all your monitors, printers, and scanners.

Control Strip

Disk Space: 65K
RAM Used: 28K
Side effects if disabled or deleted: Loss of use of Control Strip and all its modules.
Comments: If you like and use Control Strip, keep it; if you hate Control Strip and never want to see it again, trash it.

To save another 200-plus kilobytes of disk space, also trash the Control Strip Modules folder in the System Folder while you're trashing the Control Strip control panel.

Date & Time

Disk Space: 98K
RAM Used: 9K
Side effects if disabled or deleted: Loss of capability to set Macintosh internal clock.
Comments: Keep it. If your hard disk is horribly crowded, this is one of the control panels that you can copy to a floppy disk and use, even if it wasn't in the Control Panels folder at startup.

Desktop Pictures

Disk Space: 98K
RAM Used: 14K
Side effects if disabled or deleted: Loss of capability to change desktop pattern and/or pictures.
Comments: Keep it; it's fun.

DialAssist

Disk Space: 32K
RAM Used: 0
Side effects if disabled or deleted: Loss of dialing assistance for Apple Remote Access.
Comments: Keep it if you use ARA; otherwise, feel free to dump it.

Editor Setup

Disk Space: 68K
RAM Used: 0
Side effects if disabled or deleted: Loss of ability to choose OpenDoc parts editors.
Comments: If you use OpenDoc (or Cyberdog), leave it alone. Otherwise, you don't need it.

Energy Saver

Disk Space: 228K
RAM Used: 0
Side effects if disabled or deleted: No automatic screen dimming and sleep (on Energy Star compliant models only).
Comments: If it works with your Mac and monitor and you like it, keep it. If not, trash it. But I warn you: Trashing it is not ecologically correct. See also "Energy Saver Extension" in the next section.

Extensions Manager

Disk Space: 195K
RAM Used: 0
Side effects if disabled or deleted: Loss of capability to enable and disable individual control panels and extensions.
Comments: You need it. Keep it.

File Sharing

Disk Space: 650K
RAM Used: 1K
Side effects if disabled or deleted: Loss of capability to turn file Sharing (and Program Linking) on or off.
Comments: You only need it if you use file sharing. If you never use file sharing, make sure it's turned off before you delete it.

General Controls

Disk Space: 95K
RAM Used: 14K
Side effects if disabled or deleted: Too numerous to mention.

Comments: Keep it. If 95K of hard disk space or 14K of RAM makes a difference to you, you've got bigger problems, and disabling or trashing the General Controls control panel isn't going to help you.

You can get along without General Controls, but you won't be able to change any of its settings without first putting it back in the Control Panels folder and restarting your Mac. It won't run if you try to launch it from a floppy; it has to be in the Control Panels folder when you start up, or it won't work.

Keyboard

Disk Space: 65K
RAM Used: 0
Side effects if disabled or deleted: Loss of capability to specify key repeat speed and rate or choose foreign-language keyboard layouts.
Comments: Keep it.

Launcher

Disk Space: 69K
RAM Used: 0
Side effects if disabled or deleted: Loss of Launcher window.
Comments: You've already heard what I think about Launcher (Chapter 6, if you've forgotten already). I trashed mine.

Location Manager

Disk Space: 325K
RAM Used: 0
Side effects if disabled or deleted: Loss of Location Manager functions on a PowerBook.
Comments: Delete it unless you use a PowerBook and want to create custom locations.

Mac OS Easy Open

Disk Space: 162K
RAM Used: 14K
Side effects if disabled or deleted: Loss of capability to configure Macintosh Easy Open (see Chapter 12).
Comments: Keep it.

MacLinkPlus Setup

Disk Space: 65K
RAM Used: 0
Side effects if disabled or deleted: Loss of ability to configure MacLinkPlus translators.
Comments: If you never deal with files from DOS or WinDoze computers, or never see messages that say "An application can't be found for this document," you don't need it. Still, I'd keep it if I were you.

Map

Disk Space: 65K
RAM Used: 0
Side effects if disabled or deleted: Loss of map.
Comments: Big deal. Trash it.

Memory

Disk Space: 65K
RAM Used: 0
Side effects if disabled or deleted: Too numerous (and awful) to mention (see Chapter 9 for details).
Comments: Do not delete!

Modem

Disk Space: 228K
RAM Used: 0
Side effects if disabled or deleted: Possible loss or disruption of modem services.
Comments: If you use a modem, keep it.

Monitors & Sound

Disk Space: 195K
RAM Used: 0
Side effects if disabled or deleted: Loss of capability to switch monitor color depths, alert sounds, and sound volume. Loss of additional capabilities if you have more than one monitor or a multisync monitor.
Comments: Keep it.

Mouse

Disk Space: 32K
RAM Used: 0
Side effects if disabled or deleted: Loss of capability to change mouse tracking or double-click speed.
Comments: Keep it.

Numbers

Disk Space: 33K
RAM Used: 0
Side effects if disabled or deleted: Loss of capability to change thousands of separators, decimal separators, and symbols for currency.
Comments: I've never used it.

OpenDoc Setup

Disk Space: 65K
RAM Used: 0
Side effects if disabled or deleted: Loss of control over starting and stopping OpenDoc and allocating memory to it.
Comments: If you don't plan to use OpenDoc (or Cyberdog, which requires it) you can trash the control panel. You can also move it to a floppy, if you like.

PC Exchange

Disk Space: 358K
RAM Used: 18K
Side effects if disabled or deleted: Loss of capability to mount PC-formatted (DOS-formatted) floppy disks.
Comments: If you never get or use DOS disks, you can safely delete it. If you occasionally have to deal with DOS disks, disable it with Extensions Manager and save 18K of RAM.

PPP

Disk Space: 488K
RAM Used: 0
Side effects if disabled or deleted: Loss of ability to connect to Internet.
Comments: If you use the Internet, keep it; if you don't, you don't need it.

If you're on a network but don't use the Internet, check with your network administrator before trashing this (or any other) piece of System software.

QuickTime Settings

Disk Space: 33K
RAM Used: 0
Side effects if disabled or deleted: Loss of AutoPlay features for CDs and CD-ROMs and some MIDI (Musical Instrument Digital Interface) configuration options.
Comments: Your call. If you need it, you probably know it.

Remote Access Setup

Disk Space: 65K
RAM Used: 8K
Side effects if disabled or deleted: Loss of ability to access this Mac remotely.
Comments: Like the old doctor joke, if you want to make remote connections to this Mac, don't trash it. Conversely, if you never dial in to this computer, trash that puppy.

Speech

Disk Space: 130K
RAM Used: 27K
Side effects if disabled or deleted: Loss of ability to use Talking Alerts and Text-to-Voice.
Comments: Your call. It does use a little RAM, and its 3-megabyte Voices folder, which you'll find in the Extensions folder, takes up a bit of disk space. I think the voices are cute and I am keeping them.

Startup Disk

Disk Space: 33K
RAM Used: 0
Side effects if disabled or deleted: Loss of capability to choose a startup disk if more than one disk with a System Folder is connected at startup.
Comments: You may need it someday, especially if you're going to add an additional storage device — external hard disk, SyQuest, Zip, Jaz, or magneto-optical disk drive, or whatever. I say keep it.

TCP/IP

Disk Space: 325K
RAM Used: 0
Side effects if disabled or deleted: Loss of ability to connect to Internet.
Comments: If you use the Internet, keep it; if you don't, you don't need it.

If you're on a network but don't use the Internet, check with your network administrator before trashing this (or any other) piece of System software.

Text

Disk Space: 33K
RAM Used: 0
Side effects if disabled or deleted: Loss of capability to choose Text Behaviors.
Comments: If you only run the American version of Mac OS 8, you'll probably never need it.

Users & Groups

Disk Space: 780K
RAM Used: 1K
Side effects if disabled or deleted: Loss of capability to create users and groups for file sharing.
Comments: If you don't use file sharing, you don't need it.

Web Sharing

Disk Space: 195K
RAM Used: 0
Side effects if disabled or deleted: Loss of capability to use your Mac as a personal Web server.
Comments: If your Mac isn't connected to the Internet full-time, you can't use Web Sharing, so you might as well delete it.

Control panels by RAM used

Table 14-1 is a quick-reference chart of the control panels in descending order of RAM usage.

Table 14-1	Control Panel RAM Usage
Control Panel	*RAM Used*
Apple Menu Options	43K
Speech	29K
Control Strip	28K
PC Exchange	19K
Desktop Pictures	14K
Mac OS Easy Open	14K
General Controls	14K
AutoRemounter	10K
Date & Time	9K
Remote Access Setup	8K
Users & Groups	1K
File Sharing	1K

The rest of the items in your Control Panels folder use no RAM, even if they're in the Control Panels folder at startup.

Control panels by disk space used

To see a list of items in your Control Panels folder in descending order of size, first use the View➪Views Options to turn on Calculate Folder Sizes; then choose View➪As List and View➪Sort List➪by Size. The Control Panels folder window now displays its contents in descending size order.

Extensions

There are three main types of extensions among the approximately 105 items in your Extensions folder:

- ✔ System extensions
- ✔ Chooser extensions
- ✔ Apple Guide documents

Apple Guide documents use no RAM, nor do most Chooser extensions. System extensions, on the other hand, almost always grab a bit of RAM at startup. There are also a couple of other kinds of files in the Extensions folder; I'll talk about them after I finish with the big three.

To see these items by type, open the Extensions folder and then choose View➪As List and then choose View➪Sort List➪by Kind. If the View by Kind option isn't available, choose View➪View Options and check Kind under the Show Column heading.

Let's start with the most important extensions, the ones that can save you lots of precious RAM if you disable or delete them (if, of course, you don't need them). I'm talking about your System extensions.

System extensions

EM Extension

Disk Space: 33K
RAM Used: 0
Side effects if disabled or deleted: Loss of use of Extensions Manager control panel.
Comments: Keep it.

Why is EM Extension first in an alphabetical list? Because Apple ships it with a space before the E so that it is first in alphabetical lists. Extensions load alphabetically, and because this is the extension that gives Extensions Manager its powers, it must load before the other extensions in order to turn them on or off.

Hold down the spacebar just after you power up your Mac to use Extensions Manager *before* other extensions begin to load.

Apple Appearance Extension

Disk Space: 748K
RAM Used: 318K
Side effects if disabled or deleted: Loss of ability to change window colors, system fonts, and so on.
Comments: Keep it until you're absolutely sure that you're satisfied with the way your desktop looks.

Apple CD-ROM

Disk Space: 98K
RAM Used: 40K
Side effects if disabled or deleted: Loss of use of CD-ROM drives.
Comments: If you have a CD-ROM drive, keep it.

Apple Color SW Pro CMM (QuickDraw GX only)

Disk Space: 65K
RAM Used: 0
Side effects if disabled or deleted: Possible loss of some color printing abilities under QuickDraw GX.
Comments: If you use QuickDraw GX, you need it; if not, you don't.

Apple Guide

Disk Space: 878K
RAM Used: 27K
Side effects if disabled or deleted: Loss of Apple Guide (interactive help).
Comments: Tough call. It uses a great deal of disk space (if you count all its Guide files) and a significant amount of RAM, but I think it's worth keeping. Delete or disable it only if you must.

Apple Photo Access

Disk Space: 164K
RAM Used: 0
Side effects if disabled or deleted: Loss of capability to open PhotoCD files.
Comments: PhotoCD is the Kodak format for high-resolution image storage. PhotoCD files mostly come on CD-ROM disks. If you're likely to encounter PhotoCD files, keep it. If you don't have a CD-ROM drive, you definitely don't need it.

Apple QD3D HW Driver

Disk Space: 65K
RAM Used: 0
Side effects if disabled or deleted: Loss of access to QuickDraw 3D-capable hardware.
Comments: If you use QuickDraw 3D-capable hardware, keep it. If not, delete it.

AppleScript

Disk Space: 488K
RAM Used: 40K
Side effects if disabled or deleted: Loss of use of AppleScript scripts and
Script Editor program.
Comments: You read Chapter 13, right? You know whether you want to keep
AppleScript. (I would.)

ATI Graphics Accelerator

Disk Space: 98K
RAM Used: 150K
Side effects if disabled or deleted: Loss of use of ATI-accelerated video,
found in some newer Macs.
Comments: If you don't have ATI video, trash it.

Audio CD Access

Disk Space: 33K
RAM Used: 0
Side effects if disabled or deleted: Loss of capability to play audio CDs
(that is, your Pearl Jam and Elvis Costello CDs, or at least *my* Pearl Jam and
Elvis CDs).
Comments: If you don't have a CD-ROM drive, you don't need it. If you have
a CD-ROM drive, you should probably keep it around, just in case.

Color Picker

Disk Space: 520K
RAM Used: 25K
Side effects if disabled or deleted: Loss of the new Apple Color Picker.
Comments: This whole shebang refers to which Color Picker you see in
programs that use a color picker to choose among colors (most graphics
programs).

The new Color Picker is, in my humble opinion, prettier than the old one and
probably easier to use. Trashing this extensions usually has little conse-
quence, but if you use color graphics programs of any sort, you might want
to keep it around.

ColorSync

Disk Space: 618K
RAM Used: 199K
Side effects if disabled or deleted: Loss of use of ColorSync (Apple's color
matching system for monitors, printing devices, and scanners).
Comments: You probably don't need it unless you scan or print color
images. And it uses a lot of RAM and disk space for something most people
have no need for.

Contextual Menu Selection

Disk Space: 98K
RAM Used: 173K
Side effects if disabled or deleted: Loss of support for contextual menus in applications.
Comments: Keep it. Contextual menus are a cool new feature and are available in some applications.

Desktop Printer Spooler

Disk Space: 65K
RAM Used: 0
Side effects if disabled or deleted: Loss of desktop printer support.
Comments: Lets you drag and drop documents onto desktop printer icons, and to change printers without opening the Chooser. Keep it.

Energy Saver Extension

Disk Space: 95K
RAM Used: 64K
Side effects if disabled or deleted: No automatic screen dimming and sleep (on Energy Star compliant models only).
Comments: If it works with your Mac and monitor and you like it, keep it. If not, trash it.

File Sharing Extension

Disk Space: 195K
RAM Used: 4K
Side effects if disabled or deleted: Loss of file-sharing capability.
Comments: If you don't use file sharing, you can safely delete it.

Foreign File Access

Disk Space: 65K
RAM Used: 128K
Side effects if disabled or deleted: Loss of capability to mount some CD-ROM disks.
Comments: If you have a CD-ROM drive, you need it; if you don't, you don't.

GXGraphics

Disk Space: 2.2MB
RAM Used: 3MB
Side effects if disabled or deleted: Loss of QuickDraw GX support.
Comments: If you don't use QuickDraw GX, you can safely delete it. It's a total memory-hog.

High Sierra File Access

Disk Space: 33K
RAM Used: 0
Side effects if disabled or deleted: Loss of capability to mount some CD-ROM disks.
Comments: If you have a CD-ROM drive, you need it; if you don't, you don't.

Internet Config Extension

Disk Space: 32K
RAM Used: 0
Side effects if disabled or deleted: Internet configuration options won't be shared among applications.
Comments: Cyberdog and other Internet programs may not work properly without it. If you use the Internet, keep it.

ISO 9660 File Access

Disk Space: 33K
RAM Used: 0
Side effects if disabled or deleted: Loss of capability to mount some CD-ROM disks.
Comments: If you have a CD-ROM drive, you need it; if you don't, you don't. (I'm sorry if I sound like a broken record, but that's my advice.)

MacinTalk 3 and MacinTalk Pro

Disk Space: 348K and 845K, respectively
RAM Used: 0
Side effects if disabled or deleted: Loss of speech capabilities; see Speech control panel.
Comments: If you want your Mac to talk to you, keep them; if not, don't. Don't forget to also trash the Voices folder (see next section), Speech control panel (previous section), and Speech Manager extension if you decide to trash these two.

MacLinkPlus for Easy Open

Disk Space: 293K
RAM Used: 0
Side effects if disabled or deleted: Loss of automatic substitution of applications. You may experience the dreaded "An application can't be found for this document" error.
Comments: Keep it.

Printer Share

Disk Space: 98K
RAM Used: 12K
Side effects if disabled or deleted: Loss of capability to share certain devices, such as plotters, that could not be shared previously. Also, loss of the capability to password-protect color printers that use expensive printing materials.
Comments: If you're on a network, ask your network administrator before deleting or disabling.

PrinterShare GX

Disk Space: 63K
RAM Used: 0
Side effects if disabled or deleted: Loss of capability to share certain devices such as plotters that could not be shared previously. Also, loss of the capability to password-protect color printers that use expensive printing materials.
Comments: Only required if you're using QuickDraw GX. Check with your network administrator before deleting or disabling it, though.

QuickDraw 3D

Disk Space: 1.4MB
RAM Used: 0
Side effects if disabled or deleted: Loss of use of QuickDraw 3D.
Comments: You probably installed QuickDraw 3D for a reason. Therefore, keep it. Some game you like probably needs it.

QuickTime, QuickTime MPEG Extension, QuickTime Musical Instruments, and QuickTime PowerPlug (PowerPC only)

Disk Space: 1.3MB, 293K, 488K, and 943K, respectively
RAM Used: Less than 40K
Side effects if disabled or deleted: Loss of capability to play QuickTime movies or use QuickTime applications.
Comments: I leave mine enabled all the time, but I probably have more stuff that requires QuickTime than you do. If you use QuickTime, even occasionally, leave these items alone.

QuickTime VR

Disk Space: 585K
RAM Used: 32K
Side effects if disabled or deleted: Loss of support for QuickTime VR.
Comments: QuickTime VR is a cool 3D format used on some Web sites and games. Delete it if you don't go to multimedia sites and if you're sure that you don't have any games that need it.

Remote Only

Disk Space: 33K
RAM Used: 0
Side effects if disabled or deleted: Can't access Mac from remote computer(s).
Comments: Keep it if you use Remote Access; dump it if you don't.

Serial (Built-In)

Disk Space: 98K
RAM Used: 0
Side effects if disabled or deleted: Loss of support for serial ports.
Comments: If you use your serial ports (for a printer, modem or network connection), keep it.

Shared Library Manager and Shared Library Manager PPC

Disk Space: 195K and 228K, respectively
RAM Used: 0
Side effects if disabled or deleted: Many programs and utilities will cease to function.
Comments: You need these. Don't delete them.

Speech Manager

Disk Space: 65K
RAM Used: 11K
Side effects if disabled or deleted: No speech. See also MacinTalk extensions, Speech control panel, and Voices folder.
Comments: Keep it if you want your Mac to speak.

SystemAV

Disk Space: 260K
RAM Used: 0
Side effects if disabled or deleted: Monitors & Sound control panel quits working.
Comments: Don't delete it. Keep it.

~AppleVision

Disk Space: 488K
RAM Used: 0
Side effects if disabled or deleted: Only required if you have an AppleVision monitor. If so, you need it to use the Monitors & Sound control panel.
Comments: If you don't have an AppleVision monitor, by all means dump this sucker. (By the way, in case you were wondering, the little tilde at the start of this extension's name forces it to the bottom of this alphabetical list.)

Chooser extensions

Chooser extensions are extensions that appear in the Chooser desk accessory when you open it. AppleShare is one of them; all the others are *printer drivers,* the software that your Mac requires to talk to a printer.

AppleShare

Disk Space: 293K
RAM Used: 195K
Side effects if disabled or deleted: Loss of use of file sharing.
Comments: If you use file sharing, you need it; if you don't, you don't.

Printer Drivers

The Installer puts several printer drivers into your Extensions folder for you: Color SW 1500, Color SW 2500, Color SW Pro, ImageWriter, LaserWriter 300/LS, LaserWriter 8 and StyleWriter.

Disk Space: Between 63K and 845K each
RAM Used: 0
Side effects if disabled or deleted: None, as long as you leave the driver for *your* printer(s) — that is, the printer(s) that you use — in the Extensions folder.
Comments: You only need the driver or drivers that match the printer(s) you use. If you never use any color printer, for example, get rid of every Chooser extension with the word *color* in its name. If you never use an ImageWriter, get rid of all the ImageWriter Chooser extensions. And so on.

Apple Guide documents

There may be as many as ten Apple Guide documents in the Extensions folder.

Disk Space: 63K to 1.9MB
RAM Used: 0
Side effects if disabled or deleted: Loss of use of Apple Guide interactive help.
Comments: If you don't use Apple Guide, you can safely delete all of the Guide files. But I'd leave them alone. You never know when you'll need help, and if you delete these files, help won't be available when you need it.

Other items in the Extensions folder

Desktop PrintMonitor

Disk Space: 130K
RAM Used: 0
Side effects if disabled or deleted: Loss of capability to print in background.
Comments: Keep it.

Desktop PrintMonitor is not an extension, although it lives in the Extensions folder. It is an application. Thus, it only uses RAM when background printing is taking place.

If you have problems with background printing, try increasing Desktop PrintMonitor's preferred memory size (in its Get Info window).

Ethernet (Built-In)

Disk Space: 95K
RAM Used: 0
Side effects if disabled or deleted: Can't use Ethernet.
Comments: If you're not on an Ethernet network, you don't need it.

OpenTptAppleTalkLib, OpenTptInternetLib, OpenTptModem, OpenTpt Remote Access, OpenTpt Serial Arbitrator, and OpenTransportLib

Disk Space: about 800K all together
RAM Used: about 200K
Side effects if disabled or deleted: Loss of ability to use Internet and networking features.
Comments: Leave these alone if you use a network or the Internet. Even if you don't, you may someday need these things. Disable them in Extensions Manager if you must, but leave them on your hard disk if you can.

VT102 Tool

Disk Space: 162K
RAM Used: 0
Side effects if disabled or deleted: Loss of ability to emulate VT102 terminal over modem.
Comments: Keep it.

AppleScriptLib and SOMobjects for Mac OS

Disk Space: about 250K between them
RAM Used: 67K
Side effects if disabled or deleted: Lots of stuff will stop working, including Cyberdog and any other OpenDoc programs.
Comments: If you use OpenDoc, you need both of these.

File Sharing Library

Disk Space: 130K
RAM Used: 0
Side effects if disabled or deleted: Loss of file sharing capability.
Comments: If you use file sharing, keep it. Otherwise, delete it.

Internet Access

Disk Space: 390K
RAM Used: 0
Side effects if disabled or deleted: Loss of Internet capability.
Comments: If you use any Internet applications, keep it around.

Link Tool Manager and Modem Link Tool

Disk Space: 98K and 65K, respectively
RAM Used: 0
Side effects if disabled or deleted: Apple Remote Access won't work.
Comments: Keep these if you use Apple Remote Access. Otherwise, delete them.

Memory Manager

Disk Space: 65K
RAM Used: 0
Side effects if disabled or deleted: Loss of OpenDoc support.
Comments: Keep it. If you use OpenDoc (or Cyberdog, which requires OpenDoc), keep it. Otherwise, you can delete it.

PrintingLib

Disk Space: 715K
RAM Used: 0
Side effects if disabled or deleted: Printing won't happen.
Comments: You need it for printing; don't delete it.

QuickDraw 3D, QuickDraw 3D IR, QuickDraw 3D RAVE, and QuickDraw 3D Viewer

Disk Space: 1.4MB, 293K, 325K, and 225K, respectively
RAM Used: 0
Side effects if disabled or deleted: QuickDraw 3D won't work.
Comments: If you use QuickDraw 3D, keep 'em; if not, junk 'em.

Serial Port Arbitrator, Open Tpt AppleTalk Library, Open Tpt Internet Library, Open Transport Library, OpenTpt Modem, and OpenTpt Remote Access

Disk Space: a couple of megabytes
RAM Used: 225K
Side effects if disabled or deleted: Loss of Internet or network services.
Comments: If any of these items are in your System Folder, you need them.

Folders in the Extensions folder

There are several folders in the System Folder; you may or may not need them or their contents.

Global Guide Files

This folder contains almost a megabyte of Apple Guide files for optional programs like Apple Audio, Apple Button, Apple Draw, Apple Image Viewer, OpenDoc Guide, and Apple 3DMF Viewer. Feel free to trash any that you don't need.

Location Manager Modules

This folder contains 260K of modules for the Location Manager, used with PowerBooks to customize network and Internet connections. Trash them if you don't have a PowerBook.

Modem Scripts

This folder contains over 3MB of modem stuff, most of which you don't need. You can trash all the scripts except for the one whose name matches your modem if you need the disk space.

MRJ Libraries

This folder contains over 2.6MB of Java-related stuff. You'll need it if you use MRJ (Macintosh Runtime for Java) to view Java-enabled Internet sites. Otherwise, you can trash it.

Multiprocessing

You don't need this folder or its contents unless your Mac has multiple processors (few do, at least so far).

OpenDoc Libraries

This folder contains files used by OpenDoc. If you use OpenDoc (or Cyberdog), leave it alone.

Printer Descriptions

This folder in your Extensions folder contains printer description files for 32 Apple printers. They require from 65K to 130K of disk space and use no RAM. You can delete all but the one (or ones) that match your printer or printers.

Scripting Additions

This one contains components of AppleScript. Removing any of the files in this folder may cause AppleScript to behave erratically. If you use AppleScript, leave this folder alone. If you don't use AppleScript and never plan to, you can delete it.

Voices

This 3MB folder contains the voices used by Speech and MacinTalk. If you don't need the voices, you don't need the folder. And if you only use a couple of voices, delete the ones that you don't use.

Extensions by RAM used

Table 14-2 is a quick-reference chart of the extensions, sorted in descending order by RAM usage.

Table 14-2	Extension RAM Usage
Extension	*RAM Used*
GXGraphics	3MB
Appearance Extension	318K
OpenTransportLib	227K
ColorSync	198K
AppleShare	195K
Contextual Menu Extension	173K
ATI Graphics Accelerator	150K
Foreign File Access	127K
SOMobjects for Mac OS	67K
Energy Saver Extension	64K
Apple CD-ROM	40K
AppleScript	40K

Extension	RAM Used
QuickTime	32K
QuickTime VR	32K
Apple Guide	27K
Color Picker	25K
Printer Share	12K
Speech Manager	11K
OpenTptAppleTalkLib	5K
File Sharing Extension	4K
QuickTime PowerPlay	1K
QuickTime MPEG Extension	6K

All other extensions use 5K or less of RAM.

Extensions by disk space used

To see a list of items in your Extensions folder in descending order of size, first use the View⇨Views Options to turn on Calculate Folder Sizes; then choose View⇨As List and View⇨Sort List⇨by Size. The Extensions folder window now displays its contents in descending size order.

The Rest of the Stuff in Your System Folder

The installer installed more than just control panels and extensions. Here's what the rest of it does:

Apple Menu Items

The Apple Menu Items folder, covered extensively in Chapter 4, contains some folders, some desk accessories, and some applications.

The items in your Apple Menu Items folder only use RAM after you open them. So don't get rid of them to save RAM. If you're really short on disk space, use the old "View as list, sort by size" trick to find out how much each Apple Menu Item uses.

The difference between applications and desk accessories

I promised back in Chapter 4 that I'd explain the difference between an application and a desk accessory (DA) here in Chapter 14. Being a man of my word, here goes:

Desk accessories are a throwback to System 4 and earlier, when there was no multitasking, and there was no way to run more than one program at a time. Desk accessories were mini-programs that could be used even while other programs were open.

These days, now that opening multiple programs is the norm, desk accessories are the same as other programs — with three little differences:

✔ In list view, under the Kind category, desk accessories are listed as desk accessories (duh), not applications.

✔ You can't change a desk accessory's Minimum or Preferred Memory Requirements.

✔ Every desk accessory uses 20K of RAM (in About This Computer).

For all intents and purposes, a desk accessory is the same as an application program.

The only one that's an easy call is Jigsaw Puzzle, which is totally useless. (Wife Lisa chimes in: "Don't tell them that! I like the Mac jigsaw puzzle — the kids can't hide the pieces.") The other items are all useful in some way, and I'd recommend keeping them around.

Clipboard

Disk Space: Varies
RAM Used: 0
Side effects if disabled or deleted: Loss of Clipboard contents at the moment of deletion.
Comments: This file is like a chameleon's tail — it regenerates if it's damaged or destroyed. So don't bother deleting it, it'll just grow back. Besides, why would you want to?

Control Strip Modules

Disk Space: 325K, more or less
RAM Used: 0
Side effects if disabled or deleted: Loss of use of module if it's not in this folder.
Comments: Don't delete it if you use Control Strip. Feel free to delete individual modules you don't use if you feel like it.

Claris

Contains files used by Claris Emailer Lite. If you don't use Emailer Lite to read e-mail you can delete it, but if you do, and/or if you own any other Claris software, like ClarisWorks, FileMaker Pro, or Claris Organizer, leave the folder alone.

DataViz

Contains all your important file translation stuff. Don't delete it if you use Macintosh Easy Open or MacLinkPlus.

Editors

Contains the editors you need for use with OpenDoc. If you use OpenDoc, leave this folder alone.

Finder

Disk Space: 3.4MB
RAM Used: Not applicable
Side effects if disabled or deleted: Loss of use of Mac.
Comments: Don't even think about it. Your Mac won't boot without a Finder.

Fonts

Contains your fonts; leave it be.

Launcher Items

Contains the items that show up in Launcher; you need it if you use Launcher. So if you use Launcher, leave this folder alone. If you don't, feel free to trash it.

MacTCP DNR

Contains information used by TCP/IP. You'll need it if you use the Internet. If you're not planning to log on, you can delete it.

Preferences

The Preferences folder is where all programs, extensions, control panels, and desk accessories store their preferences files. These files store information that the program (or extension, control panel, or desk accessory) needs to remember between uses.

Most preferences files regenerate themselves when deleted, so trashing them is usually a waste of time.

When you get rid of a program, extension, control panel, or desk accessory, there's a good chance that it has left behind a preferences file in the Preferences folder. It's not a bad idea to go into your Preferences folder every so often and trash any files that appear to belong to software no longer on your hard disk.

For example, if you decide that you never want to use the Launcher control panel again, you can delete the Launcher Preferences file. Though Launcher Preferences only uses a few K of disk space, after a while, your Preferences folder may become quite crowded with preferences files that belong to software you don't even have on your hard disk any longer.

Ack! I just looked at the Preferences folder on my main Mac and discovered almost 200 preferences files, at least half from programs that I no longer have or use.

I'll be right back — I'm going to practice what I preach and clean it up by trashing unneeded and unwanted prefs files.

I'm back. While I was doing my spring cleaning, I remembered another good tip having to do with preferences files: Trashing a program's preferences file can sometimes fix problems with the program itself.

If you have a program, extension, control panel, or desk accessory that's acting strange in any way — crashing, freezing, quitting unexpectedly — look in the Preferences folder and see if it's got a preferences file. If it does, try deleting it. Then restart your Mac.

This tip doesn't always work, but it's worth a try if a program that used to work starts acting funky.

By the way, some programs store all your customized settings (key combinations, macros, window positions, and so on) in their preferences files. If you delete these files, you may have to reset some of your customized settings in these programs. In most cases, that's no big deal, but in the case of, say, my Microsoft Word preferences, I'd have to spend about three hours recustomizing all my menus and keyboard shortcuts. Not fun. In fact, I keep a backup copy of my Word prefs on a floppy just in case the file gets corrupted or somebody comes along and changes things when I'm not around.

Scrapbook File

Disk Space: Varies
RAM Used: 0
Side effects if disabled or deleted: Loss of contents of Scrapbook.
Comments: If you don't use Scrapbook, you can delete it. But if you have anything you care about in the Scrapbook, you'll lose it when you trash this file.

Scripting Additions

Contains files used by AppleScript. If you don't intend to use AppleScript, it's safe to trash this folder.

Shared Libraries

This folder is empty (and therefore harmless) when you install Mac OS 8 for the first time. Files used by the many shared library extensions live here. Leave the folder alone.

System

Disk Space: 4.4MB
RAM Used: Not applicable
Side effects if disabled or deleted: Loss of use of Mac.
Comments: Don't even think of it. Your Mac won't boot if this file isn't in the System Folder.

Chapter 15

Internet-Working

● ●

In This Chapter

▶ An overview of the Internet

▶ The Internet Setup Assistant

▶ Cyberdog

▶ Surfing with Netscape and Company

● ●

*T*he Internet, sometimes referred to as the Information Superhighway, is a giant worldwide network of computers. With an Internet connection, you can view text and graphics on your computer, even if the text and graphics are sitting on a computer in Tokyo. The Internet enables you to send and retrieve messages and computer files to and from almost anywhere in the world — in milliseconds. Simply put, the Internet connects your Mac to a wealth of information residing on computers around the world.

Internet Overview (Brief)

The Internet, which is really nothing more than a giant conglomeration of connected computers, offers many kinds of services. This chapter covers the top three: World Wide Web, FTP (file transfer protocol), and electronic mail.

Other services offered on the Internet include live online chatting, bulletin board discussions called newsgroups, and video conferencing. After you've got your connection set up (something I cover in a moment), I urge you to check out these nifty features. Unfortunately, while this is way-interesting stuff, it's also beyond the purview, so that's all I'm going to say about them.

The most interesting part of the Internet, at least in my humble opinion, is the World Wide Web, the part of the Internet that lets you *surf* to *Web sites* and view them on your computer with software called a *browser*.

Mac OS 8 offers built-in Internet connectivity right out of the box. While most previous versions provided some of the plumbing, in the form of MacTCP, it was still up to you to assemble appropriate programs — browsers, PPP client (you don't need to know what that means yet, but you will in a moment), FTP client, e-mail program, and so on — on your own. Mac OS 8 comes with its own PPP client and Cyberdog, a pretty nifty little piece of software (actually, a collection of pieces of software; see the sidebar "What's Open, Doc?" for details) that allows you to browse the World Wide Web, send and receive electronic mail, download remote files via File Transfer Protocol, and more.

Because Mac users always want a choice, Mac OS 8 also has a few other Internet tricks up its sleeve: copies of Netscape Navigator, Claris Emailer, and a cool piece of software called Internet Setup Assistant to help you get and configure an account with an Internet Service Provider. You can use either Cyberdog or Navigator to cruise the Internet. I'll tell you a little bit about both, and you can decide for yourself, once you've spent some quality time with each. Hey, you can use both if you like!

But before I can talk about Cyberdog or Navigator, I must first discuss the underlying technology — Open Transport, OpenDoc (no relation), PPP, and TCP/IP — and then help you configure your Internet connection. When all that is done, you can play with Cyberdog or Navigator to your heart's content.

So with no further ado, let's get your Internet connection set up so that you can play with the dog.

What's Open, Doc?
(or, Everything you need to know about OpenDoc in one page or less)

OpenDoc is Apple's plug-in software architecture. OpenDoc uses software components — called parts — that can be dragged and dropped into documents created by any OpenDoc-aware application. You can combine parts from different Mac OS software developers to add tables, graphs, outlines, and even live Internet resources into your documents. Because OpenDoc is a cross-platform technology, documents created with OpenDoc can work across different computer platforms, including Mac OS, Windows, UNIX, and OS/2.

Unfortunately, Apple has shelved further OpenDoc development, so it's unlikely that third parties will develop parts to support it.

Installing OpenDoc adds the following stuff to your Power PC computer (note that you can only install OpenDoc on Mac OS systems with PowerPC processors):

✔ OpenDoc system software (in the Extensions folder)

✔ The Stationery folder (at the root level of your hard disk)

When you install an OpenDoc part, a stationery file is placed in the Stationery folder. You can either double-click the Stationery icon to create a new document or drag the stationery into another document to add functionality to any OpenDoc-aware application or document.

When you install OpenDoc parts, the part editors are placed in the Editors folder. Editors are like miniapplications that handle different types of data, such as text, graphics, or Internet information. When an editor is installed, it works something like a system extension: Its functionality is available, but you don't open or use the editor itself. To use an editor, you need to locate the editor's stationery (in the Stationery folder on the root level of your hard drive).

To get OpenDoc parts, contact your favorite application developers to find out if they support OpenDoc, or visit Apple's OpenDoc Web site at http://opendoc.apple.com.

Getting Set Up for Surfing

If you're a typical home user, there are three things you need to surf the Internet:

✔ A modem

✔ An account with an ISP (Internet service provider)

✔ Cyberdog, Apple Internet Access software, Open Transport PPP, and OpenDoc installed on your Mac

If you use your Mac in an office setting, you may use something called a net modem instead of a regular modem, or you may have an altogether different (and probably much faster) way of connecting to the Internet: ISDN or T1 lines. Your network administrator (the person you run to when something goes wrong with your computer) is going to have to set up your Mac if you connect to the Internet using something other than a modem.

It starts with the modem

A *modem* is a small, inexpensive device that turns data (that is, computer files) into sounds and then squirts them across phone lines. At the other end, another modem receives these sounds and turns them back into data (that is, your files).

There are two things to know if you're going out to buy a modem.

✔ Make sure it runs at 28.8 Kbps or higher, or you'll be very unhappy with the speed at which you surf.

✔ Make sure it includes a Mac cable. WinDoze computers require a different kind of modem cable, so be sure to ask.

Now plug a phone line into the modem and plug the modem cable into the modem port on the back of your Mac. It's the one with the little phone icon next to it.

That's it. Now let's set up an account with an ISP.

Your Internet service provider and you

Now that you have a modem, you need to select a company to provide you with access to the Internet. It's kind of like choosing a long-distance company — prices and services offered vary, often from minute to minute.

The going rate for unlimited access to the Internet is $19.95 per month. If your service provider asks for considerably more than that, find out why.

Anyway, first select a provider. Several national online services that you've probably heard of provide Internet access. They include CompuServe, America Online, and Prodigy. There are also pure Internet service companies like Earthlink and Netcom. AT&T and perhaps even your cable company are in the Internet business, so shop around for the deal that works best for you.

Mac OS 8's Internet Setup Assistant can even help you choose an ISP from a list of national companies. The advantage of this method, if you're looking for a new ISP account, is that the software configures your whole setup automatically. The drawback is that you only have a few companies to choose from. Let's give it a try, shall we?

Choosing an ISP with Internet Setup Assistant

You need to install two bundles of software to get connected to the Net for the first time. The first is Open Transport PPP. Basically, this is the software that dials the phone and makes your connection to the Internet. Next, you'll need to install Internet Access.

Once you've installed the Internet Access portion of Mac OS 8, you'll find the Internet Setup Assistant in the Internet folder on your hard disk. It will take you through the process of choosing an ISP and getting your account set up. You can also use it to configure or modify an existing account. We'll talk about that a bit later. For now, let's concentrate on choosing an ISP.

The Internet Setup Assistant consists of a series of screens. You answer questions about yourself and your modem, then choose an ISP from a list prepared by Apple and Netscape. Of course, you don't have to choose one of these ISPs, but learning about their pricing and services will help you compare them to other ISPs you might be considering.

1. Click the Register button on the first Internet Setup Assistant screen (see Figure 15-1).

2. After a few moments, another Internet Setup Assistant screen appears, with more information about the process of choosing an ISP. Click the right arrow at the bottom of the screen to move to the next one.

3. Enter your name and phone number and move to the next screen.

4. Choose your modem from the list and move to the next screen.

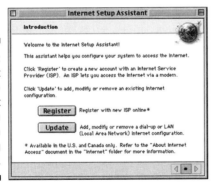

Figure 15-1:
The Internet
Setup
Assistant
walks you
through
picking
an ISP.

5. Enter any dialing prefixes (like 9, to get an outside line) that you'll need to make a toll-free phone call. Click Go Ahead when you're ready. Oh, and make sure your modem is connected and turned on.

When you click Go Ahead, Netscape Navigator (which was installed when you installed Internet Access software) launches, and the Internet Setup Assistant dials up Netscape's ISP server. Navigator presents a page listing at least three national ISPs for you to choose from.

6. Click one of the ISP logos. Soon you will see a page that looks very much like Figure 15-2. It describes the ISP's services, prices, tech support hours, and more.

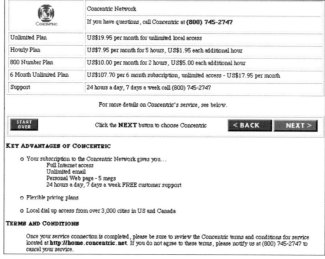

Figure 15-2: You'll find almost everything you might want to know about the ISPs on Netscape's site on this page.

	Concentric Network
	If you have questions, call Concentric at **(800) 745-2747**
Unlimited Plan	US$19.95 per month for unlimited local access
Hourly Plan	US$7.95 per month for 5 hours, US$1.95 each additional hour
800 Number Plan	US$10.00 per month for 2 hours, US$5.00 each additional hour
6 Month Unlimited Plan	US$107.70 per 6 month subscription, unlimited access - US$17.95 per month
Support	24 hours a day, 7 days a week call (800) 745-2747

For more details on Concentric's service, see below.

START OVER — Click the **NEXT** button to choose Concentric — < BACK   NEXT >

KEY ADVANTAGES OF CONCENTRIC

o Your subscription to the Concentric Network gives you...
   Full Internet access
   Unlimited email
   Personal Web page - 5 megs
   24 hours a day, 7 days a week FREE customer support

o Flexible pricing plans

o Local dial up access from over 3,000 cities in US and Canada

TERMS AND CONDITIONS

Once your service connection is completed, please be sure to review the Concentric terms and conditions for service located at **http://home.concentric.net**. If you do not agree to these terms, please notify us at (800) 745-2747 to cancel your service.

From the ISP page, you can start the process of getting signed up for an Internet account. You can also go back to the main ISP page by clicking the Back button.

The best way to compare ISPs is to look at their features and prices side-by-side. Instead of choosing one right now, print out the page of info you're reading, and do the same for each featured ISP. Then pick the company you like best and go back to the ISP page on the Web.

Signing up

Assuming that you decide to go with one of the ISPs featured here, it's time to sign up. Click the ISP of your choice from Netscape's main ISP-listing page. The ISP's info page (the one with the ISP's prices and services) appears; click Next. You'll be asked to choose a type of account (how many hours per month do you plan to use?) and to choose a user name and password (see Figure 15-3). Some boxes are already filled in for you based on the information you've given the Internet Setup Assistant. But you can change it. I could, for example change my username from blevitus to bobl, bigbob, or something else that suits me.

Figure 15-3:
Fill out this
form to set
up your
new
Internet
account.

When you've entered all of the information the ISP asks for, including your credit card number, you're in business. You have an Internet account — and best of all, the software you need to use it is all configured and ready to go. Congratulations. You can skip the next section and start teaching Cyberdog some tricks.

If you opted not to choose an ISP from the Netscape list, or if you already have one, there's still some work to do before you can get out there and surf. (Funny, that's what my mom used to say to me.)

Go configure: More fun with Internet Setup Assistant

You need four pieces of information to configure your Internet connection:

- Your username
- Your password
- The local phone number that your modem dials to make a connection to your provider
- Your ISP's server name and address

When you have all these pieces assembled, you're ready to do some configuring.

Actually, with Internet Setup Assistant, "configuring" is an awfully strong way to put it. Sure, you'll enter all the information you'll need to connect to the Internet, but you don't have to get lost in a maze of jargon and control panels to do it. Just open up Internet Setup Assistant and follow the arrows. What could be simpler?

1. Open Internet Setup Assistant. You'll find it in the Internet folder.

2. Click the Update button to configure your account. Even if you have a brand-spanking-new Internet account, Update is the right choice. Register is used to pick an ISP from the Netscape ISP page, as described earlier.

3. The next screen you see reminds you of the info you'll need before you can configure your account. Assuming you've got everything you need, click the right arrow at the bottom of the window. If something's missing, call your ISP.

4. Now Internet Setup Assistant wants to know whether you're starting from scratch or modifying a configuration that's already on your system. Leave the default button checked.

5. It's time to name your Internet account. I called mine Bob's Account (see Figure 15-4). You'll want to leave the Modem button selected. Go to the next screen.

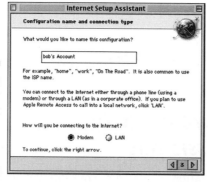

Figure 15-4:
Give your
Internet
account a
logical
name.

6. Choose your modem from the list and move to the next screen.

7. Now we'll do some real configuring. Enter your ISP's phone number, your username, and your password, just like I did in Figure 15-5. Next screen, please.

Figure 15-5:
Tell your
Mac where
to call and
who you
are with
this Internet
Assistant
screen.

Everyone who connects to the Internet uses an *IP address,* a set of unique numbers that identifies your computer. Sometimes an ISP will assign you an IP address to use with your account. Most providers, though, assign you an IP address each time you connect. It really doesn't matter how you get an IP address, as long as you get one. The only time you have to worry about it is the first time you configure your account. That would be right now.

8. If your ISP gave you an IP address, choose Yes. If not, leave No checked. Next.

Even if your ISP didn't give you an IP address of your own, you probably did get what's called a DNS address. Basically, that's the IP address of your ISP. Often, there are several. Look at Figure 15-6 to see how a DNS address (sometimes called a server address) should look. You'll also see a blank for a domain name. That's the equivalent of the DNS address in words. For my provider, it's earthlink.net.

Figure 15-6:
This is
where you
enter your
ISP's DNS
address
and domain
name.

9. Enter the DNS address and domain name, and go to the next screen.

   There are a couple of steps to getting your e-mail address configured. First, you'll tell Internet Setup Assistant your e-mail address and password, and then you'll enter your account info, as seen by the ISP's mail server.

10. Enter your e-mail address and password. This is the address you'll give to people who want to send you e-mail, and the address that appears at the top of messages you send. Go to the next screen.

11. Now you'll need to enter the e-mail account and SMTP server address (see Figure 15-7). Sometimes, the account is the same as your e-mail address. Sometimes it's a little different. In this example, my e-mail address is levitus@earlthlink.net, but my e-mail account is levitus@mail.earthlink.net. The SMTP server is the machine that processes mail for your ISP. Go on to the next screen.

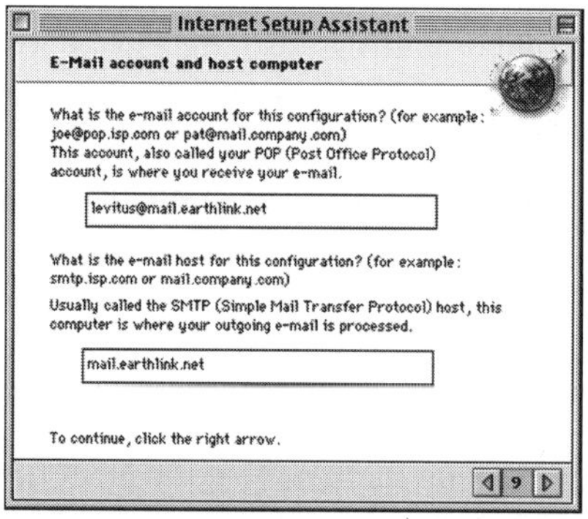

Figure 15-7: Enter your e-mail account and SMTP server information here.

12. We're on the home stretch now. On this screen, enter the name of your ISP's news server. It's also called the NNTP (Network News Transfer Protocol) server, and it makes it possible for you to read Usenet newsgroups. Moving right along to the next screen. . . .

13. The last Internet Setup Assistant screen gives you the chance to review your work, enable your new configuration, and get online right away. If you'd like to see what you've done, click Show Details. When you're happy with your new configuration, click Go Ahead. The Setup Assistant updates a few control panels while you wait.

That's it. You're good to go. Let's move on and meet your new puppy, Cyberdog.

One Cool Puppy: Meet Your New Cyberdog

Here's Apple's official description of Cyberdog: "Cyberdog is a suite of Internet components that allows you to browse the World Wide Web, receive and send e-mail, read articles from Usenet newsgroups, browse AppleTalk zones and servers, exchange files with FTP, and log into other computers with Telnet. Cyberdog provides tight integration between these components, and with other OpenDoc applications. Cyberdog also allows you to customize your use of the Internet."

That works for me. The nice part is you don't have to go out and find any software of your own; the downside is that other software — such as Netscape Navigator, Microsoft Internet Explorer, and others — may be more powerful and robust than Cyberdog.

If you decide that Cyberdog isn't for you, move on to the next section, where I explain some other Internet tools Apple has included with Mac OS 8, including a copy of Netscape Navigator.

I'm not fudging about Cyberdog. Its just that Apple isn't really committed to Cyberdog, as evidenced by the "no further development" status of its enabling technology OpenDoc. Right this second, the other products I mention above have some advantages over Cyberdog. By the time you read this, they'll probably have even more. Or not.

Cyberdog requires a Power Macintosh and at least 16 megabytes of RAM. (If less than 16MB of RAM is installed in your computer, use the Memory control panel to turn on virtual memory. Then set the amount of memory to 32MB and restart. For more details on virtual memory, see Chapter 9.)

Install OpenDoc *before* installing Cyberdog, or Cyberdog won't work.

Logging on

Before you can use Cyberdog, you must log on to your ISP's network. Here's how:

1. Choose Apple menu⇨Control Panels⇨PPP to open the PPP control panel.

2. Click the Connect button or press Return or Enter.

That's it. Your modem shrieks and squeals, and pretty soon the Status area of the PPP control panel shows that you are connected, as illustrated in Figure 15-8.

Figure 15-8:
The PPP control panel. Note the information in the Status area when you're connected to the net.

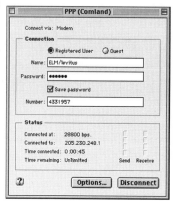

In case you're wondering how your username, password, and ISP phone number found their way into the PPP control panel, I'll tell you. When you configured Internet Setup Assistant, the information you entered was transferred to the PPP control panel, and to a couple of others (TCP/IP and Modem). Fortunately, you won't have to mess with those two unless you change ISPs or modems. PPP, on the other hand, has some cool features that I'll talk about shortly.

Leave the PPP control panel open while you're online. The little boxes above the words Send and Receive flash when information is going or coming. It doesn't tell you much, but it's fun to watch, and it does let you know that you're still connected.

If you want your connection to be made automatically when you launch Cyberdog in the future, click the Options button in the PPP control panel, and then click the Connection tab at the top of the window. Check the box next to Connect automatically when starting TCP/IP applications (see Figure 15-9).

While we're in the PPP options window, let's take a look around. If you're following along at home, it's not necessary to be connected to the Internet to change PPP's options. It won't take long.

Figure 15-9:
Do this
and you'll
make a
connection
automatically
whenever
you launch
Cyberdog
(or any
other
Internet
application
such as
Netscape
Navigator
or Internet
Explorer).

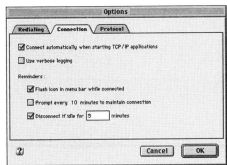

Under the Connection tab in the Options window, you'll see several check boxes. They are:

- ✔ **Use verbose logging:** Keeps track of every connection attempt and other action of your PPP software.

- ✔ **Flash icon in menu bar while connected:** Flashes an icon to remind you that you're connected and using online time.

- ✔ **Prompt every X minutes to maintain connection:** Reminds you that you are connected and disconnects automatically if you don't respond to the warning.

- ✔ **Disconnect if idle for X minutes:** Lets you set a maximum length of time to stay connected when there's no activity.

Meet your pup

Now that you've configured everything and you're connected to the Internet, you're finally ready to have some fun. Really. Here we go:

Launch Cyberdog. The Cyberdog notebook opens automatically, as shown in Figure 15-10.

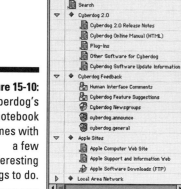

Figure 15-10:
Cyberdog's
notebook
comes with
a few
interesting
things to do.

Your Cyberdog notebook

Apple has taken the liberty of providing you with a few entries in your new Cyberdog notebook to get you started.

Whenever you visit a site on the Internet that you like and would like to remember, create an entry for it in your notebook by choosing Notebook⇨New Item.

Your notebook can store many kinds of Internet addresses. It can store Web page addresses (such as the ones shown in Figure 15-8: Cyberdog Software Update Information, Cyberdog Home Page, Cyberdog Net Station, Feedback, Plug-ins, and so on). You can tell that these items are Web pages by their icons, which look like little pages with a little triangle next to them.

Puttin' on the dog

Let's pay a quick visit to the Cyberdog home page. Double-click its icon in the Notebook window, and you'll soon see a browser window that displays the Cyberdog home page, which looks something like Figure 15-11.

It'll probably look a little (or a lot) different because Web pages are dynamic and constantly changing.

Figure 15-11:
Cyberdog's
Web
browser
window,
connected
to the
Cyberdog
home page.

Now for the really cool part. Web pages are, by their nature, hyperlinked to other Web pages. Web *hot links* appear as blue text with an underline, which means that with a single click, you can view a related document.

When your cursor is over a hot link, it turns into a paw print, as shown in Figure 15-11. Most links are in blue text and underlined, but graphics can also be hot links. If your cursor turns into a paw print when you move it over a graphic, that graphic is a link to another page.

When I click in Figure 15-11, the browser magically takes me to a page listing the cool things you can do with Cyberdog.

Cyberdog keeps a history of each page you visit in a pop-up menu (see Figure 15-12). To return to a page you visited previously, choose its name from this menu. But remember that this history is erased when you quit Cyberdog, so if you visit a site you like, make sure to save its address in your Cyberdog notebook.

Figure 15-12:
The pop-up
History
menu
remembers
where
you've been
since you
started
Cyberdog
for this
session.

I highly recommend that you visit all the Cyberdog-related sites in your notebook. There's so much more to say about the Internet . . . that I could write a book about it. (And I have. Several, in fact.) Meanwhile, my editor is hounding me to finish this chapter without exceeding my page budget, so I'm going to be mercifully brief in the rest of my tour. Suffice it to say that this chapter barely scratches the surface.

Cyberdog can also send and receive electronic mail. Notebook addresses such as Human Interface Comments and Cyberdog Feature Suggestions are e-mail addresses. You can tell by their icons, which look like a person on top of postcard.

If there's a feature you want to see in upcoming versions of Cyberdog, just double-click the Cyberdog Feature Suggestions item and send Apple an electronic mail message (see Figure 15-13). Choose your letterhead, type a few words, and then press the Send Now button. In a few moments, your message will arrive at Apple's Cyberdog laboratory, where it will be passed around and shared by dozens of geeky engineers with pocket protectors.

Cyberdog also does *FTP* (File Transfer Protocol), which lets you access FTP sites where you can download files to your Mac. Go the Cyberdog Notebook and double-click the entry for Apple Software Downloads (FTP), and you'll see a window offering the latest and greatest software files for your downloading pleasure, as shown in Figure 15-14.

Folders in Cyberdog windows act just like folders in the Finder; they can contain documents, subfolders, or both. When you double-click a file, however, it is automatically downloaded to your desktop and placed in a folder named Cyberdog Downloads.

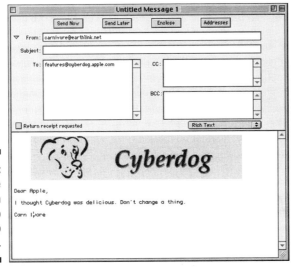

Figure 15-13:
A feature
suggestion
ready to
send to
Apple.

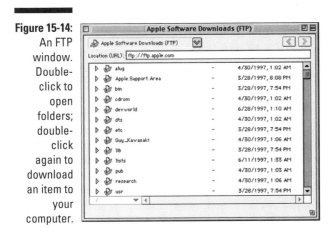

Figure 15-14:
An FTP
window.
Double-
click to
open
folders;
double-
click
again to
download
an item to
your
computer.

Finally, your notebook can store *newsgroups,* discussion bulletin boards where conversations between users can take place. Double-click the cyberdog.general item under the Cyberdog Feedback heading to sample the newsgroup dedicated to your favorite Web-surfing pup, Cyberdog (see Figure 15-15).

Unfortunately, that's all I have time for. Rest assured I've shown you just enough to be dangerous.

```
┌──────────────────── cyberdog.general ───────────────────┐
│ 255 articles, 255 unread    Subject           Author        Posted       │
│ ▷  4    Re: Grabbing pictures off WWW pages   Lou Hom      6/18/1997  │
│ ▷  2    OpenDoo                               Lou Hom      6/18/1997  │
│ ▷  3    Can't view counter image - why?                    6/18/1997  │
│ ▽  2    Re: problem with mail enclosures      Chris Johnson 6/18/1997 │
│         Re: problem with mail enclosures      David vanWert  6/20/1997 │
│ ▽  2    Re: I want an invisible CyberDocument Chris Johnson 6/18/1997 │
│         I want an invisible CyberDocument     Bret Marion    6/18/1997 │
│ ▽  3    Re: Exporting Cyberdog mail           John A. Vink   6/18/1997 │
│         Re: Exporting Cyberdog mail           Andrew P Sch... 6/21/1997 │
│         Re: Exporting Cyberdog mail           Brad Hutchings 6/21/1997 │
│         Re: Apple & third party support for Cd John A. Vink  6/18/1997 │
└─────────────────────────────────────────────────────────┘
```

Surfing with Netscape and Company

When Apple put Mac OS 8 together, it took a look around at the Internet tools it had, and the tools people were already using. Of course, there was that rascally Cyberdog, with lots of integrated access to the Web, e-mail, FTP and news. But most Macintosh-using surfers had already settled on a browser from Netscape (Navigator) or Microsoft (Internet Explorer). Apple decided to include Navigator, Claris Emailer, and Peter Lewis's nifty Internet Config.

Like Cyberdog, the Netscape Navigator software suite relies on TCP/IP and PPP to make a connection. If you've checked the Connect automatically when starting TCP/IP applications check box in the PPP control panel, PPP will dial your ISP when you launch Navigator. There's an even simpler way to get started: When you installed Apple's Internet Access tools, the installer dropped an application on your desktop called Browse the Internet (see Figure 15-16). When you double-click its icon, the little application looks for a Web browser on your hard disk. It will find Netscape Navigator and open it.

When PPP has connected you to the Internet, Navigator will display an Apple Web page designed especially for new Net surfers. When I wrote this chapter, though, it was still under construction (see Figure 15-17). By the time you read it, the page will look a lot better.

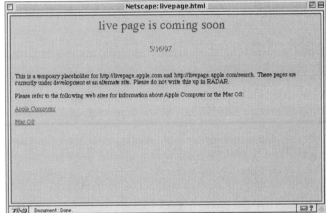

Figure 15-17: The placeholder for Apple's live home page.

Navigating in Navigator

Okay, so the live home page isn't much to look at right now. Fortunately, your copy of Netscape Navigator comes with some pointers to other nifty Mac sites you'll want to check out.

Pull down the Bookmarks menu and take a look at the list your pals at Apple have put together. You'll find pointers to Apple sites (see Figure 15-18), hardware and software vendors, and more.

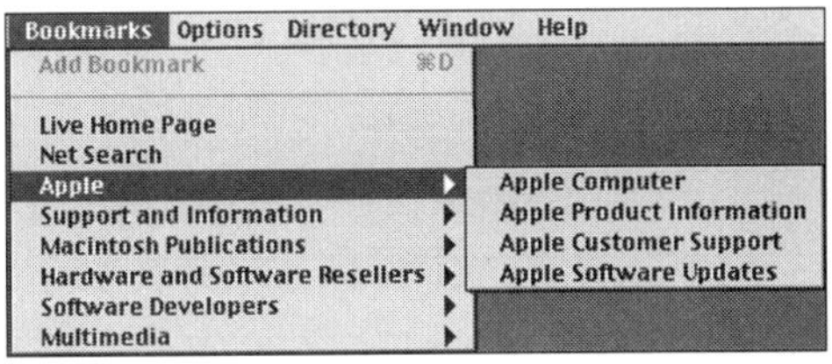

Figure 15-18: Your copy of Netscape Navigator comes with a set of useful bookmarks.

There's a lot more to Navigator that I don't have time to describe, but I'll hit the highlights.

If you've seen Netscape Navigator before, you may wonder what became of the toolbar and buttons that usually adorn the top of a Navigator window. You can turn Navigator's toolbar on by selecting Show Toolbar from the Options menu. The toolbar gives you access to navigation commands and other basic stuff like printing.

If you want to see the *URL* (the Internet address) for the Web pages you visit, check Show Location.

The Directory buttons (Options➪Show Directory Buttons) lead to search engines and other tools that will help you find stuff on the Internet.

Figure 15-19 shows a full complement of navigation bars, and Apple's home page to boot. If you don't like looking at all those bars, just uncheck the appropriate item on the Options menu.

Figure 15-19:
Apple's
home
page and
Netscape
Navigator's
tool and
directory
bars, in all
their glory.

Now that you know your way around Navigator, you can check out some of the sites from the bookmark list or search for a Web site dedicated to your favorite pastime with the Internet directory buttons.

Get your mail with Claris Emailer

You can use different applications to read Internet mail. Even Netscape Navigator has a built-in mail reader. But the easiest and best mail reader around (that means, the best one on your hard disk right now) is Claris Emailer Lite.

Remember the handy Browse the Internet icon that got Netscape Navigator up and running? Well, you'll find another icon on your Mac OS 8 desktop. This one looks like a folder and is called Mail (see Figure 15-20). Double-click the Mail icon.

Figure 15-20:
The Mail alias opens Claris Emailer.

Emailer is fast and easy to use. You'll be able to send and receive messages and create an address book that includes the addresses of your friends and family. The Emailer browser window looks like Figure 15-21.

Figure 15-21:
The Emailer browser window.

It's time to create your first message.

1. Choose New from the Mail menu.

2. Type a subject for your message and press the Tab key twice.

3. Enter the name of the person you'd like to send a message to. Press Tab. Once you've finished addressing a mail message, you can add the recipient to your Emailer address book. From then on, you'll be able to type the first few letters of the recipient's name, and Emailer will fill out the address for you. Neat, huh?

4. Now, type the e-mail address of your recipient. I've always been a fan of the dogcow that gave Claris its name (see Chapter 7), so in Figure 15-22 I'm writing to thank him for Emailer.

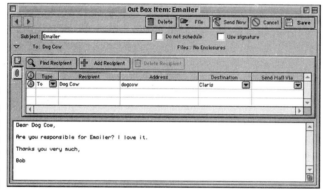

Figure 15-22:
Using
Emailer to
compose a
message.

5. Press Tab and enter a destination, or choose one from the pop-up menu. When I addressed my message to dogcow@claris.com, Emailer filled in the destination field for me. That's because claris.com is one of the Internet domains Emailer knows about, right out of the box. Others include CompuServe, Netcom, and Sprint. Choosing a destination from this list, or adding your own, makes it even faster to address mail.

6. Ignore the Send via field and press Tab again. Now you're ready to type your message.

7. When the note says just what you want it to say, click Save. It will be sent the next time you check your mail.

Now, I know what you're thinking: How do I check my mail? Easy. Just choose Connect Now from the Mail menu.

I love Claris Emailer and have upgraded to the deluxe version. Check it out at http://www.claris.com.

Part IV
The Infamous
Part of Tens

The 5th Wave   By Rich Tennant

Karl Malden as a young man

Are you gonna keep your nose glued to that screen all day again today?

In this part . . .

We're in the home stretch now. Just three more chapters and you're outta here.

These last three are a little different — they're kind of like long top ten lists. I'd like you to believe that it's because I'm a big fan of Dave Letterman, but the truth is, IDG Books has always put "Part of Tens" in books with *...For Dummies* in their titles, and this book must continue the tradition. Because IDG pays me, I'm doing these chapters their way. (Actually, it's kind of fun.)

First, I'll briefly describe ten items that weren't installed with Mac OS (but you might need someday). I'll show you what they do, how to install them, and why you might need them. A couple of them might actually be useful to you someday.

I'll then move on to a subject near and dear to my heart: Ten awesome things for your Mac that are worth spending money on.

Finally, you'll take a tour of Dr. Mac's top ten troubleshooting tips, for those times when good System software goes bad.

Chapter 16

Ten Optional Pieces of Mac OS 8 That You Might Someday Need

• •

In This Chapter

▶ Mac OS Runtime for Java

▶ Personal Web Sharing

▶ QuickDraw 3D

▶ OpenDoc

▶ MacLink Plus

▶ Apple Location Manager

▶ Cyberdog

▶ QuickDraw GX

▶ Text-to-Speech

▶ Apple Remote Access

• •

*T*here's a bunch of stuff that's not installed when you perform a noncustomized install, and it's all covered in this chapter. Maybe you won't need them, maybe you will, but there's no way to tell until you know what each option is and what it does.

The custom options for Mac OS 8 are:

✔ Mac OS Runtime for Java, to use programs written in the Java computer language.

✔ Personal Web Sharing, to share documents using the World Wide Web.

✔ QuickDraw 3D, to view and manipulate 3D images (requires a PowerPC computer).

✔ OpenDoc, to take advantage of software written for the OpenDoc environment.

✔ MacLink Plus, to easily open Mac OS, DOS, and Windows documents. These translators work with the Mac OS Easy Open control panel.

✔ Apple Location Manager, to quickly switch between different settings on your PowerBook computer.

✔ Cyberdog, to access the Internet using the OpenDoc environment.

✔ QuickDraw GX, to use programs with advanced graphics and typography features.

✔ Text-to-Speech, to have your computer read text and alert messages aloud.

✔ Apple Remote Access, to connect to a remote Mac OS computer using a modem.

Unfortunately, due to space limitations, I can't really explain how to *use* each of these potentially useful, optionally installed goodies. Instead, I'll briefly describe each one, then provide some insights on whether you need it or not. (To find out how to install and uninstall components, and what exactly is installed on your hard disk when you do, see Appendix A.)

Mac OS Runtime for Java

Mac OS Runtime for Java (MRJ) is Apple's version of Java. Java is a programming language (or a platform, depending upon who you ask) that is most frequently used in Web pages you view on the Internet. Stand-alone Java programs, mostly called *applets,* are beginning to become available as well.

MRJ lets you run programs written in Java on your Mac with the included Applet Runner program, with most popular Web browsers, or with any other Java-enabled Mac OS application

Bob sez:

If you use the Internet (and who doesn't these days), use stand-alone Java applets, or use a Java-enabled Mac OS program, this is the implementation of Java you want.

Personal Web Sharing

Mac OS Personal Web Sharing lets you host Web pages on an intranet or on the Internet. It provides a very easy (and somewhat limited) way to share your own Web page and/or files with remote users, even if they have a

WinDoze or UNIX computer. That's the good news. Unfortunately, it requires a continuous TCP/IP connection as well as a permanent IP address. Which means that if you access the Internet via modem, you probably don't qualify. That's the bad news.

Bob sez:

If you meet the qualifications and want to publish a simple Web page or share some files with a remote user, it doesn't get any easier than this. Otherwise, don't even bother to install it.

QuickDraw 3D

QuickDraw 3D lets your Mac run programs written to take advantage of it (mostly games, so far). It is required if you have a plug-and-play 3D accelerator card. (Check your hardware manual if you're not sure whether your computer has one; more and more models are including this feature.)

QuickDraw 3D also provides a common file format for 3D documents called QuickDraw 3D Metafile format (3DMF). I know you just had to know that.

Bob sez:

Because QuickDraw 3D–enabled games as well as plug-and-play 3D acceleration cards are relatively rare, you probably don't need QuickDraw 3D today. But I expect you will. So because it doesn't use any additional memory until a QuickDraw 3D-enabled program is launched, I recommend you install QuickDraw 3D, especially if you sometimes run games.

OpenDoc

OpenDoc lets you run OpenDoc software such as Apple's own Cyberdog. Because Apple has announced that OpenDoc won't be part of their next-generation operating system, code-named Rhapsody, there's very little OpenDoc software available, and most people have no need for it.

Bob sez:

Unless you love Cyberdog, which most Macintosh users don't, or use some other piece of OpenDoc software, which most Mac users also don't, you don't need OpenDoc.

MacLink Plus

MacLink Plus is a set of translators that let your Mac open documents created by programs you don't have on your hard disk and documents created by non–Mac OS computers.

MacLink Plus works in conjunction with Mac OS Easy Open, which was installed with Mac OS 8.

Bob sez:

MacLink Plus doesn't use any memory and requires only a few megabytes of disk space. Unless you never get files from other people, never download files from the Internet, and never get files created by other types of computers, you should definitely install it.

Apple Location Manager

Apple Location Manager is for PowerBook users (it won't work with desktop models, so unless you have a PowerBook, don't even bother) who use their computers in multiple locations. It stores location-specific information, such as Chooser and printer settings, AppleTalk on-off settings, TCP/IP settings, and more, which makes configuring your PowerBook to work in different locations quick and easy.

Bob sez:

If you don't have a PowerBook, you definitely don't need Apple Location Manager. If you have a PowerBook but only use it in one place, you probably don't need it. If you have a PowerBook and use it all over the country, continent, or world, you're going to love it. In other words, Apple Location Manager is a way-cool thing, but only useful for true road-warriors.

Cyberdog

Cyberdog is Apple's home-grown suite of Internet tools. It includes Web browser, e-mail, newsgroup, and FTP services, and it requires OpenDoc.

Bob sez:

Because Netscape Navigator is on your hard disk (it's part of a normal, noncustomized Mac OS 8 install in the Internet: Internet Applications folder), try that Web browser first. If it works fine for you, as it does for most people, don't bother to install Cyberdog or OpenDoc. (See previous section on OpenDoc.)

QuickDraw GX

QuickDraw GX was Apple's advanced printing architecture, but it has been discontinued. This installer appears to help ease the transition for those few people using programs that require QuickDraw GX.

Bob sez:

Unless you're one of the unlucky few who depend upon a program that requires QuickDraw GX, you don't need it.

Text-to-Speech

Text-to-Speech lets many Mac programs, including SimpleText, read typed text aloud.

Bob sez:

It's clever and kind of fun, but it uses a bit of RAM (about 300K) and a few megs (5) of hard disk space. Still, it's kind of neat, so install it if you have enough memory and disk space.

If you do install it and then discover that you never use it, don't forget to turn it off using Extensions Manager — or uninstall it.

Apple Remote Access

Apple Remote Access (ARA) is a one-trick pony that lets you share files between two Macs over a modem.

Bob sez:

If you need to do that (share files between two Macs via modem), install ARA on both computers and go to town. Otherwise, you don't need it.

Two More Things You Should Know About

There are a few items that are (usually) not installed when you choose the Easy Install option in the Mac OS 8 Installer program. I talk about them in Appendix A, but two of these custom-install items are so well worth knowing about that I'm going to violate the *Dummies* "Part of Tens" rule and include them here.

Easy Access

Easy Access (shown in Figure 16-1) is a control panel designed primarily for people with impaired mobility. That doesn't mean it might not come in handy for anyone.

Easy Access lets you do three things:

- Use the numeric keypad on your keyboard (instead of the mouse) to control the cursor on the screen.
- Type keyboard shortcuts without having to press both keys at the same time.
- Type very slowly.

Mouse Keys

When you turn on Mouse Keys, the numeric keypad, instead of the mouse, controls the cursor. The 5 key is the mouse button; the 0 key is the click and hold button. The rest of the numbers control the cursor direction (see Figure 16-2).

Figure 16-1:
The Easy
Access
control
panel may
come in
handy for
any user.

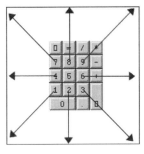

Figure 16-2:
The
numeric
keypad
controls the
cursor. The
5 key is a
click; the 0
key is a
click and
hold.

The keyboard shortcut Command-Shift-Clear toggles Mouse Keys on and off.
If you have the audio feedback option checked, you'll hear a whoop when
Mouse Keys is turned on and another when it's turned off.

The Mouse Keys radio buttons control the delay before movement occurs
(after you press the key) and the speed at which the cursor travels across
the screen.

Slow Keys

Slow Keys delays the Mac's recognition of keystrokes. In other words, if the
acceptance delay is set to Long, you would have to hold down a key for
almost two seconds for it to be recognized. This feature is designed to filter
out inadvertent and accidental key presses.

Sticky Keys

Sticky Keys lets you type keyboard shortcuts one key at a time. In other words, to open an icon, you'd ordinarily press the Command and O keys simultaneously. Sticky Keys makes it possible to press the Command key first and then the O key after it.

The keyboard shortcut for turning Sticky Keys on and off is to press the Shift key five times in rapid succession. To lock the modifier key down, press it twice in rapid succession.

As illustrated in Figure 16-3, when you press the modifier key, you'll see a little icon in the upper-right corner of your menu bar that gives you visual feedback on the state of Sticky Keys.

Figure 16-3:
Sticky Keys turned on (left); modifier key pressed and waiting for keystroke (center); and modifier key locked (right).

My take: It can come in handy. For example, in programs that don't have a nudge command for moving objects one pixel at a time using the arrow keys, Mouse Keys makes a decent substitute. It might be worth keeping around for this feature alone. You can always turn it off using Extensions Manager.

CloseView

CloseView blows up your screen. No, it doesn't make it explode; it enlarges the image, and it can all be done with keyboard shortcuts.

The CloseView control panel appears in Figure 16-4. The white frame around it is the area that will be displayed when I turn magnification on (in Figure 16-5).

Figure 16-4:
If I turn on magnification now, the area in the frame will be blown up to fill my screen . . .

Figure 16-5:
. . . like this. This image fills my entire monitor.

CloseView uses a lot of memory — from a few hundred K to more than a thousand K. If you can afford the RAM, it's a useful little doohickey to have around. It can give you a zoom feature in programs that don't allow zooming. On the other hand, hundreds of K is a lot of RAM to waste if you don't use CloseView often.

My take: Install it but turn it off using Extensions Manager. If you need it, enable it in Extensions Manager and restart.

One Last Real Good Tip

Almost everything in this chapter includes Mac OS Help and/or Balloon Help. Use them to learn more about how these goodies work.

Chapter 17

Ten Ways to Make Your Mac Better by Throwing Money at It

●●

In This Chapter

▶ Stuff I think you ought to buy

●●

*T*his is my favorite part. As you've probably figured out by now, I love
souping up my Mac. I live to find ways of working smarter, saving time,
and saving hand motion. And I revel in tweaking my Mac and Mac OS 8. So it
gives me great pleasure to share this chapter, my personal top ten (actually,
eleven, but don't tell my editor) things you can buy for your Mac to tweak it
and make it faster, easier to use, and (I hope) more fun.

The items listed in this chapter are things I have, use every day, love dearly,
and would buy again.

- ✔ **RAM:** It's worth every penny. If you have anything less than 16MB in
  your Mac, you'll like it a lot better if you upgrade to 32MB or more. If
  you like to do a few things at once, 64 or more megs of RAM is worth
  considering. (For what it's worth, RAM has never been cheaper than it
  is today.)

- ✔ **Backup software:** There are only two kinds of Macintosh users: Those
  who have lost data and those who are going to. If your work means
  anything to you, get something that helps automate the task of backing
  up your files. Retrospect or DiskFit, both from Dantz Development, are
  the names to trust. Remember these words: "If you don't back it up, you
  will someday lose it."

- ✔ **CD-ROM Drive:** Turn your boring Mac into a multimedia entertainment
  and education center. If you don't have one, you absolutely need one.
  And then buy a few . . .

- ✔ **CD-ROMs:** There are some great games, references, and educational
  titles out there. You'll love 'em, and so will your kids.

✔ **Games:** I just love Titanic, Bad Mojo, Alley 19 Bowling, The Last Express, FA-18 Hornet, and You Don't Know Jack. Gaming on the Mac has never been better. And by the way, all of the above come on CD-ROM only.

✔ **Big monitor:** You'll spend less time scrolling and rearranging windows. You'll spend more of your time getting actual work done, which is a good thing, right? I use a multisync Sony 20sfII and love it to death.

✔ **Modem:** Your capacity to communicate will increase tenfold. Join an online service, surf the Internet, e-mail your friends, and much, much more. Get a modem that can do 28.8 or 33.6 Kbps. 14.4 Kbps doesn't cut it anymore. If you're a real Internet hound, check out ISDN or cable modems for even faster Net access.

✔ **Now Utilities:** It puts Mac OS 8 on steroids. Use it for a week, and you'll wonder how you lived without it. SuperBoomerang, which makes the Open and Save dialog boxes almost usable, is worth the price of the entire package, but there are eight other excellent utilities included as well. A must-have.

✔ **QuicKeys:** This utility creates macros called *shortcuts* that can perform a task or a series of tasks (a *sequence*) with a single command. It's like AppleScript, only better. Another must-have.

✔ **Retrieve It:** This little-known utility from MVP Solutions searches for text within documents and even across the Internet. It's a great addition to Find File. My final must-have.

✔ **A New CPU:** If you've got any money left, consider upgrading to a newer, faster Mac or clone. They've never been faster, cheaper, or better-equipped.

So there you have it: 11 awesome ways to spend a big chunk of change. So ladies and gentlemen, start your checkbooks. Go forth, throw money at your Mac, and most of all, have fun.

Chapter 18

At Least Ten Things to Try When Good System Software Goes Bad

● ●

In This Chapter

▶ The dreaded Sad Mac
▶ The flashing question mark
▶ Startup crashes
▶ Reinstallation

● ●

1 said Chapter 14 was "easily the most useful chapter in the book." It is. Unless you wake up one morning to find your Macintosh sick or dying. Then (and only then) is this chapter more useful because it's the one that is going to save your bacon.

As a bleeding-edge Mac enthusiast with almost eleven years of Mac under my belt, I've had more than my share of Mac troubles. Over those years, I've developed an arsenal of tips and tricks that I believe can resolve more than 90 percent of Macintosh problems without a trip to the repair shop.

Disclaimer: Of course, if your hardware is dead, there's nothing you or I can do about it. But if your hardware is okay, there's a 90 percent chance that something (or a combination of things) in this chapter will get you up and running.

I know that there are *more* than ten things in this chapter. My editor, Tim Gallan, says it doesn't matter, that the "Part of Tens" in *Dummies* books is sort of just for show, and I don't really have to have ten of anything as long as I use the word *ten* in the chapter name. Cool, eh?

Think of this chapter as yet another occasion where I give you more than your money's worth.

Dem Ol' Sad Mac Chimes of Doom Blues

One thing we all dread is seeing the Sad Mac icon (see Figure 18-1) and hearing that arpeggio in G minor, better known as the Chimes of Doom.

The Sad Mac usually indicates that something very bad has happened to your Mac, often that some hardware component has bitten the dust. But Sad Macs are rather uncommon — many users go years without seeing one. If you've got one, don't despair. Yet. There is something you can try before you diagnose your Mac as terminal — something that just might bring it back to life. Try this:

1. Shut down your Mac.

2a. If your Mac came with a Disk Tools floppy disk, insert it.

or

2b. If your Mac has an internal CD-ROM drive and came with a bootable CD-ROM System Software disk, insert that or the Mac OS 8 CD instead.

3. Restart your Mac.

4. If you are using a CD, you probably have to hold down the C key on your keyboard during startup.

If you see the Mac OS startup screen when you boot off your Disk Tools or CD-ROM, there's hope for your Mac. The fact that you could boot from another disk indicates that there's a problem with your hard disk or your System Folder. Whatever it is, it will more than likely respond to one of the techniques discussed throughout the rest of this chapter, so read on.

If the forthcoming techniques don't fix the problem, or you still see the Sad Mac icon when you start up with Disk Tools or CD, your Mac is toasted beyond my help and needs to go in for repairs (usually to an Apple dealer).

Before you drag it down to the shop, you might try 1-800-SOS-APPL. They may well suggest something else you can try.

Flashing Question Mark Problems

Go through these steps in sequence. If one doesn't work, move on to the next.

Now would be a good time to reread the "Question Mark and the Mysterians" section of Chapter 1, which explains the flashing question mark and why Disk Tools or a bootable CD-ROM are the ultimate startup disks. Both are things you need to know before you continue.

1-800-SOS-APPL

This is a very good number to know. It's Apple's technical support line, and it's good for all Apple-branded products. If nothing in this chapter brings you relief, call Apple before you lug the box down to the repair shop. Maybe they know something I don't.

In the bad old days, Apple's stance on technical support was "Ask your Apple dealer." That position, as you might guess, wasn't very satisfying — at least not to users. So a few years ago, Apple saw the light and instituted direct, toll-free technical support via the aforementioned 1-800-SOS-APPL, a big win for Macintosh users.

I have, since the line opened up several years ago, called a few times a year, often with an obscure problem. I have to say that they are very well informed at Apple tech support — they are batting close to 1,000, believe it or not. These guys and gals do know their stuff.

There is a drawback to this service: You may have to wait a bit. Some days it takes 30 minutes to get a live person on the phone. And some products are now covered only by "pay-to-use" support. Still, it's worth giving this number a try before you proceed any further.

Call using a speaker phone. Enjoy the soothing music and continue with your work until you hear a live person.

On the other hand, I've often had my call answered on the first ring. I think it's easier to get through first thing in the morning; they're open from 6 to 6, Pacific time.

The Disk Tools disk or bootable Mac OS 8 CD-ROM is *soooo* important, it's a good idea to have more than one copy around. That way, if one gets misplaced, damaged, eaten by the dog, accidentally formatted, exposed to a strong magnetic field, or otherwise rendered useless, you won't be totally out of luck. An older version of Mac OS or the CD that came with your computer are examples of "extra" bootable CDs you might have hanging around. The Mac OS 8 CD is bootable as well.

I keep a copy of Disk Tools in my middle desk drawer and several bootable CDs on the bookshelf.

If you have a removable media drive like a Zip or a Jaz or a SyQuest, it's a good idea to create a bootable cartridge (by installing Mac OS 8; see Appendix A) and stash it someplace safe, just in case. If you can't find a Disk Tools disk or a bootable CD, you can use this disk to start up your Mac.

If your copy of Mac OS 8 came on floppies, it's a good idea to make copies of all the Mac OS master installer disks and then use the copies to install. Luckily, most of you got Mac OS 8 on a CD.

But if you don't have a bootable CD-ROM, you can't do the rest of the stuff in this chapter. So if you don't have one handy, go find it now.

Start with something easy: Rebuild the desktop

Before attempting more drastic measures, try rebuilding the desktop.

Actually, rebuilding the desktop should go under the heading of preventive maintenance. Apple recommends rebuilding the desktop once a month, and so do I.

Another good time to rebuild the desktop is if you notice icons disappearing, changing or being replaced by generic icons (see Figure 18-2). This problem is usually a result of a desktop that needs rebuilding.

The desktop you're rebuilding is an invisible database that keeps track of every file on your hard disk, manages what icon goes with which file, and manages which program launches when you open a document.

More strictly speaking, the desktop is a pair of invisible files called Desktop DB and Desktop DF. They're stored at root level, but you can only see them with special software designed to work with invisible files. Leave them alone.

Figure 18-2:
If your formerly colorful icons turn generic, like these, try rebuilding the desktop.

Another good time to rebuild the desktop is if you start getting "An application can't be found for this document" errors when you know that you have the application or have assigned a substitute using Macintosh Easy Open.

How to actually do it

Anyway, to rebuild the desktop, hold down the Command and Option keys during startup until you see the dialog box in Figure 18-3.

Figure 18-3:
Yes, you do want to rebuild the desktop. Click OK.

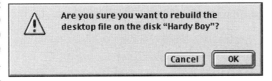

After you click OK, you'll see a progress window as the desktop is rebuilt. In a moment or two, it disappears and you're off and running.

If you have more than one hard disk or hard disk partition, a dialog box like the one shown in Figure 18-3 will appear for each disk that mounts on the desktop at startup. Click OK for every disk.

Oh yeah. You don't need to rebuild the desktop of the Disk Tools disk, so you can click Cancel for that one. You need to deal with your hard disk, and rebuilding the desktop on the Disk Tools disk won't do you any good.

If you booted from a CD, you won't be asked if you want to rebuild its desktop 'cause it's not a recordable device. Its desktop, like the rest of the data on it, can't be changed.

Just remember to rebuild your desktop monthly to keep your Mac in tip-top shape. And rebuild it again if you see the flashing question mark.

You're going to attempt to boot from your hard disk now, so remove the Disk Tools disk or bootable CD from the drive and restart.

If you still see the flashing question mark, it's time to . . .

Send for the ambulance: Run Disk First Aid

The next step in the program is to run the Disk First Aid application from your Disk Tools disk or Mac OS 8 CD-ROM.

The desktop isn't the only place where hard disks store information about themselves. There are BTrees, extent files, catalog files, and other creatively named invisible files involved in managing the data on your disks. Disk First Aid is a program that checks all those files and repairs ones that are damaged.

How to actually do it

If you haven't done so already, restart your Mac with the Disk Tools disk in the floppy drive or the Mac OS 8 CD in the CD-ROM drive (hold down the C key if you have to).

1. Launch the Disk First Aid application (see Figure 18-4).

Figure 18-4:
It's Disk
First Aid to
the rescue!

Disk First Aid

2. Click the icon for your hard disk at the top of the Disk First Aid window (see Figure 18-5).

3. Click the Repair button.

Your Mac will whir and hum for a few minutes, and the results window will tell you what's going on (see Figure 18-6).

Ultimately, Disk First Aid will tell you (you hope) that the disk appears to be okay. If so, restart your Mac without the Disk Tools disk or CD-ROM in the drive. If everything is okay, then go back to work.

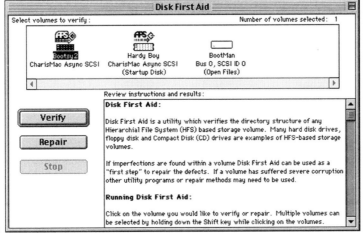

Figure 18-5:
Click your hard disk's icon and then click Repair; Disk First Aid does the rest.

Figure 18-6:
Disk First Aid runs some tests and offers its diagnosis.

If Disk First Aid finds damage that it's unable to fix, a commercial disk-recovery tool such as Norton Utilities for the Macintosh may be able to repair the damage.

If the software *can't* repair the damage, you'll have to initialize your disk. But that's okay, right? You have that backup software and you use it.

If everything checks out with Disk First Aid, try to boot from your hard disk again. If you still get the flashing question mark, try . . .

Installing new hard disk drivers

This section applies to Apple-brand hard disks only. If you have a third-party hard disk, the procedure is different. Read your hard disk's manual before you continue. Sorry.

What you're going to attempt next is to install (update) your hard disk drivers.

Drivers are little invisible bits of code that tell your hard disk how to communicate with a Mac. They occasionally become damaged and need replacing. Done properly, the technique is completely harmless and can make the flashing question mark disappear. Mac OS 8 installs new drivers automatically (on Apple-brand hard disks) when you first install it.

How to actually do it

1. Restart your Mac using Disk Tools or your Mac OS 8 CD-ROM as startup disk.

2. Launch the Drive Setup application. It doesn't matter which, so launch whichever one you find first; they both do the same thing, as far as we're concerned for this lesson.

3. Choose Functions⇨Update Driver (Figure 18-7).

Figure 18-7: To update (install new) hard disk drivers using Drive Setup, choose Functions⇨ Update.

You should see a message telling you that the new driver won't be available until you restart your computer.

Do not click Initialize or choose Functions⇨Initialization Options! If you initialize your hard disk, it will be erased completely and irrevocably.

You get a warning or two first, but if you're not paying attention, a few false clicks (or presses of the Return or Enter key) and your hard disk is blank.

So update, don't initialize, okay?

If that solution doesn't get you up and running, and you're still seeing that danged flashing question mark when you try to boot from your hard disk, don't despair. There are still a few things you can try, such as . . .

The latest dance craze: zapping the PRAM

Sometimes your parameter RAM (PRAM) becomes scrambled and needs to be reset.

The PRAM is a small piece of memory that's not erased or forgotten when you shut down. It keeps track of things like printer selection in the Chooser, sound level, and monitor settings.

Try zapping your PRAM if your Monitors & Sound control panel or your Chooser seem to forget their settings when you shut down or restart.

Restart your Mac and hold down Command-Option-P-R (that's four keys — good luck; it's okay to use your nose) until your Mac restarts itself again. It's kind of like a hiccup. You see the smiling Mac or flashing question mark for a second, and then that icon disappears and your Mac restarts.

Zapping the PRAM returns some control panels to their default settings (but, interestingly, not the date or time), so you may have to do some tweaking after zapping the PRAM.

SCSI voodoo

It is said that connecting more than one SCSI device — an external hard disk, SyQuest, Zip, Jaz, optical disk, scanner, and so on — requires the luck of the gods.

The first bugaboo is SCSI termination. According to Apple, the first and last device on a SCSI chain must have a terminator. No devices in between should have termination. Internal hard drives are always terminated. And the total length of a SCSI chain can be no more than 22 feet.

But sometimes you can't get your SCSI chain to work by following the rules. Sometimes it requires terminating a drive in the middle of the chain as well as the first and last drives. Other times, a chain won't work if the last device *is* terminated. The physical order of devices matters. And, of course, there are those SCSI ID numbers.

So if you're seeing a flashing question mark still, and you have any external devices attached, shut down your Mac and unplug them. After they're all disconnected, try restarting your Mac using the Disk Tools disk.

Never plug or unplug SCSI devices with the power on. Turn both your Mac and the device off before you attempt to connect or disconnect any cables.

If your Mac starts up when no SCSI devices are connected, you've got a problem on the SCSI chain: a termination problem, a bad cable, or a SCSI ID conflict.

I'll be back: the terminator

A terminator is a plug that fits into the empty cable connector of the last device on your chain. Many newer external hard disks have termination built in. Consult your hard disk manual if you're not sure.

Some terminators are *pass-through* connectors, which can have a cable connected to them. Others block off that connector completely; these are known as block terminators.

If you see the flashing question mark and your last device isn't terminated, terminate it. If it is terminated, unterminate it. If you have more than one device and your terminator is a pass-through terminator, connect it to a device in the middle of the chain (instead of the end) and try to start your Mac.

If you have two terminators and two or more devices, try two terminators, one in the middle and one at the end. This trick isn't recommended, but sometimes that's what it takes to make it work.

If all this terminator juggling isn't working for you, try changing the physical order of the devices. If right now your Mac is connected to the hard disk, which is connected to the Zip drive, then try connecting the Zip drive to the Mac and the hard disk to the Zip drive.

I add and subtract SCSI devices more often in a year than most people do in two lifetimes. I'm always firing up some new storage device that someone wants me to check out. And I've had good luck since switching to a drive with Digital Active Termination.

Digital Active Termination senses how much termination your SCSI chain requires and then supplies it automatically. It's almost a miracle, and it's included on almost all storage devices from APS Technologies. Just put any device with Digital Active Termination at the end of your chain, and you are virtually guaranteed perfect termination, regardless of the number of devices in the chain or the physical order of the devices.

Cables: cheap is bad

When troubleshooting SCSI problems, you should check your SCSI cables. If you can borrow others, try that option. Cheap cables, usually ones that are thin and flexible, are more prone to failure than heavy, shielded cables. Again, APS has excellent thick cables at fair prices.

Gotta have some ID: unique SCSI ID numbers required

If you have multiple SCSI devices, don't forget that each must have a unique SCSI ID between 0 and 7. Your internal hard disk has ID 0, so external devices can have numbers from 1 to 6. Internal CD-ROM drives are frequently assigned the ID number 3.

You usually select the ID number using a wheel or button on the back of the device. Just make sure that each drive in the chain has a unique number and you're all set.

Try again to restart without the Disk Tools disk.

If nothing so far has cured the flashing question mark, you have to suspect damage to the System software on your hard disk.

So now you're going to try to replace your old System software with fresh, new System software.

Reinstalling the System software

The reason that this procedure comes last in this section is that it takes the longest. The procedure is detailed at great length in Appendix A, affectionately known as "Anyone Can Install Mac OS 8."

Read it and follow the instructions.

If nothing has worked so far

If none of my suggestions have worked, if you've rebuilt the desktop, run Disk First Aid, installed new hard disk drivers, zapped your PRAM, disconnected all SCSI devices, and reinstalled your System software, and you're still seeing the flashing question mark, then you've got big trouble.

You may have any one of the following problems:

- ✔ Your hard disk is dead and so is your floppy drive.
- ✔ Your hard disk is dead but your floppy drive is okay.
- ✔ You have some other type of hardware failure.
- ✔ All of your startup disks — your Disk Tools and Install Disk 1 floppies and/or your System software CD — are defective (unlikely).

The bottom line: If you're still seeing the flashing question mark after trying all the stuff in the previous pages, you almost certainly need to have your Mac serviced by a qualified technician.

If You Crash at Startup

More of a hassle to solve than flashing question mark problems, but rarely fatal, startup crashes are another bad thing that can happen to your Mac.

A *crash* is defined as a System Error dialog box, frozen cursor, frozen screen, or any other disabling event.

At startup is defined as any time between flicking the power key or switch (or restarting) and having full use of the Finder desktop.

A startup crash may happen to you someday. If it does, here's what to do.

Restart without extensions and control panels

The first thing you need to do is establish whether an extension or control panel is causing the crash by starting up with all of them disabled.

If your Mac is already on, choose Special⇨Restart, holding down the Shift key until you see "Extensions Disabled" in the Welcome to Mac OS window. After you see "Extensions Disabled," you may release the Shift key.

If your Mac is off, power it up and hold down the Shift key until you see "Extensions Disabled" in the Welcome to Mac OS window. Again, you can release the Shift key after "Extensions Disabled" appears.

If your Mac starts up successfully when you hold down the Shift key but crashes or freezes when you don't, you can deduce that one (or more) of your extensions or control panels is responsible for the crash. Read the section "Resolving extension and control panel conflicts" below.

If your Mac still crashes when you hold down the Shift key, you can deduce that something is wrong with your System or Finder. Read the section "How to perform a clean System reinstallation" later in this chapter.

Resolving extension and control panel conflicts

If you're reading this section, you have an extension or control panel that is causing your Mac to crash at startup. The trick now is to isolate which one (or, occasionally, more than one) is causing your troubles. Chances are, it's a third-party extension or control panel, but you can't rule out Apple extensions and control panels either. They too can conflict with other extensions or control panels or become corrupted and not function properly.

Because you know that your Mac will start up with the Shift key down, you use Extensions Manager to track down the rogue extension or control panel file.

I'm so happy Apple included Extensions Manager as part of System 7.5 and improved it a lot for Mac OS 8, I could turn backflips. You'll see why when I show you how to resolve your difficulties with Extensions Manager. Just imagine what a hassle it would be without EM.

The first step is to establish whether any of the Apple Mac OS 8 extensions or control panels is causing problems.

1. Launch the Extensions Manager control panel.

2. Choose Mac OS 8 all from the pop-up menu (see Figure 18-8) and then click the restart button.

Situation 1: You can now boot successfully, which means that the culprit must be one of your third-party extensions or control panels.

Situation 2: You still crash at startup, which means that the culprit must be one of the Mac OS extensions or control panels.

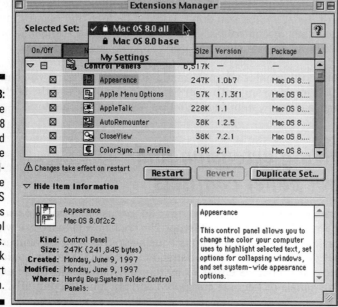

Figure 18-8:
Choose
Mac OS 8
all to load
only the
standard-
issue
Mac OS
extensions
and control
panels.
Then click
the Restart
button.

In Situation 1, repeat these steps until you crash again:

1. Power up or restart your Mac and then press and hold the spacebar until the Extensions Manager window appears.

2. Add one extension or control panel to the enabled list by clicking it so that a check mark appears.

3. Click the Continue button to begin the startup process.

If you start up successfully, you know that the extension or control panel you just added is not the culprit. Repeat these three steps, enabling one new item each time you restart, until you crash. When you do, the last extension or control panel you enabled is the culprit.

See the section called "Dealing with recalcitrant extensions and control panels" for possible solutions.

In Situation 2, repeat these steps until you stop crashing:

1. Power up or restart your Mac and then press and hold the Spacebar until the Extensions Manager window appears.

2. Disable one of the currently enabled extensions or control panels by clicking it so that its check mark disappears.

3. Click the Continue button to begin the startup process.

Repeat these three steps, disabling one item each time you restart, until you stop crashing. When you do, the last extension or control panel you disabled was the culprit.

See the next section, "Dealing with recalcitrant extensions and control panels," for some things you can try.

Sometimes you can tell which extension or control panel is causing your crash by looking carefully at the little icons that appear on the bottom of your screen during startup. Each icon you see represents a control panel or extension loading into memory. If you can determine which icon was the last to appear before the crash, you can try disabling it before going through the iterative and frustrating process of determining the culprit as described above. You might get lucky and save yourself hours of boring detective work.

If you have a good memory, enable or disable a few at a time in Step 2. Just keep track of what you're doing and you can reduce the number of restarts it takes to find your offender.

Dealing with recalcitrant extensions and control panels

In the previous section, you determined which particular extension or control panel was giving you fits. In this section, I have a couple of suggestions — replace and reorder — that may let you use the offending item anyway.

How to replace a recalcitrant file

1. Delete the guilty control panel or extension from your hard disk by dragging it to the Trash.

2. Open the Preferences folder in your System Folder and delete any preferences file with the same name as the guilty file.

3. Replace the guilty file with a fresh copy from a master disk.

If it's an Apple extension or control panel, use the Mac OS installers as described in Appendix A. If it's a third-party product, follow the installation instructions in its manual.

Restart and see if the problem reoccurs.

If it does, you may *still* be able to use the recalcitrant extension or control panel by diddling with the loading order of extensions and control panels at startup.

How to reorder a recalcitrant file

To understand how to reorder, you must first understand why you need to reorder.

In some cases, extensions and control panels crash only if they load before or after another extension. Ergo, by diddling with the loading order, you can force one file to load before another.

How do you diddle the loading order, you ask? When extensions and control panels load at startup, they load in alphabetical order by folder. To wit:

1. The Extensions folder's contents, in alphabetical order

and then

2. The Control Panels folder's contents, in alphabetical order

followed by

3. Control panels or extensions loose in your System Folder (that is, not in the Extensions or Control Panels folders), in alphabetical order.

So, if you have a recalcitrant extension or control panel, try forcing it to load either first or last. This trick works more often than not.

To force an offending control panel or extension (Snapz Pro in this example) to load first, precede its name by several spaces and move it into the Extensions folder if it's a control panel. It will then load before any other extensions or control panels (Figure 18-9).

Figure 18-9:
The first
item to load
will be the
control
panel I
renamed
" Snapz
Pro."

Name	Date Modified	Size	Kind
Snapz Pro	Thu, Jan 23, 1997, 4:54 PM	247K	control panel
EM Extension	Mon, Jun 9, 1997, 12:00 PM	19K	system extension
About Apple Guide	Thu, May 15, 1997, 12:00 PM	38K	Apple Guide docume
Appearance Extension	Mon, Jun 9, 1997, 12:00 PM	722K	system extension
Apple CD-ROM	Today, 11:27 AM	95K	system extension
Apple Color SW Pro CMM	Wed, Apr 26, 1995, 12:00 PM	57K	system extension
Apple Guide	Mon, Jun 9, 1997, 12:00 PM	874K	system extension
Apple Photo Access	Mon, Jun 19, 1995, 12:00 PM	171K	system extension

Extensions — 106 items, 96.1 MB available

By putting the Snapz Pro control panel in the Extensions folder (so that it loads before items in the Control Panels folder or System Folder) and preceding its name with several spaces, I ensured that Snapz Pro would be the first to load.

Going the other way, to force an extension or control panel to load last, precede its name with several tildes and move it out of the Extensions folder and into the System Folder itself (see Figure 18-10).

Figure 18-10:
The last item
to load will
be the
control panel
I renamed
"~~~~Snapz
Pro."

	Name	Date Modified	Size	Kind
▷	Shutdown Items	Yesterday, 9:06 AM	—	folder
▷	Shutdown Items (Disabled)	Today, 11:45 AM	—	folder
▷	Startup Items	Yesterday, 9:48 AM	—	folder
▷	Startup Items (Disabled)	Today, 11:45 AM	—	folder
	System	Yesterday, 1:14 PM	6.1 MB	suitcase
▷	System Extensions (Disabled)	Today, 11:45 AM	—	folder
▷	Text Encodings	Mon, Jul 14, 1997, 1:07 PM	—	folder
	~~Snapz Pro	Thu, Jan 23, 1997, 4:54 PM	247K	control panel

System Folder — 29 items, 96.2 MB available

By preceding the item's name with tildes and moving it out of the Extensions folder and into the System Folder itself, as shown, I've ensured that Snapz Pro will be the last extension or control panel to load.

More sophisticated startup managers, such as Now Utilities' Startup Manager and Casady & Greene's Conflict Catcher 4, let you change the loading order of extensions and control panels by dragging them around, avoiding the inconvenience of renaming or moving them manually. I wish Extensions Manager had this capability. If you find yourself resolving many conflicts with extensions or control panels, one or the other of these programs is a good investment.

Both programs also perform the conflict resolution three-step boogie automatically. You just restart, tell the software whether the problem is gone, and then restart again. The software does all the enabling and disabling and keeps track automatically. At the end, it tells you which file is the culprit. If you have many of these conflicts, one of these two programs is a worthwhile upgrade to the bare-bones Extensions Manager.

If you're still reading and your problem hasn't been resolved, there's one last thing you can try; namely, a clean System software installation.

How to perform a clean System reinstallation

This is a drastic final step. If nothing so far has fixed your startup problems, a clean System reinstallation, a.k.a. *clean install,* very well may. I saved this solution for last because it's the biggest hassle, and you don't want to go through the trouble if something easier can fix you up. So if you're doing a clean install, it's more or less your last hope.

Don't worry. This solution will most likely get you back on your feet. This one will fix all but the most horrifying and malignant of problems. So let's get to it.

The easy way to perform a clean install

Prior to System 7.5, clean installs were performed manually and were much harder to explain.

Thankfully, there is now a barely hidden shortcut in the Install Mac OS program that lets you perform a clean install automatically, with no muss or fuss. Here's how:

Clean versus regular installation

To understand why you need to do a clean install, or even what a clean install is, you have to understand a little about how the Install Mac OS program works and what *resources* are.

Resources are the building blocks from which all programs, control panels, extensions, and so on, are built. The Install Mac OS program is, technically, a resource installer. It installs the resources that become programs, control panels, extensions, and so on.

And the Install Mac OS program is very smart about which resources it installs. It looks at your hard disk; then, if it sees a System Folder containing a System and a Finder, it installs only the resources it thinks you need. So, for example, if the Install Mac OS program sees a System and Finder, it looks to see if they contain the proper resources. If they do, it doesn't install anything, even if the resources are damaged.

Therein lies the rub. The Install Mac OS program can sometimes outsmart itself. If the reason your Mac is crashing is that a resource inside the System, Finder, a control panel, or an extension has become damaged or corrupted, the Install Mac OS program may not replace the defective resource if you perform a Regular Install.

A clean install, on the other hand, ensures that every single file and every single resource is replaced with a brand spanking new one. In fact, a clean install gives you a brand new System Folder.

1. Start up or restart your Mac with Install Disk 1 in your floppy drive or the Mac OS 8 CD in your CD-ROM drive.

2. Launch the Install Mac OS 8 program.

3. Click Continue in the first screen you see.

4. The Select Destination screen, as shown in Figure 18-11, appears. Click the check box for Perform Clean Installation, then click the Select button.

5. Continue the installation as usual, feeding floppy disks if requested.

Figure 18-11: It's never been easier to perform a clean install.

When the Install Mac OS program is through, you have a brand spanking new System Folder on your hard disk. Your old System Folder has been renamed Previous System Folder. Nothing has been removed from it.

The folder called Previous System Folder contains all your old third-party extensions, control panels, and fonts. Because it's possible, even likely, that one of these items contributed to your problem, I recommend that you reinstall them one item at a time. In other words, move one extension or control panel from Previous System Folder onto the new System Folder's icon. Then restart and work for a while to see if any problems occur before reinstalling another.

It's a good idea to trash the System and Finder in the Previous System Folder as soon as possible after performing the clean install.

It's simply a bad idea to have two System Folders on one hard disk, and as long as Previous System Folder has a System and a Finder in it, your Mac could confuse Previous System Folder with the real System Folder, and that confusion could cause you major heartache.

So delete the old System and Finder files, the ones in the Previous System Folder, now. Just in case. Thanks.

Don't forget that the System Folder is smart. If you drag a control panel or extension onto its icon (but *not* into its open window), it puts the file in the proper folder for you.

Part V
Appendixes

The 5th Wave   By Rich Tennant

©RICHTENNANT

FROM
ORIGINAL
VAN-GOGH-OF-THE-MONTH
CLUB

"SINCE WE BEGAN ON-LINE SHOPPING, I JUST DON'T KNOW WHERE THE MONEY'S GOING."

In this part . . .

I saved some important topics for last because, as an intelligent Mac user, you already know much of what I cover in these appendixes.

First, I cover installing Mac OS 8. The whole process has gotten quite easy with this version of the System software. You may wonder why I bothered to write about it.

Second, I deal with the whole process of backing up. You know that your files are important, and I'm sure that you already know how to copy files from your hard disk to a floppy or someother form of media. But just in case you don't, you'd better read this appendix.

Appendix A
Anyone Can Install Mac OS 8

● ●

*T*he Mac OS 8 CD-ROM can install more than just System software. So in the first section, I discuss the plain vanilla installation that'll happen if you just keep clicking OK and Continue and Agree. . . .

An easy install includes the basic system software, Mac OS Info Center, Internet Access, Open Transport PPP, Mac OS Runtime for Java, Personal Web Sharing, OpenDoc, QuickDraw 3D, and MacLink Plus. If for some reason you don't want to install those components (read about them elsewhere in the book), uncheck them as shown in Figure A-1.

Figure A-1:
To avoid installing Mac OS Runtime for Java, Personal Web Sharing, OpenDoc, QuickDraw 3D, and/or MacLink Plus, uncheck them in the Install Software window.

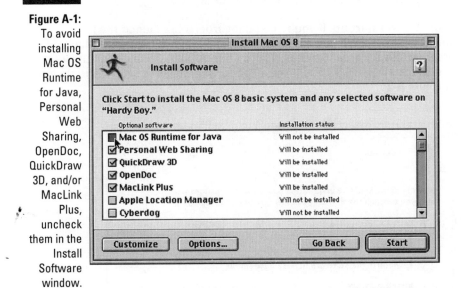

After that, I explain how to install each item that requires a separate installation.

Finally, there are several other optional pieces of System software — such as Easy Access and CloseView (see Chapter 17) — that require a separate custom installation process in the main Mac OS installer program. I cover them in the final section.

If the reason you're installing (actually reinstalling) Mac OS 8 is that your Mac is acting up, you may need to perform a *clean install.* See the section in Chapter 18.

The procedure for installing Mac OS 8 is the same regardless of whether you're upgrading from an earlier version of System software or installing Mac OS 8 on an empty hard disk.

Ready? Take a deep breath.

Installing Mac OS 8

Shut down your Macintosh if it's turned on. Insert the Mac OS 8 CD-ROM or the floppy disk called Install Disk 1 and turn on your Mac. If you're starting up from a CD, hold down the C key on your keyboard.

Your Mac will start up. If you're installing from a CD, launch the Install Mac OS 8 program. If you are installing from floppies, the Install Mac OS 8 program should launch automatically. (If it doesn't, double-click the icon named Install Mac OS.) You'll see a comforting welcome screen like the one in Figure A-2.

Figure A-2:
The opening screen of the Install Mac OS 8 program.

(Are you beginning to detect a pattern? Macs are warmer and fuzzier than other personal computers?)

Click the Continue button. The Select Destination window appears. Choose a disk to install Mac OS 8 onto from the pop-up Destination Disk menu. Of course, if you only have one hard disk it will be automatically selected for you by the nice installer program.

Click the Select button. Now read some important information about this software.

Print it and read it. Really. It's important, and I'm not going to repeat it all here.

When you're done, click the Continue button. The License Agreement window appears. Read it if you like. Then click the Continue button. You may have to click an Agree button now (I did with some versions of the installer and didn't with others).

Eventually the Install Software screen appears (see Figure A-3).

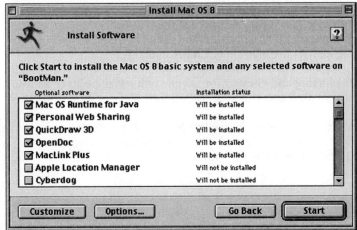

Figure A-3:
The Install
Software
window,
ready to
rock.

This is where you choose what software you want installed. For a normal (easy) install, just click Start. Or if you want to add optional components now, check them in the list. (Refer back to Chapter 16 to find out what they are and what they do.)

Click the Start button. The installer checks your destination disk with Disk First Aid to make sure it's in tip-top shape. It then updates your hard disk drivers automatically if you have an Apple hard disk.

If you have more than one hard disk, or a hard disk that's wasn't made by Apple, you may see a warning that the installer is not going to try to update these disks. That's okay; it's what you want.

Hard disk drivers are little bits of computer code installed by the software that formatted your hard disk. They manage how the disk talks to the Mac. Old disk drivers may be incompatible with new system software, so it's always a good idea to check with the manufacturer before installing a new version of Mac OS if you have a non-Apple hard disk. Apple hard disks, of course, have their drivers updated automatically as part of the installation process.

If you have a non-Apple hard disk, you should contact its manufacturer before installing Mac OS 8. This could be important. You need to know whether you need to update your hard disk drivers. Though you might be able to install Mac OS 8 without updating your hard disk drivers, it's a bad idea. Your Mac may not boot after the installation if your current hard disk drivers are incompatible with Mac OS 8.

If you're installing from a CD-ROM, just kick back and relax for a few minutes.

If you're installing from floppies, your Mac asks you to insert Install Disk 2. Do it. Later it asks for Install Disk 3, 4, 5, and so on, up to Disk 100 or so. Pay attention, 'cause it may not ask for them in order (depending upon what you are installing). Eventually you'll be asked to insert Install Disk 1 again. That's the signal that installation is almost over.

After whirring and clicking for a while, your Mac politely informs you that the installation was successful. Quit, restart your Mac, and away you go.

That's it. Your hard disk now has Mac OS 8 installed. Piece of cake. The hardest part is moving your arm if you had to feed floppies, and waiting if you installed from the CD. Onward!

Custom Installs

To install Mac OS Info Center, Internet Access, Open Transport PPP, Mac OS Runtime for Java, Personal Web Sharing, OpenDoc, QuickDraw 3D, and MacLink Plus, check their names and follow the directions in the previous section right up until the part where you clicked the Start button.

Don't forget that Mac OS Info Center, Internet Access, Open Transport PPP, Mac OS Runtime for Java, Personal Web Sharing, OpenDoc, QuickDraw 3D, and MacLink Plus were probably installed when you first installed Mac OS 8. Unless you manually deselected them when you first installed Mac OS 8, they're already installed. The instructions that follow show you how to install them if you haven't already.

Follow the instructions in the first section of this chapter right up to the part where you click the Start button. Then, instead of clicking the Start button, click the Customize button. The Custom Installation and Removal window appears. Click next to the names of the options you want to install.

You can quickly check items' installation status (as shown in Figure A-4); it changes depending on whether or not their box is checked.

In this example, the Mac OS 8, Mac OS Info Center, Internet Access, and Open Transport PPP installers will run in sequence when I click Start.

Figure A-4:
Custom installation; Mac OS 8, Mac OS Info Center, Internet Access, and Open Transport PPP will be installed when I click the Start button.

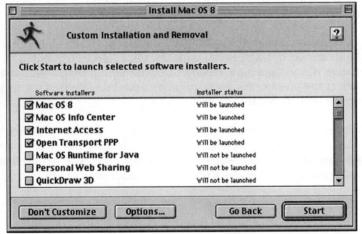

The Install Mac OS 8 program is nothing more than a little launcher program that launches the installer for each piece of the System software. Don't believe me? Look in the folder called Software Installers. ARA Client Install, Cyberdog, English Text-to-Speech, InfoCenter, Internet Access, Location Manager Install, Mac OS Runtime for Java, MacLink Plus, Open Transport/ PPP, OpenDoc, Personal Web Sharing, QuickDraw 3D, QuickDraw GX, and System Software each have their own personal installer program. If you want to save time, you can launch these installers separately and avoid dealing with the Install Mac OS 8 program completely.

Optional Mac OS Items

Some Mac OS components — including useful ones such as Easy Access and CloseView — require separate installation using the Custom Install feature.

To install these optional components, follow the directions in the first section of this appendix right up until the part where you click the Start button.

Instead of clicking the Start button, deselect everything but Mac OS 8.

Now click the Start button, or press Return.

You could avoid everything I've said so far in this section by opening the System Software Installer folder and launching that installer instead of the main one at root level.

The "Welcome to Mac OS" splash screen appears. Click the Continue button. Yet another license agreement appears. Click Agree. The Install System Software window appears. Finally. Click the Switch Disk button if necessary to select the proper disk for installation and then choose Custom Install from the pop-up menu.

Click the check box next to items you want to install and then click the Install button or press Return. After some whirring and clicking (and inserting floppy disks if you are installing from floppies), you're told that the installation was successful. Click the Quit button.

Appendix B
Back Up Now or Regret It Later

••

Although Macs are generally reliable beasts, someday your hard disk will die. I promise. They all do. And if you haven't backed up your hard disk, there's a good chance that you'll never see your files again. And if you do see them again, it'll only be after paying Scott at the DriveSavers data recovery service a king's ransom, with no guarantee of success. DriveSavers is the premier recoverer of lost data on hard disks. They do good work and can often recover stuff nobody else could. They charge accordingly.

I'm going to give you DriveSavers' phone number. It's 415-883-4232. Now pray you never need it. Back up often, and you won't. If, somehow, none of this sinks in, tell Scott I said Hi.

In other words, you absolutely, positively, without question MUST BACK UP. Just as you've adopted the Shut Down command and made it a habit, you must learn to back up your hard disk and back it up often.

How often is often? That depends on you. How much work can you afford to lose? If the answer is that losing everything you did yesterday would put you out of business, you need to back up daily, or possibly twice a day. If you'd only lose a couple of unimportant letters, you can back up less frequently.

Backing Up Is (Not) Hard to Do

There are lots of ways to back up your hard disk. Some are better than others.

The manual, "brute force" method

Drag your files a few at a time to floppy disks.

Yuk. If it sounds pretty awful, trust me, it is. It takes forever; you can't really tell if you've copied every file; and there's no way to copy only the files that have been modified since your last backup. Almost nobody sticks with this method for long.

Commercial backup software

There's nothing else in this book that I insist that you buy, but you must buy backup software if you don't already have some.

For some unfathomable reason, Apple has almost never seen fit to provide backup software with new Macs or include it with System software releases. I know some Performas have a crummy backup program, but Apple has left millions of Mac owners clueless.

Mac owners get nothing more than a brief passage regarding backing up in the *Macintosh User's Guide.* It ought to be in big red letters, in the first chapter, and include a warning from the Surgeon General or something. And it wouldn't kill them to provide a backup utility either. Sheesh, even DOS has a backup command, albeit a lousy one.

C'mon, Apple, give Mac owners a fair shake. At least include the lame Apple Backup program some Performa owners got.

Fortunately, plenty of very good backup programs are available for well under $100, including the excellent DiskFit Pro and DiskFit Direct from Dantz Development. If you want the best, most flexible, most powerful, top-of-the-line backup software, spend a little more and pop for Retrospect.

Backup software automates the task of backing up. The backup software remembers what is on each backup disk and only backs up files that have been modified since the last backup. Your first backup with commercial software should take no more than 90 minutes and use a few dozen 1.4MB floppy disks. (Better: Zip, Jaz, SyQuest, Bernoulli, or magneto-optical disks.) Subsequent backups, called *incremental backups* in backup-software parlance, should only take a few minutes.

Be sure to label the disks that you use for your backups because, during incremental backups, the backup software is going to ask you to "Please insert backup disk 7." If you haven't labeled your disks clearly, you have a problem.

Why You Need Two Sets of Backup Disks

You're a good soldier. You back up regularly. You think you're immune.

Now picture this: One day you take a floppy disk to QuicKopyLazerPrintz to print your resume on their laser printer. You make a few changes while at QuicKopyLazerPrintz and take the floppy home and stick it into your Mac.

Unbeknownst to you, the floppy became infected with a computer virus at QuicKopyLazerPrintz. (I discuss viruses in the "Virus trivia" sidebar later in this appendix.) When you insert the disk into your Mac, the infection spreads to your hard disk like wildfire.

Then you back up. Your backup software, believing that all the infected files have been recently modified (well, they have been — they were infected with a virus!), proceeds to back them up. You notice that the backup takes a little longer than usual, but otherwise, things seem to be okay.

A few days later, your Mac starts acting strangely. You borrow a copy of that excellent virus-detection software, Disinfectant, and discover that your hard disk is infected. "Aha," you exclaim. "I've been a good little Mac user, backing up regularly. I'll just restore everything from my backup disks."

Not so fast, bucko. The files on your backup disks are also infected.

This scenario demonstrates why you need multiple backups. If you have several sets of backup disks, chances are pretty good that one of the sets is clean.

I keep three backup sets. I use one set on even-numbered days, one on odd-numbered days, and I update the third set once a week and store it in my bank's vault. This scheme ensures that no matter what happens, even if my office burns, floods, is destroyed by a tornado or hurricane, or is robbed, I won't lose more than a few days' worth of work. I can live with that.

Virus trivia

A computer virus, in case you missed it in *Time* or *Newsweek,* is a nasty little piece of computer code that replicates and spreads from disk to disk. Most viruses cause your Mac to misbehave; some viruses can destroy files or erase disks with no warning.

If you use disks that have been inserted in other computers, you need some form of virus-detection software. If you download and use files from Web and FTP sites on the Internet, you need some form of virus detection as well.

Don't worry too much if you download files from commercial online services such as America Online or CompuServe. They are very conscientious about viral infections. Do worry about that Web site called Pirate's Den that an unsavory friend told you about.

John Norstad's excellent virus-detection-and-eradication software, Disinfectant, is widely available and is freeware. Just make sure that you have the latest version because new viruses appear on the scene every so often, and Disinfectant (and all antivirus software) requires updating to be able to detect and fight them.

On the commercial front, Virex and SAM (Symantec Anti-Virus for Macintosh) have their fans. I'm using Virex right now, but I've used others at one time or another and have never gotten a virus.

The big advantage of buying a commercial antivirus program is that the publisher will contact you each time a virus is discovered and provide you with a software update to protect you against the new strain. Or, for a fee, the publisher can send you a new version of the software every time a new virus is found.

If you only use commercial software and don't download files from Web sites with strange names, you have a very low risk of infection. On the other hand, if you swap disks with friends regularly, shuttle disks back and forth to other Macs, use your disks at service bureaus or copy shops, or download files from various and sundry places on the Internet, you are at risk.

If you're at risk, either download a new copy of Disinfectant each time a new virus is discovered or buy a commercial antivirus program.

Index

IDG BOOKS WORLDWIDE REGISTRATION CARD

Visit our Web site at http://www.idgbooks.com

ISBN Number: 0-7645-0271-9

Title of this book: Mac® OS 8 For Dummies®

My overall rating of this book: ❏ Very good [1]　❏ Good [2]　❏ Satisfactory [3]　❏ Fair [4]　❏ Poor [5]

How I first heard about this book:

❏ Found in bookstore; name: [6]

❏ Advertisement: [8]

❏ Word of mouth; heard about book from friend, co-worker, etc.: [10]

❏ Book review: [7]

❏ Catalog: [9]

❏ Other: [11]

What I liked most about this book:

What I would change, add, delete, etc., in future editions of this book:

Other comments:

Number of computer books I purchase in a year:　❏ 1 [12]　❏ 2-5 [13]　❏ 6-10 [14]　❏ More than 10 [15]

I would characterize my computer skills as: ❏ Beginner [16] ❏ Intermediate [17] ❏ Advanced [18] ❏ Professional [19]

I use ❏ DOS [20]　❏ Windows [21]　❏ OS/2 [22]　❏ Unix [23]　❏ Macintosh [24]　❏ Other: [25]

(please specify)

I would be interested in new books on the following subjects:

(please check all that apply, and use the spaces provided to identify specific software)

❏ Word processing: [26]

❏ Data bases: [28]

❏ File Utilities: [30]

❏ Networking: [32]

❏ Other: [34]

❏ Spreadsheets: [27]

❏ Desktop publishing: [29]

❏ Money management: [31]

❏ Programming languages: [33]

I use a PC at (please check all that apply): ❏ home [35] ❏ work [36] ❏ school [37] ❏ other: [38]

The disks I prefer to use are ❏ 5.25 [39]　❏ 3.5 [40]　❏ other: [41]

I have a CD ROM:　❏ yes [42]　❏ no [43]

I plan to buy or upgrade computer hardware this year:　❏ yes [44]　❏ no [45]

I plan to buy or upgrade computer software this year:　❏ yes [46]　❏ no [47]

Name:　　　　　　　　Business title: [48]　　　　　　Type of Business: [49]

Address (❏ home [50] ❏ work [51]/Company name:)

Street/Suite#

City [52]/State [53]/Zip code [54]:　　　　　　Country [55]

❏ **I liked this book!** You may quote me by name in future IDG Books Worldwide promotional materials.

My daytime phone number is _____

IDG BOOKS WORLDWIDE

THE WORLD OF COMPUTER KNOWLEDGE®

☐ # YES!

Please keep me informed about IDG Books Worldwide's
World of Computer Knowledge. Send me your latest catalog.